The New York Times

SWEET SUNDAY CROSSWORDS
75 Puzzles from the Pages of *The New York Times*

Edited by Will Shortz

ST. MARTIN'S GRIFFIN ☙ NEW YORK

The New York Times

SMART PUZZLES

PRESENTED WITH STYLE

Available at your local bookstore or online at www.nytimes.com/nytstore

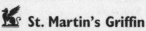 St. Martin's Griffin

Taking Half-Steps

ACROSS

1 Knives, forks and spoons
6 Jackson and Reno
12 Where a plant or animal thrives
20 Shakespearean nobleman
21 Wipes out
22 Spanish conquistador who searched for the Seven Cities of Gold
23 Taking too much
24 Reassure that one's joking, in a way
25 Aesthete
26 Little shavers at school?
28 Northern sympathizer
29 ___ moment's notice
30 Tucker out
31 Bone: Prefix
32 Just recently
35 Maternally related
37 Knoll
39 Like trenchant wit
45 Paper tray size: Abbr.
46 Mercedes sedan
48 Potpourri
50 Burrowing rodents
51 Home in the woods
52 Kin: Abbr.
53 Radiohead frontman Yorke
55 Cockamamie
57 Extraordinary and unexplainable
59 Play sentinel
61 Fix, as a fairway
62 "The Clan of the Cave Bear" author
63 Southern university whose campus is a botanical garden
64 Table scraps
65 Economic woe
69 Burns, e.g.
73 Ones pictured in corp. reports
74 Newspaper units: Abbr.
75 Body of water in a volcanic crater, for one
76 Group that doesn't believe in revolution?
82 #2 or #3
84 "Get it?"
85 "Lohengrin" soprano
86 Fixed price
87 Quick inning enders, for short
88 Walled city of Spain
89 Key
91 Modernize the plant
93 Trademarked marker
94 Spheres
96 ___-Alt-Del
98 Gusto
99 Draft inits.
100 Goddess with a headdress depicting a throne
102 Killed, as a test
104 Former transportation regulation agcy.
106 Dangers for children and klutzes
111 Immigrant's opposite
116 1994 Schwarzenegger film
117 Judge in Judges
118 Neighbor of a Turkmen
119 Cactuslike plant of the Southwest
120 Doorway jamb
121 Remark after an awkward silence
122 Vocal skeptic
123 Hockey team, say
124 Nobelist Bohr

DOWN

1 Aircraft carrier
2 "Open ___"
3 Cruel Ugandan
4 Veg-O-Matic company
5 Planned
6 Instrument played in the mouth
7 Short operatic solos
8 Kid minders
9 Glacial ridge
10 Render
11 Retired boomers
12 There's no foul play when one passes by these
13 Brass
14 More pretentious
15 Vaquero's neckwear
16 ___ a secret
17 Rikki-tikki-___
18 Some punches
19 Slander or libel
27 Cavalry member
31 2005 biography subtitled "The Making of a Terrorist"
32 Seasoned hand
33 Sycophant
34 Repeated film title role for Jim Varney
36 Organic food label
38 Links chain
40 Orly bird?
41 Pass (out)
42 Potpourri
43 Lens solution brand
44 Fixed at an acute angle
47 Guide
49 Fox hunter's cry
54 Shapes studied by Dr. Watson and his partner
56 Frequent answer to "When?"
58 Set-___
59 Letter after pee
60 Wrinkly-faced dogs
62 Lhasa ___
65 Dastardly laughs
66 Mario's dinosaur sidekick
67 Like some cigarettes
68 Way to refuse
69 Pavement caution
70 Bottom dealers, perhaps
71 Cousins of giraffes
72 Tightens (up)
73 Backups for backups
75 "The Origin of Species" concept
76 Part of a freight train
77 Something a dome lacks
78 Samoan port
79 Former Connecticut governor Jodi
80 Welsh, e.g.
81 Robert of "The Sopranos"
82 "___ Andromeda" (British sci-fi series)
83 10th-century pope
86 F major has just one
90 Kind of kick
92 Former surgeon general C. ___ Koop
95 It's found near the toe of a boot

by Timothy Polin

ACROSS

1 Natives of the land known as Aotearoa
6 One with eyes for a cook?
10 Implied
15 Silken construction
18 Pasty
19 Share a view
20 Split
21 Plant's grain-bearing part
22 Dislike of the son of Mary, Queen of Scots?
25 Prefix with bar
26 It's hard to understand
27 Heavy metal rock?
28 Springtime calendar hunk
30 Suffragist Carrie Chapman ___
31 Catwalk no-show?
33 March sisters' creator
37 Threatened ferociously
39 Conservative
40 Take the plunge
41 Southwest natives
42 "No introduction needed" phrase
45 Soft-spoken prayer ending?
48 Build a publishing empire?
53 Mosaicist, e.g.
54 First Arab country to have sanctions imposed on it by the Arab League
56 Poet Pablo
57 Radioactivity unit
59 Mag space seller, e.g.
62 Golf cup name
63 Not just my
66 Practical joke used on squirrels?
70 Things may be picked up with this
71 Cohesion
74 Brown, maybe
75 Highlighter colors, often
78 Catholic university in Philly
80 County on one side of the Golden Gate Bridge
83 Hauled, in a way
87 What sweaty dancers create at annual awards show?
90 Rush to get on the train?
92 Jewish mourning period
93 Dwarf with a purple hat
94 Arm part
95 Mein ___
98 Like some cookware
101 "Lumber" collector in a park
103 Where worms don't last long?
106 It's found between the shoulders
108 Rubber man?
109 Lunch inits.
110 "Consider it done!"
115 Air pump setting: Abbr.
116 What black holes swallow to bulk up?
119 "Horatio, thou art ___ as just a man . . ."
120 "___ ride"
121 10E and 40 long, e.g.
122 Former Red Sox star Garciaparra
123 Lines with crossings: Abbr.
124 Utopias
125 Mai ___ (drinks)
126 Purchase that's canceled

DOWN

1 Fashion
2 "No guarantees"
3 "Yikes!"
4 Mil. unit below a division
5 Give a shot
6 A to Z, e.g.
7 University of ___, where Andrea Bocelli earned a law degree
8 Italian article
9 Engulfs
10 It may get stuck in an eye
11 Small batteries
12 Desert and rain forest
13 Material in old mah-jongg sets
14 Common break hour
15 Kook
16 Less stressful
17 Brit's bumbershoot
19 Neglect
23 Trapped like ___
24 Shore bird
29 Some terra cotta
31 Precipitating
32 Drink for a toddler
33 Unwanted swimming pool bit
34 What rakes may do
35 Tilt
36 Kind of disc
38 Unidentified people
41 Marx Brothers, e.g.
43 Yahoo! alternative
44 FEMA part: Abbr.
46 The Tigers of the N.C.A.A.
47 Tombstone figure
48 2000 musical with the song "Every Story Is a Love Story"
49 Singer Anthony
50 Bro
51 13th, at times
52 40 million-member org. founded in 1958
55 Not so prevalent
58 Cleanup org.
60 Gigayear
61 Fairly
63 Unseat
64 "For ___ us a child . . ."
65 Rembrandt van ___
67 Shoe named for a cat
68 LAX data
69 Romance novelist Roberts
72 Geoffrey the Giraffe's store
73 "I suppose so"
76 Core
77 Paid sports spectator
79 Title of veneration
81 Justin Bieber and others
82 Ponytail locale
84 Newsman Marvin or Bernard
85 Cube creator Rubik
86 When Juno and Gold Beach were assaulted
88 Think too much of
89 "Look ___ hands!"
91 They're often sold by the dozen
93 One who works with canines
95 Hold back
96 It gets the lead out
97 Prepares a bow, with "up"

by Patrick Merrell

AIN'T HE SWEET?

ACROSS

1 Arthur Honegger's "A Christmas ___"
8 Staring intently
13 "Scrooged" actor Robert
20 Add a musical track to, e.g.
21 Destroyed
23 Noted bride of 1969
24 Model for an art class, say
25 "Stop stalling!"
26 Approach like an eagle
27 Baptism, e.g.
28 Kid's block
30 Cozy footwear
31 "I could ___ horse!"
33 Japanese stringed instrument
34 Journalist Joseph
36 Clearly happy
39 Goes for the gold?
40 Spice organizers
43 Lose intensity
44 Fencing position
47 Crunchy snack bit
50 Storage units
51 Piccadilly movers
55 Roman "olive"
56 "Make ___!"
58 "Unto us ___ is given"
59 Salt flats locale
60 Carnivore's love
62 Components
68 Getaway planner?
70 Newfangled
71 Actress Andie
73 Like some lines
74 Pola of the silents
76 Decoration on a 91-/100-Across
77 Mistreat
79 Predispositions
82 Score after deuce
84 "Hairspray" role
86 Young business partner?
90 Bay Area airport, in shorthand
91 With 100-Across, image revealed by connecting the circled letters alphabetically
95 Mozart's birthplace: Abbr.
96 "Miracle on 34th Street," e.g.
99 Medium skill
100 See 91-Across
101 Cold war fighter
102 2001 film in which 91-/100-Across is a character
104 Horsed around?
106 Shake up
109 Special ___
111 Chess champ Mikhail
112 "Honey in the Horn" trumpeter
113 "___ framed!"
115 Some toy batteries
116 Beta preceder
119 Tone quality, in music
121 Stuck
123 Wall St. deal
126 Singer Mitchell
128 Bronx and Central Park attractions
129 ___ good turn
132 Prepare, as eggnog
133 Partridge's preferred tree
134 Navigational aid
136 Fictional planet in "Flash Gordon"
138 "Incidentally . . ."
140 Drive-thru sandwich order
141 Crudités platter centerpiece
145 Delicious
146 Org. in Tom Clancy novels
147 Maternity ward figures
149 Coffee order
151 Stipulations
153 Pacino and Bundy
154 Eponymic town of Cambridgeshire
155 Mediterranean capital
156 Skip across the water's surface
157 Certain pass: Abbr.
158 Radio abbr.
159 Guinness suffix
160 1-Down's warning
161 Mandatory coll. course
162 Capt.'s guess

DOWN

1 Hooded menace
2 Benefit
3 "Drat!"
4 91-/100-Across, often
5 Nabokov novel
6 Rock's Jethro ___
7 Proficient
8 Year in San Juan
9 "The Little Mermain" fellow
10 Cafeteria variety
11 Mineral in healing crystals
12 Rocker Brian
13 Video game island
14 W.W. II battleship
15 Ref's decision
16 Aid for making a 91-/100-Across
17 Cyclist's offer
18 Merge
19 Vintage records
21 Fan's fixation
22 Popeye's ___' Pea
29 Fun-house sounds
32 Elves, to Santa: Abbr.
35 ___-12
37 Part of many a science course
38 "___ Misérables"
39 '70s TV production co.
41 Mao contemporary
42 "Santa Baby" singer
45 Camaro ___-Z
46 Paradise
47 Bulbous plant part
48 Butter alternative
49 Actor Foxx
52 Bickering
53 High praise
54 Storage unit
57 Friend ___ friend
58 Deaf talk: Abbr.
61 You are: Sp.
63 Serving well?
64 Public health agcy.
65 French pronoun
66 Have
67 Composer Max
69 Sit still?
71 Calf-length dresses
72 Hawaiian porch
75 Stormed
78 Star of "Gunsmoke"?
79 Cellar, in classifieds
80 Get an ___ effort
81 De ___ (anew)
83 How Santa's reindeer are harnessed
85 Slights, say
87 Buster?
88 Winter bird feeder food
89 Terse reproofs
92 Radiate
93 Mob turncoat
94 ___ B'rith
97 Cousin ___
98 Californie, e.g.
102 Tunisian seaport
103 Males
105 16th-century monarch credited with presenting 91-/100-Acrosses to guests

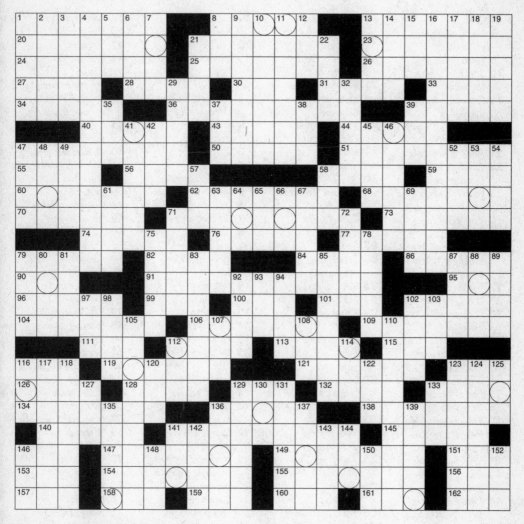

by Elizabeth C. Gorski

ADDENDUM

ACROSS

1 Many college profs
5 Food preserver
10 Sandwich choice, for short
13 Crosswise to the keel
18 Pool ball's "Watch this!" comment?
21 Arles affirmative
22 Onetime first name in Israeli politics
23 High-mounted window you can't stop looking at?
25 "Come ___?"
26 Steely Dan album featuring "Deacon Blues"
27 Traveled by bus
28 Thin blue line?
29 Resisted a job offer, say
30 Go downhill
32 Part of a watch touching the breastbone?
35 End of many a list
36 Camper's canful
38 She's entertaining
39 Heist planner's concern
41 Wedding part
42 Ceiling
45 Strong winds
46 "You don't have to be busy to look busy," e.g.?
54 Squished bug, e.g.
56 [I'm so funny!]
57 Go all to pieces
58 Antipasto tidbit
59 Pill that relieves computer-related anxiety?
63 High
64 Bring in
65 History topic
66 "I think," to texters

68 Empire State Building climber, for short
69 Holds under the tap
71 Inhuman group of golfers?
76 Behaved
77 1988 Summer Olympics site
79 Handbag monogram
80 "A Love Like ___" (Barbra Streisand album)
81 Sultan's wife, perhaps?
83 Sends up
85 Thank you for waiting
86 Reed of rock
87 "1984" superstate
89 Desperately want
94 Bad experience
96 Late sixth-century year
99 Jungle king's jeans and overalls?
102 Looked intently
104 Knocked on the noggin
105 Rainy day planner?
106 Twelve Oaks neighbor
108 Pac-12 athlete
109 Restaurant greeter's option
110 Ennui among quantum physicists?
114 Go on a shopping spree
115 Savings plan, briefly
116 Dessert delivered over the Internet?
117 Brouhahas
118 Cowlick fixer

119 Monster of Jewish folklore
120 The Big Board, for short

DOWN

1 "What a load of hogwash!"
2 Jimi Hendrix's debut single
3 Set out
4 Stray from righteousness
5 Refuse to release
6 Low-pH compound
7 Go to the tape?
8 "___ hath an enemy called Ignorance": Ben Jonson
9 Negative conjunction
10 Conjecture
11 It's good in Italy
12 Pal of Huck Finn
13 Swirly marbles
14 "The Big Sleep" co-star, 1946
15 Funny Boosler
16 They're exchanged in France
17 Candy eaten in handfuls
19 "Praying" part of a praying mantis
20 Master
24 Pixar title character
29 Best-selling author who wrote "I did not write it. God wrote it. I merely did his dictation"
31 Downswing
32 They're heavy during storms
33 Sample
34 Injury symptom
36 Reception room in a mansion

37 Rare craps roll
40 Sharp nails
41 Through
42 "The Big Bang Theory" network
43 Sports Illustrated's Sportsman of the Century
44 Creamy Italian side dish
46 One taking a bow in Japan
47 Smoothie ingredient
48 Homme's partner
49 Travel by car
50 ___ Quijano (Don Quixote's real name)
51 Deleting
52 "___ got a feeling . . ."
53 What's in an Rx
55 Leaning
60 Words to live by
61 Garden spot
62 Lash of old westerns
63 Hides in the shadows
67 In olden times
69 When doubled, ardent
70 Diamonds, to a yegg
72 Einstein's birthplace
73 NATO alphabet vowel
74 Hosp. diagnostic aid
75 Ability to identify Zener cards
77 Lacking a coat, maybe
78 ___ de vie
82 Fill, and then some
83 Big name in Champagne
84 Easily drawn gun

by Patrick Berry

87 One of the music industry's Big Four
88 Kick out
89 If everything goes your way
90 Cut-rate
91 Fierce, as an argument
92 Weather Channel newsmaker
93 Wicked ones
94 About ready to drop
95 Square
97 Badly made
98 Says no to
100 Catch
101 R. J. Reynolds brand
102 Like three of golf's four majors
103 "Philadelphia" director
106 Greenish blue
107 Having the knack
110 Chinese zodiac animal
111 Smoke
112 Sort who's a natural leader, supposedly
113 Great time

ACROSS

1 A person can take big strides with this
6 Hannibal's foil in "The Silence of the Lambs"
13 Museum piece
20 Forum fashions
21 Glade, e.g.
22 Hue akin to olive
23 ___-Itami International Airport
24 "Just do drills for now"?
26 Undo
28 Back to Brooklyn?
29 Slaughter
30 Disturb one's neighbors at night?
37 Comic strip "___ and Janis"
38 Inflation-fighting W.W. II org.
39 A pop
40 Former bill
42 Handful
44 Table saver
47 Don Quixote's love
52 Duffer's feeling toward a putting pro?
54 Meeting one's soul mate, perhaps?
56 Bogart's "High Sierra" role
57 Clive Cussler novel settings
59 Weight allowance
60 "Behold," to Brutus
61 Represent with a stick figure, say
63 Words on a Wonderland cake
65 Nonentities
67 Successfully perform a download?

71 Who wrote "A true German can't stand the French, / Yet willingly he drinks their wines"
75 Chamber exit
76 One who discriminates?
81 Naysayer
82 Fr. title
83 Fen-___ (former weight-loss drug)
86 Grow dark
87 Applied foil at the Hershey's factory?
91 One man's declaration to an upset party planner?
93 Sewing aids
94 Rider on a crowded bus, maybe
96 "I knew it!"
97 Relations
98 Shoppe modifier
99 Foreign football score
101 Blue shade
105 Drive by the United Nations?
113 Ponders
115 Upton Sinclair novel on which "There Will Be Blood" is based
116 Slum-clearing project, say
117 Impostor's excuse?
124 "Me, Myself & ___"
125 Tainted
126 Part of some Tin Pan Alley music
127 Went into la-la land, with "out"
128 Take control of
129 Original
130 Twisty curves

DOWN

1 Bundle bearer
2 "I'll have ___"
3 Response to a pledge drive request
4 Glen Canyon reservoir
5 Get a bit misty
6 Academy enrollee
7 Constellation whose brightest star is Regulus
8 Prince Valiant's eldest
9 Bunkum
10 EarthLink, e.g., for short
11 Actor Firth
12 Thrill
13 One may be overhead
14 "Little" singer of the '60s
15 Coll. elective
16 Capital city on the Atlantic
17 Pundit Bill
18 Model
19 Vodka drink, informally
25 "Definitely!"
27 Go into la-la land, with "out"
31 Strong cast
32 2010 Emma Stone comedy set in high school
33 Highway sign abbr.
34 Was audibly surprised, maybe
35 Shake
36 Holiday season event
41 Loos
42 Animal house, say
43 Creepy: Var.
45 Start
46 Hovel

47 Removal of restrictions, informally
48 Path of Caesar
49 One-named singer for the Velvet Underground
50 Suffix with depend
51 They might have it
52 Some appliances
53 Nag's call
55 ___-shanter
58 Tarot user, maybe
62 New York's Tappan ___ Bridge
64 Flat: Abbr.
65 Kill quickly
66 "South Pacific" hero
68 Diplomatic efforts
69 Hindu spring festival
70 French income
71 Exclaim breathlessly
72 Ready for service
73 Conseil d'___
74 Sports contest
77 Men of La Mancha
78 4-Down locale
79 Actress Sofer
80 Goal
82 Food in Exodus
84 Language from which "bungalow" and "jungle" come
85 Saxony seaport
88 Bad response upon first seeing one's new haircut?
89 Insomnia cause
90 Adaptable aircraft
92 From now on
95 Khan man?
100 Take charge?
101 Drivers of some slow-moving vehicles

by Tony Orbach

102 Allotment
103 Kind of nerve
104 One way to go, betting-wise
106 Word after an ampersand, maybe
107 Body cavity
108 Eccentric
109 What Oliver asked for more of
110 Berlin Olympics star
111 Rajah's partner
112 Malamutes' burdens
114 "Auld Lang ___"
118 Musician Montgomery
119 Things that may be 65-Downed
120 Cadge
121 Inventor Whitney
122 Itch
123 Motor finish?

WEATHER REPORT

ACROSS

1 DNA testing might reopen one
9 Uses a 13-Across on
13 "Star Trek" weapon
19 Person who's a zero?
20 What will the French think of next?
21 Troop group
22 Dream setting
24 After-dinner choices
25 PC key
26 Some online communications, for short
27 QB Tebow
28 Thérèse de Lisieux, for one
30 :D, e.g.
33 Battle-ax
37 Grp. that coordinates E.T.A. and E.T.D.
40 Letter-shaped girder
42 Basis of a lawsuit
43 "By __!"
44 Slip-on
46 Places for rings, maybe
48 Humble response to praise
50 Organ repair sites, briefly
51 Polished
52 __ B. Driftwood ("A Night at the Opera" role)
53 Org. that may assess violence levels
54 PBS flagship station
55 Part of a pinochle round
56 Former U.N. secretary general Kofi __
58 Get ready to drive
59 x, y and z
60 Scot's "not"
61 Ousted from the ring, for short
62 TV station, e.g.
64 Cicely or tarragon
66 Weather comment represented visually by this puzzle's circled letters
72 Major artery through San Antonio
73 Plant tissue
74 Hunted
75 TV tavern keeper
76 Bud
78 Feel (for)
80 The Mediterranean has a warm one
82 Shade of a swan's bill in a Keats poem
83 Kindergarten stuff
84 Gravitate
85 Not cheating
86 Many wonks
88 Scat syllable
89 One of the Everly Brothers
90 Fate
91 Fictional Simon
92 Esteem
94 Rolling __ (rich)
96 Kaput
98 Overseas Mr.
99 Austrian physician who lent his name to an English word ending in "-ize"
100 Propose
102 "True Colors" singer, 1986
104 Roam
105 Letters on some N.Y.C. luggage
108 Actress Tyler
111 Subject of a Vatican investigation
114 Artificial plot device
118 "The Conqueror," e.g.
119 "__ it" ("Understood")
120 Some bills have them
121 Dolls
122 Brit's teapot cover
123 Like some boards

DOWN

1 Chewed stimulant
2 Precious girl's name?
3 In the event that
4 2000 title role for Richard Gere
5 LL Cool J's "Going Back to __"
6 "Lemme __!"
7 "That is quite clear"
8 Directional suffix
9 "Shut your trap!"
10 Nudists
11 Nascar Hall of Fame architect
12 Part of a security system
13 It's lowered to hear music
14 Taft's partner in a 1947 act
15 Light reflection ratio
16 R.S.V.P. facilitator: Abbr.
17 Tolkien creature
18 Pharmacies fill them, in brief
21 Fourth letter after 49-Down
23 Leaf pores
29 You probably raise your arm for this
31 It's north of the South
32 Stock page listings: Abbr.
34 Big Apple team
35 Side (with)
36 Heroic deeds
37 __ Hall (site on many a campus)
38 Attacked
39 Shows that can be racier than their network counterparts
40 Nest maker
41 Cheating
45 Angry Birds, e.g.
47 Manipulate to one's advantage
49 Fourth letter before 21-Down
53 Track __
54 Prison unit
57 Security Council veto
58 Mine transport
61 __ kwon do
63 Put away
65 Big name in frozen desserts
67 72-Across and others: Abbr.
68 "Cagney & Lacey" org.
69 Bazooka, e.g.
70 Yokel
71 Martial arts master
76 Lady
77 Villa, e.g.
79 Portuguese king
81 Tart drink
82 Doc's reading
85 Battle wear
87 Bond
89 Tediously didactic

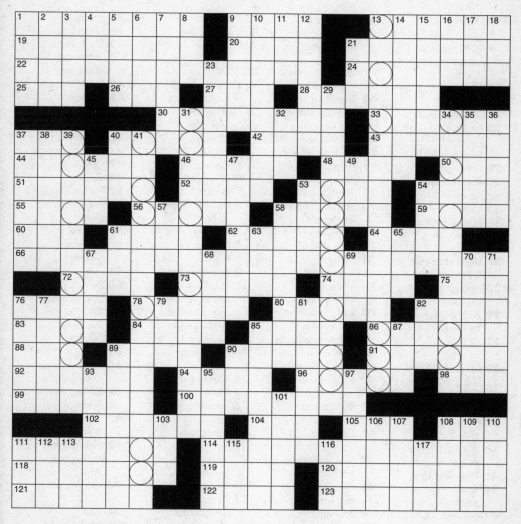

by Finn Vigeland

SNOW WHITE'S EMPLOYMENT AGENCY

ACROSS

1 Colo. ___, Colo.
4 1040 preparer, for short
7 Heartbeat
13 Plied with spirits
18 Shakespeare
20 National Forensic League skill
22 Rare violin
23 Royal house until the early 20th century
24 Bad occupation for Sleepy?
26 One
27 Head of ancient Sparta?
28 Hardest to ship, say
29 Bad occupation for Happy?
31 Bit of wear for a fop
32 Hero who debuted in Weird Tales magazine in 1932
33 M.A. hopeful's ordeal
34 Like Oscar Wilde's humor
37 Ruler in a robe
41 Touch while running
42 Home of two M.L.B. teams
44 Villains in 1939's "Stagecoach"
48 Last ___
50 Ones running away with the game?
54 Mrs. Robinson's daughter
55 Having hands, maybe
57 Bad occupation for Sneezy?
59 More than a quarter of the earth's crust, by mass
61 Longtime Yankee nickname
62 Spot for a flame
63 Bad occupation for Grumpy?
69 2000 musical with the song "Fortune Favors the Brave"
70 Diplomatic, say
71 Some juices
73 Bad occupation for Dopey?
79 Grippers
80 Spanish dish
81 Classic figure in a top hat
83 It needs to be fed frequently
84 Best in the market
86 Last word of "Finnegans Wake"
87 ___ Canals
89 Gives a darn?
90 Bridge maker's deg.
91 Biblical mount
93 Singer John
95 Common tattoo spot
98 Bad occupation for Doc?
105 Hippocampus hippocampus, e.g.
108 Mishmashes
109 Employee of the month award, say
110 Bad occupation for Bashful?
112 Waldorf salad ingredients
113 Sports anchor Rich
114 Attacked ground units, in a way
115 Honchos
116 Lands in a puddle, maybe
117 Accent
118 ___-Magnon
119 ___-la-la

DOWN

1 Kerri ___, U.S. gymnastics star at the 1996 Olympics
2 45 player
3 Pay up
4 Cave ___
5 One going to market
6 Daily or weekly: Abbr.
7 "Friends" role
8 (0,0), on a graph
9 Eruption sight
10 "___ Frome"
11 A picky person may pick one
12 Trailer attachment
13 Bananas
14 "Somebody shot me!"
15 Questionnaire blank
16 Airport postings, for short
17 Force
19 Subject of dozens of Degas paintings
21 Vertigo symptom
25 Group with the 1995 #1 hit "Waterfalls"
27 Honor like a troubadour
30 Bar that shrinks
33 Miss
34 Like four U.S. presidents
35 Mathematician Descartes
36 River to the North Sea
37 Chapters in history
38 Half note
39 Novelist Calvino
40 Like lanterns at the start of evening
42 Log
43 Big bother
45 Degree of interest?
46 "Voilà!"
47 Fire
49 Convivial
51 Jai ___
52 Funeral song in Scotland
53 Cuts
56 Become a YouTube sensation
58 Finally edible
60 Zip
64 Duo with the 2003 hit "All the Things She Said"
65 Levi's alternative
66 Actors MacLachlan and Chandler
67 Serve up some ham?
68 Extend, in a way
72 Georgia and Moldova, once: Abbr.
73 Like two peas in ___
74 Hail
75 Is allowed (to)
76 Overhead transports
77 Tolkien's tree creatures
78 Some Jamaicans
82 "Switched-On Bach" instrument
85 Snares
88 Not a great hand for raising
92 Surgical inserts

by Adam Fromm

93 Aristocracies
94 Big name in insurance
95 [Give me the worm! Give me the worm!]
96 Hallmark of the Philadelphia sound
97 Sounds of hesitation
98 Relating to the palm of the hand
99 Apple software bundle that includes GarageBand
100 Volunteer's cry
101 "Shoot!"
102 Disgruntled worker's parting cry
103 External
104 "The Gondoliers" bride
105 Ballet bit
106 Malevolent
107 Lhasa __
111 "Either plagiarism or revolution," per Paul Gauguin
112 Fighters' org.

8 NETWORKING EVENT

ACROSS

1 Swivel on an axis
5 Cowboys' home, familiarly
9 Laughable
14 Marble, e.g.
17 One in Germany
18 Locale of St. Catherine's Monastery, said to be the world's oldest working monastery
19 Sources of many beads
21 Narrow inlet
22 Fancy footwear at a TV station?
24 Advertising department at a TV station?
26 Rugged transport, for short
27 ___ Levy, four-time Super Bowl coach for Buffalo
28 Visited
30 Western loop
31 Like some fortresses
33 Lose ground?
35 Classic toy company whose name is its founder's middle name
36 Slide show at a TV station?
41 "Puss in Boots" villain
42 "Barbarella" extras, for short
43 Person making waves?
44 "How ya doin', bro?"
47 Livid
50 River to Korea Bay
52 Insanity
53 Shave
54 Court recitation
55 Midpoints: Abbr.
56 Q&A at a TV station?
58 Lickety-split
60 Green-egg layers
61 Ruthless corporate type
62 Noted calendar makers
63 Underworld leader
64 Overflow
66 Skater Yamaguchi
68 Sort (out)
69 Instrument with a big bell
72 Expert at a TV station?
75 Cookie holders
76 Beginning of some temple names
77 Opéra part
78 Cockamamie
79 Carnal craving
80 European freshwater fish
81 Super ___
82 George nicknamed Mr. Basketball
83 "Tsk! Tsk!"
84 Baseball family surname
86 Enrollment at a TV station?
92 Shocked
95 How some stocks are bought
96 Hold fast
97 Seize
98 Playful response to a good insult
101 You might rub a knife across it
103 Country singer David Allan ___, writer of "Take This Job and Shove It"
104 Recruiters at a TV station?
106 Fish holder at a TV station?
109 It's picked in the Pacific
110 One taking the gold?
111 Meal with wine
112 Missouri relatives
113 It was dropped at Woodstock
114 "___ Got a Brand New Bag" (1965 James Brown hit)
115 Orange or olive
116 Await decision

DOWN

1 Opening word?
2 Tea merchant Sir Thomas
3 Early computer
4 Shout in a strip
5 Drink served with Brezeln
6 "What chutzpah!"
7 Miss at a hoedown
8 "The Simpsons" character with platform shoes
9 Old block deliverers
10 Gold rush town of 1899
11 Graceful horse
12 ___ a scratch
13 Utah's state animal
14 Mythical figure blinded by Oenopion
15 Do a certain dish duty
16 Zero, in slang
18 Beach umbrella, e.g.
20 Student involved in a prank, maybe
23 Appear on the scene
25 SpongeBob, e.g.
29 Sugary quaffs
32 Canine protector
34 Fishing gear
35 Blanket
37 ___ Place
38 Continental prefix
39 Primo
40 Product from Mars
44 Sahara feature
45 Push
46 One of a group of 12, say
47 World org. based in Lausanne, Switzerland
48 Bowl call
49 Leucippus and Democritus, philosophically
51 Some Dadaist works
52 Go up
53 Oil producer?
55 It brings up many ticket holders
56 "Ta-ta!"
57 Place to live in Germany
59 Prefix with -plasm
60 Give lessons
64 Sheiks' garments
65 Sidecars might go on it
66 "Star Trek II" villain
67 Houston university
68 ___ Islam
70 Meadow call
71 "Ready!" follower
73 Joiner of a team
74 Gravy holder
75 Home of ancient Bethlehem
79 One of a secretive trio
80 Dairy brand
82 Get foggy
83 ___ decay
85 One-point score, of a sort

by Ian Livengood

86 It might be batted at a knockout
87 Clerics' homes
88 Half of a title role for John Barrymore or Spencer Tracy
89 Goddess associated with witchcraft
90 Like some T-shirt designs
91 Didn't wait until Christmas, say
92 Terrible
93 Savvies
94 Entranced
98 Other, in Oviedo
99 Crate
100 Lassie of Arg.
102 S-shaped molding
105 Quick drink
107 Gen __
108 Outdo

ACROSS

1 Superfluous
6 Posed (for)
9 Follow persistently
12 Tiny blob
18 Charms
19 The Beatles' "All ___ Got to Do"
20 Old White House nickname
21 Badly beaten up
22 45-Down near Baton Rouge?
25 124-Across near Dover?
27 ___ contendere
28 Flower girl?
30 New Jersey town bordering Rahway
31 Photo ___
34 Swindle
35 Hindu title
36 ___ Brava
37 CD-___
38 117-Down near Salem?
42 When sung three times, part of a Beatles refrain
46 Bellyache
48 Seine summers
49 First name?
51 Starch-yielding palm
52 Old TV knob
54 How Shakespeare's Rosalind dresses
56 Sign by a theater ticket booth
57 Smithereens
58 1-Across near Hartford?
61 Blouse, e.g.
62 Still broken, say
65 Confirms
66 "Ancient Mariner" verse
68 Bad-mouthed
69 Bitchin'
70 Sun spots
73 Inter ___
74 Dante e Boccaccio
75 Rack for a rifle
76 Toss-up?
78 114-Down near Boise?
81 Santa ___ (desert winds)
82 Get it wrong
83 Certain implants
84 Role in "Nicholas and Alexandra"
87 TV police drama
89 Comics canine
90 11 or 12, but not 13
92 Paint choice
94 "___ teaches you when to be silent": Disraeli
95 76-Down near Springfield?
98 Mugful, maybe
99 Actor Quinn
102 Before, in verse
103 Pioneer in quadraphonic music
104 Caustic soda
105 Against
107 Badge earner
109 This and that: Abbr.
111 61-Across near Phoenix?
113 9-Across near Boston?
118 Critter whose name comes from Nahuatl
119 Cookout item
120 Roll of bills
121 Bring out
122 Assails
123 Staff ___: Abbr.
124 Whirlpool
125 Exorcism target

DOWN

1 Farm mother
2 Women's suffrage Amendment
3 Pampering, for short
4 Pull (in)
5 Regarding the price
6 Jazzy Nina
7 Boston's Mass ___
8 Lean
9 Doesn't budge
10 "Sure!"
11 E.U. member
12 "What ___!"
13 "Le Déjeuner sur l'herbe" artist
14 Expenditures
15 "The Time Machine" people
16 "___ your toes!"
17 B'nai B'rith grp.
23 Romeo or Juliet
24 French cup
26 Many a museum display
29 It might be blue, green or brown
31 Assn.
32 Like a sty denizen
33 6-Across near Indianapolis?
36 Some conifers
39 Do over, as a lawn
40 Abbr. before a colon
41 Prefix with -pod
43 119-Across near Albany?
44 Prefix with business
45 Basketball rim
47 Open
50 Housemother, e.g.
53 Passed easily
54 Weak
55 Armstrong and Sedaka
57 Pal
59 Light touch
60 Certain online request
63 Not quite right
64 Arrive at too quickly, in a way
67 "Hakuna ___"
69 In one's cups
70 Brewskis
71 How a fool acts
72 Spots
74 Bird wing
75 Knot
76 Spring time
77 Large-toothed whale
79 Paraded by
80 "Is she not down so late, ___ so early?": "Romeo and Juliet"
85 Number 2, e.g.
86 Still to be sampled
88 Shock
90 Sub
91 Site of a Greek tragedy
93 Big name in jeans
96 Respectable
97 Naval force
100 "___ the Sheriff"
101 Tidies up a bit
105 Number two
106 "Tu ___ mi amor"
107 Cozy
108 Drags
110 Give up
111 Weave's partner
112 Maternity ward workers, for short
114 Hip-hop
115 Deut.'s preceder
116 Environmental prefix
117 Perfect rating

by Charles M. Deber

10   ADDITIONAL READING

ACROSS
1 Handsome, as Henri
4 Lucky end?
7 Hyundai sedan
12 Mata ___ (spy)
16 G.P.'s group
17 Some nerve
19 They're all the same
20 Each
21 Send over some Bibles?
24 Tour org.
25 Really want
26 Largest, as a sum
27 Things that may have to be cleared
29 Mark Messier, for 12 years
30 Actress Gilpin of "Frasier"
31 Graybeards
33 Dolt's football game plans?
38 Bar, legally
39 Cinco follower
40 Drum set set
42 Huffs
45 Word affixed to web or handy
48 Police investigator: Abbr.
49 Comet rival
51 Ogle
52 Curved molding
54 The truth about a popular Internet community?
59 Reveal, in poetry
60 Put down
62 "C'est ___"
63 Sea of ___ (arm of the Black Sea)
64 Stimpy's pal
65 "The gloves are off!"
67 Jack's inferior
68 Albanian money
70 Decodes
72 Singer/actress with a simultaneous #1 album and #1 film, familiarly
73 Warden's charge
75 Fracas
77 Rathskeller vessel
79 Velvet finish?
80 Egotistical author's request to a reader?
84 Tiny bits of pasta
85 Live
86 Frees
87 Ike's W.W. II command
89 ___ T. (big name in 1960s music)
90 Like certain passages
93 Professorial
96 Start of some Italian church names
98 Avid reader
100 Annual publications for burros?
105 Monotony
108 Whence Zeno
109 Mistreatment
110 Cut down to size
111 Best in business
115 Russian retreat
116 "The Mikado" baritone
117 Dust cover made of 100% aluminum, perhaps?
121 As previously mentioned, in bibliographies
122 Comparatively stupid
123 Room in Clue
124 Diminutive suffix
125 Gobi-like
126 Showed over
127 Black ___ (some military activities)
128 Platoon V.I.P.

DOWN
1 Half of an interrogation team
2 "There's a Chef in My Soup!" writer
3 Chorus syllables
4 Lug
5 Orch. section
6 Successful swinger
7 Shampoo ingredient
8 Where the wild things are?
9 Put an ___
10 Engage again for a gig
11 Father-and-son rulers of Syria
12 One-named fashion designer
13 Aid for record-keeping at Mrs. Smith's?
14 "Copy that"
15 Bridge declaration
17 Like some flights
18 Sarkozy's predecessor
19 Film special effects, briefly
22 Actresses Dana and Judith
23 Enlighten
28 Believers
30 Mail-related
32 1987 Broadway sensation, colloquially
34 Landed estate
35 Old Spanish card game
36 The duck in Prokofiev's "Peter and the Wolf"
37 Superboy's sweetie
41 Magic, once
43 It's measured in points
44 Spotted
45 Rimsky-Korsakov's "Le ___ d'Or"
46 Christina of pop
47 Get together with your bet taker?
50 "Believe ___ Not!"
53 Some trains
55 Pamper
56 Cain raiser
57 Sign the register
58 Part of Y.S.L.
61 Ship's record
66 Film whale
68 Writer Wallace
69 Jeff Lynne's band, for short
71 Start of a Vol. I heading
72 ___ Kennedy Smith (sister of J.F.K.)
74 They come from Mars
75 Classic fragrance sold in France as Mon Péché
76 Macedonian city with Greek and Roman ruins
78 Opposite of "and"
81 Type
82 ___ forte (less loud, in music)
83 Judge's order
88 Dosage frequency, frequently
91 "Gnarly, man!"
92 Star or wolf preceder
94 Shooting match
95 Homer's home
97 Supply at a French smoke shop
99 Western evergreen
101 Hail in a loud voice

by Kurt Mueller

102 Brouhaha
103 Volume holder
104 Washington airport
105 Sushi bar servings: Var.
106 Dwelling
107 Like some energy

112 Bone under a watch
113 Govt. gangbusters
114 To be, to Benicio
118 One, in Orléans
119 Fill completely, in a way
120 Law degs.

CORE O' NATIONS

ACROSS

1 How a bug might go on a windshield
6 Opposite of neither
10 College town SW of Cleveland
17 Hunt
18 Donnybrook
19 Island group that includes Guam
21 Show of affection
23 Balletic
24 Misery causes
25 Ridiculous
27 The first letter of "tsar," in Cyrillic
28 Sweet ending?
29 Mobile camper, informally
30 Long-migration seabirds
31 Deep Western lake
33 Tied
34 Back to front?
35 Kind of rock
36 Eucharist plate
37 Half of a 1960s pop group
38 O. Henry bad guy who became a Hollywood/TV hero
41 Appropriate, in slang
42 Part of the Confederacy: Abbr.
43 The gold in them thar hills, say
44 Like "vav" in the Hebrew alphabet
45 Aussie "girl" famous for 55-Downing
49 Frizzy dos
51 Tax-free bond, briefly
52 Like leprechauns

54 Your, to Yves
55 Summarize
56 Pot builder
57 Opposite of spring
58 Ryder fleet
59 Record label for Cee Lo and Whitney Houston
60 Some payments: Abbr.
61 Roseanne's husband on "Roseanne"
62 And others
64 Former European money
65 "Dies ___"
67 Attack with snowballs
68 Lime ___
69 Not yet decided: Abbr.
70 Public
71 Middle parts of Japan?
72 Home of the N.C.A.A.'s Minutemen
73 Maximally wacky
75 "Fiddler on the Roof" matchmaker
77 One of two deliveries?
78 Rap's Dr. ___
79 Bonaventures, e.g.
80 Double, maybe
85 Pesto ingredient
87 The House of ___
88 Baba ___ (Gilda Radner character)
89 Writer Umberto
90 Titles for attys.
91 Ottoman officer
92 Noted tower locale
93 Spring
94 Pac-12 team, for short
95 Shelley's fairy queen
96 Crafter's pedal

98 Throng
99 Start for someone seeking advice
102 Place for produce stands
104 It's pushed in a park
105 Some exams
106 Sparkles
107 Areas
108 N.J. and Pa. each have a famous one
109 Hall of fame

DOWN

1 "Me too"
2 Tree trimmers
3 Drink with foam on top
4 "Jumpin' Jack Flash, it's ___"
5 X
6 Show sympathy, say
7 Stews
8 Check, as brakes
9 Halting
10 Text-speak gasp
11 Red Cross founder Clara
12 Remove
13 Wedding staple
14 New Guinea port
15 Unofficial discussions
16 Something gotten at an amusement park, maybe
17 Draper's supply
18 Real ___
20 Loads
22 X, in Roma
26 Trip up, perhaps
30 Makes an extra effort
32 Little chuckle
33 "Swans Reflecting Elephants," e.g.
36 Mischievous one
37 SAT section
39 Whodunit staple

40 "Are you in ___?"
41 Servings of 3-Down
44 Sea salvager's quest, maybe
45 One-named rapper with the 2008 hit "Paper Planes"
46 Like always
47 Turns down
48 Appraise
49 Mexican shout of elation
50 On the level
51 Colorful bird
53 Lets
55 See 45-Across
58 For immediate lease, say
61 Lord's Prayer word
63 The 82-Down in "The Lion King"
66 Hogwash
67 Film producer Carlo
70 Bottom of the ocean?
74 Bearded flower
76 Pricey hors d'oeuvre
79 Juilliard subj.
80 Pricey furs
81 Many a Justin Bieber fan
82 African mongoose
83 It's much thanked once a year
84 Common co-op rule
85 They can help worriers
86 Strengths
87 Gossip
88 Ungainly gait
91 San ___, suburb of San Francisco
92 Israel's Ehud
93 Wife of 67-Down
95 Barley product

by James F. C. Burns

97 O.K. Corral hero
98 Eclipse phenomenon
100 Mythical bird
101 Earth cycles: Abbr.
103 1991 book subtitled "When the Lion Roars"

ACROSS

1 Bulb holders
6 Part of the name of many a Spanish restaurant
12 Confabs
20 Stern taking a bow (in two senses)
21 Demands (from)
22 Eternally
23 Aide for a V.I.P. customer
25 Multiple Grammy winner who was a contestant on "Dancing With the Stars"
26 Paper nautilus, e.g.
27 Words mouthed to a TV camera
29 Like the pen or pencil you might reach for
30 P.T.A. interest
32 One of two options at a fast food restaurant
34 Sample
35 Prozac, for one
40 W.C.
42 "Oh baby!"
46 Eve's opposite
47 Work assignment
48 Gore in fiction
50 Dirty
51 Kind of switch
53 Special ___
54 It may be popped for fun
56 Metro area
57 XXX lover?
59 Freudian concept
62 Lie about
63 The "L" of S.L.R.
64 Trample
65 Inverness native
67 Funeral stands
69 Run out
72 "Tell ___ lies"
73 Jimmie Rodgers or Tex Owens, musically
75 Bun contents
76 Make ___ dash
78 Mountains, rivers, plains, etc.
82 More sinister
85 Blackjack decision
86 "The Magnificent Seven" co-star
87 Suffix with human
89 Actor Hill of "Moneyball"
90 Mind
92 Spanish winds
93 Distilled vis-à-vis tap
95 Gospel singer Winans
96 Like the "ng" sound
98 "___ who?!"
99 Fancy salad ingredient
101 Org. making grants to museums
103 Big faucet maker
105 University in North Carolina
106 Rear
110 Genealogical study
112 Articles aren't found in it
117 London transportation
119 Marlon Brando film
121 Set free
122 "Cheers" bartender Sam
123 Movie droid
124 Fastener patented in 1939
125 Pivoted
126 ___-Japanese

DOWN

1 Alternative to dieting, informally
2 "Just ___!"
3 Bartering locale
4 ___ Robles, Calif.
5 Checked (out)
6 Antecede
7 ___ Rose
8 Bills, e.g.
9 Most 17-Down
10 Plant pores
11 "You missed ___"
12 Grok
13 Sir Anthony Eden, 1st Earl of ___
14 Pulitzer winner for "John Brown's Body"
15 Brother's place
16 Early life forms?
17 See 9-Down
18 Refrain syllables
19 Send some pixxx?
24 Network connections
28 Environs
31 Incapacitate
33 Subject of the documentary "An Unreasonable Man"
35 Helter-skelter
36 Bar ___
37 Cavemen
38 Blows up
39 Eve who wrote "The Vagina Monologues"
41 Has parked
43 South Dakota memorial site
44 Modern December birthstone
45 White elephant, e.g.
48 TiVo precursor
49 "Eavesdrop" from across the room, say
52 It's felt on the head
54 "Time ___ . . ."
55 Poetic preposition
58 Only Hitchcock film to win Best Picture
60 Minnesota twins?
61 Song that starts "A winter's day in a deep and dark December"
65 Draw (off): Var.
66 Premium Cuban cigar brand
68 Nationals whose flag declares "God is great"
69 What echoes do
70 Clear the atmosphere of
71 Sod house locale
74 Min. or max.
75 Sweets
77 Capt.'s superior
79 Drew in
80 Old-timer
81 Some M.I.T. grads
83 Per
84 Korea's Syngman ___
88 Like some housecats
91 "Gone With the Wind" bad guys
93 Yammer
94 First TV show to debut at #1 in the Nielsen ratings
97 Eye up and down
99 Discordant
100 General Motors subsidiary
102 Feeling pervading Brat Pack movies
104 Towers
106 Reynolds of "Boogie Nights"
107 From the top
108 Mid fifth-century year
109 Hofbräuhaus crowd?

by Daniel A. Finan

111 Place after place
113 Home of the Norte Chico civilization
114 Part of 101-Across
115 Corp. money types
116 Switch attachment?
118 Metered praise
120 Charlotte-to-Raleigh dir.

ACROSS

1 "___ Mucho" (#1 oldie)
7 Sublime, in hip-hop slang
10 Former Mercury model
15 ___ Grand
18 Dragon slayer of myth
19 Stick on a table
20 Prayer opener
21 Big Apple baseball name
23 An elderly woman was having dinner with her husband and was . . .
27 Biblical verb endings
28 Pen pal?
29 At sea
30 Guilty ___
31 ___ polloi
32 Africa's bygone ___ Empire
34 Big tug
35 Big shots they're not
37 Geom. shapes
38 She said "After all these years . . ."
43 Foursomes
44 Squeeze (out)
45 Big name in makeup
46 Supped
47 Spanish bear
48 Destination NW of LAX
50 Colorful moths
51 Then she remarked ". . ."
58 Clock sound
60 Verbalized
61 Be sociable, say
62 Barack Obama's mama
63 Jug part
64 Card game similar to écarté

66 Domestic
69 Old despots
71 Bribe
72 Med. plan
74 ___ kiss
75 St. Pete stadium, with "the"
77 She, in Siena
78 Her husband asked ". . . ?"
83 Diplomat: Abbr.
84 "Home away from home" grp.
85 Halftime staples
86 Game cry
87 One whose star is dimmed
90 Hit sign
91 Places to find people lying
95 Then he asked "Or . . . ?"
99 Dr. Jekyll creator's monogram
100 Single
101 Botanical balm
102 Word with free or bound
103 Average
104 Architect Saarinen
106 Reminder of a sort
107 Have
108 ___ dixit
109 The woman replied ". . . "
115 Terse denial
116 Sci-fi film with an android named Ash
117 "What am ___ do?"
118 "As good as done"
119 L.A. hours
120 Man with a mission, maybe
121 Go-ahead
122 Serenaded

DOWN

1 Single, say
2 Perfect example
3 Skillful reasoner
4 Bernese ___
5 Mid 11th-century year
6 Long stretch
7 Like Steve Jobs, e.g.
8 Blockhead
9 Grazing ground
10 Maryland, once
11 Skagway locale
12 Blogger's bit
13 They make 39-Down: Abbr.
14 Courtroom words
15 Gaping mouths
16 Gil ___, original lead role on "CSI"
17 Winner of 2009's Best Supporting Actress Oscar for "Precious"
22 Places to relax
24 Underwater breathing aids
25 Smooth finish
26 Quick end to a boxing match?
32 Mazda roadster
33 Pilgrims John and Priscilla
34 Comedian Smirnoff
35 It's a wrap
36 Toe woe
39 They sometimes divide neighborhoods
40 Some royalties
41 Printing problem
42 Baseball manager Ned
47 Grab bag
48 Make some waves
49 Obsessed about
51 With no warmth

52 Deep border lake
53 Board that's disposable
54 Sported
55 Alcohol producer
56 Dinghy duo
57 ___ Minor
58 Lacking depth, in brief
59 Cairo's river
65 Bowling ball feature
67 Titan's place
68 Portfolio options, for short
70 Beach debris also known as rockweed
73 Comic British character who rarely speaks
76 J.F.K. transport
79 Hops dryer
80 Petunia Dursley, to Harry Potter
81 Raymond's mother on "Everybody Loves Raymond"
82 Christmas decoration
87 Toboggan ride's starting point
88 Stat for Steve Nash
89 When to tour Tours?
90 Like 14-Down
91 Knievel feat
92 Lacing (into)
93 Perturbed
94 Sign off on
96 Virus carrier, maybe
97 Musical star Paige who played the original Evita
98 1994 biopic
99 Pull (in)

by David J. Kahn

105 Let out
106 Declined a bit
107 ___ von Bismarck
108 Game cry
110 Select
111 ___ française
112 Game cry
113 How-dos
114 Australian runner

ACROSS

1 "Hansel and Gretel" figure
4 Collection of sketches, for short
7 Kind of port
10 Like most of the Swiss flag
13 Kind of trail
18 Gobbled down
20 Provide for
22 Give out one's address?
23 Northern bird
24 ___ nerve
25 Quidnunc
26 Saunter with style
27 American millionaire lost with the 63-Across
29 Two-time All-Star Martinez
30 Like a friendly dog's tail
31 Kind of trip
32 Medical pioneer Sir William
33 With 88-Across, 1960 musical partly about the 63-Across, with "The"
38 ___ blood-typing
41 Fraternal org.
42 Family
44 Land in Central America
45 [Like that!]
46 Dolt
47 Big name in lawn products
50 Singer Winans
51 Recover, as a sunken ship
52 Old PC screen
53 Takes the crown in
54 Plays, with "in"
55 Cager Baylor
56 Letter earner
58 Generation ___
60 Collect dust
61 Science fiction author Frederik
62 Start of a children's rhyme
63 Theme of this puzzle
65 Transmitted, as an S O S
66 Wise off to
67 Landscaper's buy
68 Monopoly token
69 Like tsunami-affected areas
72 Nobelist poet Neruda
73 Classic black-and-white film featuring gigantic irradiated ants
75 Peeved
77 Some tubes carry them
78 Arrive by plane
79 Prefix with plane
80 Gushes
81 Cartoon canine
82 Detective's assignment
83 What scattered things are said to be all over
85 "Don't think so"
86 Maritime danger
87 Radical '60s org.
88 See 33-Across
91 Some reuniongoers
93 Summer cooler
94 "___ Walked Into My Life" ("Mame" song)
95 Moon feature
96 What the 63-Across crossed to begin her 88-/13-Down
103 Does the hair just so
106 Toast in Toledo
107 College voter
108 Birth announcement
109 Washington, but not Adams
110 Be behind schedule
111 Clinks
112 Bygone
113 Bowflex target
114 École ___ arts
115 "Piers Morgan Tonight" airer
116 Collecting a pension: Abbr.

DOWN

1 Unwelcome reception
2 Title girl on "Introducing . . . The Beatles"
3 2003 James Cameron documentary about the 63-Across
4 Ferris's girlfriend in "Ferris Bueller's Day Off"
5 63-Across's destination on her 88-/13-Down
6 "Bad" cholesterol, for short
7 Not yet planted
8 "For example . . . ?"
9 "Give me your best shot!"
10 Actress Lee of "Funny Face"
11 Novelist Ambler
12 1920s–'30s style, informally
13 See 88-Down
14 Kindergarten comeback
15 Big huff?
16 Hall-of-Fame QB Graham
17 Stern
19 For some time
21 Atlantic City casino, with "the"
27 Short outings
28 Banjoist Fleck
32 Some modern museum designs
34 One-named singer/actress associated with Warhol
35 Continues
36 Frigid
37 Seaport in western France
38 1955 Walter Lord book about the 63-Across
39 Spaghetti sauce seasoning
40 ___ seas
41 It's about 20 miles north of Lauderdale
43 Actress Skye
45 Permanent sites?
47 "Benson" actress
48 Work in wildlife preservation?
49 Put back, in a way
51 Second go-rounds
57 Comic actor Nielsen
59 Cry with the shake of a pompom
63 Close behind
64 Spends some time out?
65 Where the 63-Across's 88-/13-Down began
66 Word with bar or fork
67 "60 Minutes" correspondent
69 Mrs. Dithers of "Blondie"
70 Professes

by Victor Fleming and John Dunn

71 Director Fritz
72 Some basic training grads
74 Biblical kingdom where Moses died
76 Mole's work
83 A lot
84 Newspaper or magazine offering
86 Early stage of a time capsule project
88 With 13-Down, disastrous event for the 63-Across
89 Distinguished
90 "___ the love?"
92 "The Far Side" cartoonist
93 Champagne holder
96 Canadian station
97 Like some parks: Abbr.
98 Joyful
99 Queen of myth
100 Wood or iron
101 Brooding types
102 Frequently injured knee part: Abbr.
104 Go (over)
105 Method: Abbr.
108 1887–1996 govt. watchdog

ACROSS

1 Many a download
4 "___ well"
8 Certain bias
14 Some storage places
19 Emu, e.g., to a chef
21 This second
22 Put down
23 A woman went . . .
25 Tricks
26 Expressionist artist James
27 Suffer vertigo
28 Fast-skating #4
29 Scratch
30 Cause of delay
31 In his office, she noticed a . . .
36 A superstar might have a big one
37 Thin overlays
38 No-goodnik
39 Michelle on a fairway
40 Not allowing
42 She remembered having a high-school crush on a handsome, dark-haired boy with . . .
47 What's that, José?
48 ___ Khan
51 BP gas brand
52 Voting side
53 However, this man was balding, gray-haired and . . .
59 North end?
60 Plains tribe
61 Had room for
65 Michelle's predecessor
68 She thought he was much too old to have been her . . .
73 Debussy piece
74 Lands' End rival
76 Bodes
78 Zero
79 Nevertheless, she asked him if he had attended her high school, and after he said yes, she asked ". . . ?"
86 Carry
89 Stew
90 "One Mic" rapper
91 Actor McKellen
92 He answered "In 1971. But . . ."
95 The Dow and the Nikkei 225
99 Object
100 Turndowns
101 Go-aheads
105 1969 newlywed in the news
106 The woman exclaimed ". . . !"
111 Chorus girl
112 Spice holder
113 See 48-Down
114 Breather
115 Divorce
116 Hall-of-Famer with 10 World Series rings
118 He looked at her closely, then asked ". . . ?"
121 "The Second Coming" poet
122 Thoroughly enjoys
123 One wearing cuffs
124 "Family Ties" mom
125 Check line
126 Shipped
127 Feminine suffix

DOWN

1 Not the way it was
2 Some servitude
3 1994 Sondheim musical
4 From the States: Abbr.
5 ___ Michele of "Glee"
6 Midwest capital
7 Plain
8 TV Guide's Pennsylvania headquarters
9 From ___ Z
10 Brown shade
11 Emcee's words
12 Disdain
13 113-Across, in France
14 Exhaust
15 Father of the bride, say
16 One who goes free?
17 With 34-Down, kind of pie
18 Yearbook div.
20 Superbright
24 Trick
29 Soft leather
31 From the top
32 Phoenix hrs.
33 Tail
34 See 17-Down
35 Some jeans
37 Big name in plastic
41 Still
43 Space movie villain
44 Rock genre
45 ___ Canals
46 Bother a lot
48 With 113-Across, landlocked waters
49 Blown away
50 Mellows
53 Come together
54 Russian/Kazakh river
55 Brush-off
56 Laptop key
57 Time piece?
58 At birth
62 Sushi fish
63 Take out, maybe
64 Take out
66 Say "I do" again
67 Spa reaction
69 Unstable particle
70 Río contents
71 Canal boats
72 Mess up
75 Rome's home
77 Symbols of piety
80 Hanging piece
81 Joanne of "The Pride of St. Louis"
82 Org. in "The Crying Game"
83 Bad: Prefix
84 Pops
85 Valve opening?
86 Bob ___, 1986 P.G.A. Player of the Year
87 One of the Three Rivers
88 Nine-time world champion rodeo cowboy
93 24 bottles of beer
94 Mary ___ cosmetics
95 Coming up
96 Sort
97 Attracts by design
98 Palliates
102 Cruise lines?
103 Runner's place
104 Snap courses
107 ___ and all
108 Bandleader Jones of the 1920s–'30s
109 "Cool!"
110 Island near Quemoy
111 Goons

by David J. Kahn

115 Opposite of
64-Down
116 "TTYL"
117 Reef denizen
118 "Are __ pair?"
("Send in the
Clowns" lyric)
119 Bug for payment
120 Table server

ACROSS

1 Little reminders
8 Bad record, e.g.
14 Coiled killers
18 Home of Elaine, in Arthurian legend
19 Pirate's support
20 Donne piece
22 "Should I say 'Come here often?' or 'Hey, babe!'"?
24 Recite, as a prayer
25 See 23-Down
26 Area banning pub regulars?
28 Heartache
30 "Before I forget . . ."
32 Losing tic-tac-toe row
33 Actor Penn of "Van Wilder"
34 Kind of jelly
37 Connecting word
38 Pirate's support?
41 Capitol Records' parent co.
42 Lines on a Dan Brown best seller?
48 "Riddle-me-___"
49 Like some yoga
50 Sworn secrecy
51 Settled (on)
53 E.T.'s ability to use the lower part of a keyboard?
58 Carpet option
61 Subject for gossip
62 Easily swayed
63 ___ Dan (Israeli archaeological site)
64 Guidebook recommendation
67 Not in the country
70 N.Y.C. avenue
71 "Welcome to the Jungle" rocker
73 Support provider
74 Crux
75 Where dimwitted people pay to drink?
82 Won
83 Some potatoes
84 Smoothie ingredients
88 Starts of some reproductions
90 Like a former 97-pound weakling?
93 It's bad to be over it
94 To be, to Augustus
95 Chemical suffix
96 When Macbeth asks "Is this a dagger which I see before me?"
97 "Holy smokes!," to a teen
98 Montréal's ___ des Soeurs
100 No. 2: Abbr.
102 Little guy
103 Dramatic production about Ivory or Dial?
108 1974 hit whose title is sung twice after "Como una promesa"
113 Horn of Africa native
114 Certain cases of the munchies?
118 Early online forum
119 Author of the 2009 book subtitled "A Plan to Solve the Climate Crisis"
120 Protest sign
121 Quagmire
122 Midday meeting
123 Chic

DOWN

1 Mitt
2 Kyrgyzstan city
3 Attica, e.g., informally
4 Carry-on
5 Lund of "Casablanca"
6 Headwear worn over dreadlocks
7 Eye problem
8 Day ___
9 Coastal fliers
10 Home under the midnight sun
11 Silver-tongued
12 Actress Suvari
13 New ___
14 DreamWorks's first animated film
15 Where an Englishman might get a break?
16 George Orwell, e.g.
17 Agate alternative
20 Storage spot
21 Jet black
23 With 25-Across, a puzzle
27 Picture, commercially
28 Small bit of power
29 Injury-monitoring org.
31 High-end French retailer
35 Aid in lost and found
36 Co-worker of Homer on "The Simpsons"
37 Underworld activities
38 Singer Anthony
39 El Prado hangings
40 Union deserter, maybe
43 The King Henry who founded the Tudor dynasty
44 Push
45 Show of pride
46 "Our Gang" girl
47 Spanish hero of yore
52 Subj. of Form 1040's line 32
54 Tiny complaint
55 How to address a maj.?
56 Small part of a pound?
57 Modern communication
58 Opposite of leg., in music
59 Prefix with -pod
60 Annual baseball events
64 Some campfire makers
65 Home of Kansai International Airport
66 Special delivery on Sun.
67 Divide up
68 Some sweet wines
69 Rembrandt van ___
72 Fraternity chapter #17
73 Bruised, say
74 Big initials in news
76 Cries of disgust
77 Betting line
78 Broccoli ___
79 Japanese port
80 Stat for Seaver or Santana
81 "Ta-___ Boom-de-ay"
85 Score on a night out
86 Lamb not found on a farm

by Ian Livengood

87 Tried to make it home, say
88 Pouch bearer
89 Skedaddle
91 Tack
92 A.T.M. button
98 Suffix with contempt
99 Bébé's need
100 Match play?
101 Buffalo N.H.L.'er
104 Roasts
105 Home of the Bahla Fort and nearby oasis
106 Arizona's ___ Verde Nuclear Generating Station
107 Hence
109 Eastern blueblood
110 School near the Royal Windsor Racecourse
111 Radio choices: Abbr.
112 Strained
115 ___ Lingus
116 Kenan's old partner on Nickelodeon
117 D.C.-to-Va. Beach direction

ACROSS

1 Words before a discounted price
7 TV network force
13 Pickle juices
19 Go-getter
20 Hometown of old radio's Fibber McGee and Molly
21 Noted parent in tabloids
23 Not level
24 Did sleight of hand with
25 Food often dipped in soy sauce
26 Band whose 1998 song "One Week" was #1 for one week
29 Tennis's Ivanisevic
30 Astrologer to the rich and famous
33 Softens
34 More furtive
36 PC key
37 Lab instructor?
39 Reduced amount?
40 1950s pinup queen ___ Page
42 Spartan walkway
43 Bridge position
44 ___ generis
45 "After you"
46 Pear variety
48 Milky Way, for one
50 Didn't accept, with "on"
53 One way for drivers to turn
55 NASA recruiting site
56 In the past, once
60 "Give ___ rest!"
61 ___-ray Disc
63 Gift from above
65 Shreve who wrote "The Pilot's Wife"
66 Onetime head of the Medellín drug cartel
69 Mattel announced their breakup in 2004
71 Name in 2000 headlines
72 Set up
76 Alphabet trio
77 Tapping site
78 Big name in lens care
79 Dernier ___
80 Sandler's "Spanglish" co-star
82 With good order
84 Classic western slugfest
87 It's just below a B
89 Really use an opportunity well
92 CPR pro
93 Slinky, e.g.
94 Togo's capital
98 Writer/philosopher Hannah
99 General name on a menu?
100 Three-stringed instruments
102 Roman 1,002
103 Children's song refrain
105 "Death of a Salesman" role
106 Best Buy buy
107 Wars, in ancient Rome
109 Plan on ordering a drink, say
112 Loose
114 Actress Dolores of the silent era
115 Brand advertised with a cow
119 Member of an assaulting party
120 Leveling tool
121 Blue boys?
122 Fervid
123 Choir supports
124 Currency replaced by the euro

DOWN

1 Rushing stat: Abbr.
2 Popeye's gal
3 Juan's one
4 New Year's Eve wear
5 Egyptian god of the universe
6 "Star Wars" guru
7 Beseeches
8 Resolved
9 Suitcase convenience
10 "Aunt ___ Cope Book"
11 Multicolored
12 Really mean
13 Giving orders
14 Pioneer in quadraphonic records
15 "I love this!"
16 Big Apple neighborhood
17 Gulf state
18 Civil war locale beginning in 1991
22 Made, as money
27 Sharply reprimanded
28 Just
30 Takes too much
31 Witty saying
32 Fifth word of the Gettysburg Address
35 W.W. II craft
38 Etui item
39 Jails, in British slang
41 Finis
44 Drop
45 Quiet transportation
47 Simon of Duran Duran
48 ___-Magnon
49 Present opener?
50 Parade tooter
51 Dickens title opener
52 Vaccine pioneer
54 "The Killing Fields" actor Haing S. ___
57 "___-Tikki-Tavi"
58 Word with plate or plant
59 Like grapefruit juice
62 Grp. whose seal has the words "This we'll defend"
64 Irving Bacheller novel "___ Holden"
65 Caper
67 Ralph ___ né Lifshitz
68 Steal
70 Equal in height
73 Avis alternative
74 Lizard look-alike
75 Football score abroad
79 South American animal with a snout
81 Quarantine advocates
83 Part of the next-to-last line of the Lord's Prayer
85 "My stars!"
86 Mend, in a way, as a metal joint
88 Lounge in many a hotel
89 Fearsome snakes
90 Mozart's "Un bacio di mano," e.g.
91 Garrison in Minnesota

by Elizabeth C. Gorski

93 More like Bette Midler stage shows
95 Green-lights
96 Common middle name for a girl
97 Biblical verb ending
99 Cravat holder
100 Recurring Matt Damon title role
101 Not out
104 "The Great Movies" author
105 Actor Waggoner and others
108 Product of fatback
110 Italian author Primo
111 Recipe abbr.
113 Brig. ___
116 Rap's Dr. ___
117 Little amphibian
118 Hush-hush grp.

ACROSS

1 Desert Storm transports
8 Is sociable
13 Annoyed with persistent petty attacks
20 Qualify
21 Contest site
22 1994 Red Hot Chili Peppers album
23 Rabbi or mullah
24 Like most Western music
25 Went over completely
26 March ___
27 John McCain and John Kerry
30 Dog command
31 Gig for a deejay
33 Sped
34 For-EV-er
35 Steeplechase, e.g.
36 Idle
38 Emulated a hungry wolf
40 Common rolls
42 River crossed by the Longfellow Bridge
44 Clogs at the bottom?
45 Arrive at by air
46 Repair shop figs.
47 British P.M. after Lloyd George
49 Ward, to the Beaver
50 Payday, often: Abbr.
51 Crash-investigating org.
52 Striped stones
55 What "Arf! Arf!" or "Meow!" may mean
57 "The Real World" airer
60 2009 hit film with subtitled scenes

62 Earn
63 Word on either side of "à"
66 Contributes
68 Transfer, as at a nursery
70 "The Charge of the Light Brigade" figure
72 Block component
73 "Wedding Crashers" co-star, 2005
76 Evolutionary chart
77 Key of Chopin's "Polonaise-Fantaisie"
79 Tina Fey and Amy Poehler, once, on "S.N.L."
80 "Spider-Man" director
81 "Get lost!"
83 Ft. Collins setting
84 Abbr. on a currency exchange board
85 Toy company behind yo-yos
86 Entered carefully
88 Canyonlands National Park features
90 Bands on the run?
91 Aircraft control surface
93 Good name for a surveyor?
94 Some Muslims
95 Those near and dear
98 Quality of new-fallen snow
101 "___ Pieces" (Peter and Gordon hit)
102 Congolese river
104 Nondemocratic rule
105 Short answers?
106 Kind of scan, for short

107 Keepers of the flame?
111 E.R. readout
112 Old nuclear watchdog: Abbr.
113 Dutch city ESE of Utrecht
114 Toil
115 The Beavers of the N.C.A.A.
116 QB's miscue
117 Newcastle-to-London dir.
118 Play that introduced the word "robot"
119 Anathematic
120 Break, of a sort
121 Some Windows systems

DOWN

1 Eighth Hebrew letter
2 Discovers
3 Post-flood locale
4 The other way around
5 Old verb ending
6 About 16,900 ft., for 3-Down
7 Letter's end?
8 The situation
9 Tree with very hard timber
10 TV title character who said "I'm not an Amazon"
11 Covered, as cookware
12 Some gunfire
13 Overhead ___
14 Cadence syllables
15 "Let's make ___ true Daily Double"
16 Plant with purple flowers
17 Name of 13 popes
18 Gold and silver, but not bronze
19 ___ City, Fla.

28 Antiquity, poetically
29 Demise
32 Course for new U.S. arrivals
35 King on un trono
36 A-one service?
37 Setting for part of 2005's "Munich"
39 Royal name in Norway
40 Use for skating
41 Break down
43 Infernal
45 Big name in mustard
48 Sloppy, as a kiss
50 Sword: Fr.
53 ___-X
54 "Oh, joy!," e.g., typically
55 Inane
56 ___ Miller (Julie Christie title role with 57-Down)
57 Warren Beatty title role with 56-Down
58 Group with a board of governors
59 Weekly since 1955, with "The"
61 Type in again, as a password
62 "After you"
63 Vessel seen just below the surface?
64 Hired gun, in gang slang
65 Coils
67 Clotting agent
69 Plastic used in piping
71 Subs
74 Marcel Marceau, e.g.
75 [This makes me mad!]

by Peter A. Collins

78 Satisfied, for a while at least
80 #2's
82 Home recorder
85 Repair shop job
87 Teetotaler
89 U.S.S.R. part: Abbr.
90 What may help one live and learn?
92 Classic hair removal brand
94 Catch some flies
95 Some beans
96 Meanies
97 Hack
98 Overly caffeinated
99 Pooped
100 Some NCOs
103 "___ Enchanted" (2004 film)
104 V
108 U.R.L. ender
109 Brewhouse fixture
110 Code-breaking grp.

ACROSS

1 Thicken
10 Pirates' home
17 Venezuelan's "very"
20 1994 biography of Calvin Klein
21 1937 Cole Porter tune
22 Serpent's tail?
23 Be willing to apprehend Mr. Bradley at any cost?
25 Original "I Love Lucy" airer
26 "What ___!"
27 Doo-wop syllable
28 "Oh, baloney!"
30 One awaiting a shipment, maybe
31 Punish Mr. Harris in a medieval way?
39 Person with a mortgage, e.g.
41 Menotti's "Lullaby," for one
42 Epitome of thinness
43 Get Mr. Koch addicted to a modern reading method?
48 Fashion's Gucci
49 To the point
50 "Pictures ___ Exhibition"
51 Down a submarine, say
53 Evade
57 Barrel in a bar
61 Kind of wave
65 Hungarian city known for its thermal baths
66 Preside over Mr. O'Neill's baptism?
69 ___ Long, Union general in the Civil War
70 "___ Carter III," best-selling album of 2008
71 Smallest member of the European Union
72 Idle
73 Criminalize
74 Letters on Ozzie Smith's cap
75 Do Mr. Sullivan's stand-up material?
79 French weapon
80 Montaigne work
82 "That seems to be the case"
83 Act of coming out
85 Madre's hermano
87 Fur fighters?
89 Opinion pieces
90 Made in France?
93 Prohibit Mr. McMahon from ever socializing again?
100 Pool organism
101 12-Down soldiers, for short
102 Set as a goal
103 Perform brain surgery on Mr. Begley?
108 Mgr.'s aide
112 Singer ___ Khan
113 Virginia ___
114 Military march
115 Suffix with Ecuador or Euclid
116 Put Mr. Meese in an Armani suit?
125 Mauna ___
126 Treater's phrase
127 Where the stars might be pointing?
128 Longtime 25-Across president Moonves
129 Brand name that used to be spelled out in commercials
130 Star Alliance member

DOWN

1 Lee of NBC News
2 U.S. president whose mother's first name was Stanley
3 109-Down portrayer in 2003's "Elf"
4 Approaches
5 Purposes
6 "Turn On, Tune In, Drop Out" subject
7 Give a leg up
8 Part of Italy where Cape Spartivento is
9 Disney doe
10 Haughty
11 "The Divorcee" actress Shearer
12 Civil War org.
13 Bud
14 Noted Cosell interviewee
15 Colorado, e.g.: Abbr.
16 Doesn't give up
17 One of the Jackson 5
18 Not yet in the oven
19 One side's retort to "No, you don't!"
24 R.M.N. served under him
29 Some clouds
31 Apiphobiac's fear
32 Grand Forks sch.
33 Auto last made in 1936
34 "99 Luftballons" singer, 1984
35 Noted John Boehner feature
36 Prefix with Cities
37 Souse's sound
38 Slip (into)
40 Mike and ___ (some jellybeans, informally)
43 Brooklyn ___
44 Trying experiences
45 Mom-and-pop grps.
46 Fit
47 Linear
49 "Mogambo" threat
52 Fax cover sheet abbr.
54 Transport on a slope
55 Greece, to Greeks
56 Retailer with a cat and dog in its logo
58 Numbers game
59 Call up
60 "___ while they're hot!"
62 Interrogate, in a way
63 Dessert menu phrase
64 Sheets and such
67 "Esmé" writer
68 Beak or beat
71 Early 12th-century year
76 Sister company of ABC
77 Title
78 Ballet leap
79 Hope
81 Take the offensive
84 Caramel-filled treat
86 Figure in Tom Thumb tales
88 Wife of Esau
90 Adipocyte
91 Elvis sings it in "Blue Hawaii"

by David Levinson Wilk

92 Household pets that need ultraviolet light in their cages
94 Buttons on the big screen
95 Geisha's accessory
96 "Top Gun" org.
97 Disgusted cry
98 Medical suffix
99 "Mayberry ___"
104 Welcomed, as a guest at the door
105 Motif
106 Epitome of hotness
107 911 responder
109 See 3-Down
110 1994 action flick with the tagline "Get ready for rush hour"
111 "The Constant Gardener" heroine
114 Sicilian city
117 Way to go: Abbr.
118 Un-P.C. suffix
119 Souse
120 TV show filmed at 30 Rock
121 ___ sort
122 You: Fr.
123 Not vert.
124 And the rest: Abbr.

ACROSS

1 Roast V.I.P.'s
4 Overall composition?
9 Military funeral concluder
13 Cars with floor-mounted ignitions
18 Density symbol, in physics
19 By itself
20 Kaaba visitor's faith
22 Say grudgingly
23 "I suppose it might seem odd that a reverend like myself would suddenly begin ___ . . ."
26 Top-___ (golf ball brand)
27 "Dirt cake" ingredients
28 Equine-related
29 Gun it
31 ". . . but I've always thought ___ had a more fun job than I do"
35 "For an avid philatelist like me, sorting envelopes is thrilling - I might spot a ___!"
37 Kind of ceremony
38 Show no modesty
39 Marvin of "Cat Ballou"
40 Friday's rank: Abbr.
43 Had
44 Poor writer's scribbling?
45 Indo-Europeans
48 "When a man is nervous about shipping breakables, I tell him, '___ carefully, sir' . . ."

52 Domino's order
53 Whirlybird
54 Actress Peeples
55 Big name in rum
59 Round-trippers, in sports lingo
60 ". . . and I write '___' on the box, which seems to reassure him"
64 Cambridgeshire's ___ Cathedral
65 Viking's destination
66 Don Juan's mother
67 "___ had enough"
68 "The best part of the job, of course, is when I'm out on the street ___"
73 Drawers of war?
76 Mesabi Range export
77 Tee-___
78 Remote place
79 Food label no.
80 "I'm a bit leery of dogs - it's unsettling to enter a yard and hear some ___ at me . . ."
84 From scratch
87 Lover of light
88 Distress
89 Old inits. in telecommunication
90 Vegas casino hotel, with "the"
91 The Bahamas' Great ___ Island
93 Novel for which Sartre declined the Nobel Prize
96 ". . . but dogs can't spoil how much I enjoy driving around in the ___"
99 "Homeowners get excited when they see me opening their ___ . . ."

104 Least bright
105 Eighty-eight
107 Dry out
108 "The Hot Zone" topic
109 ". . . and when I hand-deliver a package, the recipients are positively ___ - it's very satisfying!"
114 Fountain drinks
115 Berry of "Frankie and Alice"
116 Histrionics
117 Poetic preposition
118 Daisy variety
119 Ugly situation
120 Matches timewise, informally
121 Acid

DOWN

1 1983 Michael Keaton comedy
2 Single-named "Hollywood Squares" regular
3 Results of chafing
4 Place to get a facial
5 Film director Roth
6 Tours turndown
7 Having one sharp
8 Manner
9 Ziggurat features
10 Interviews
11 Finishes
12 ___ ammoniac
13 More guarded
14 Onetime Freud collaborator
15 Queen in the "Star Wars" saga
16 Asphalt ingredient
17 Open terrain
21 Desert landforms
24 Flummery
25 ___ de combat
30 It comes from the heart

32 Comes to
33 Forest flutist
34 Palm phone
36 Hit with a charge
38 Flapper's wrap
40 Bookish type
41 Soviet foreign affairs minister during the Cuban missile crisis
42 Answering machine insert
44 2010 Apple release
46 Rolling in green
47 Triumphant cry
49 Revivalism?
50 Leave weaponless
51 Bygone Tide rival
53 French sweetie
55 Industry, slangily
56 Wardrobe items
57 Fork
58 Dunne of "My Favorite Wife"
60 Small island
61 It's closeted
62 Put the kibosh on
63 Film director Craven
65 Title for de Staël: Abbr.
69 On the subject of
70 Moves a head?
71 Golden ___ (General Mills product)
72 "Forget it!"
73 Striking player
74 Symbol of Athena
75 Lincoln while in Congress, e.g.
78 Babel
80 Car financing inits.
81 Where prisoners swing picks
82 Ear: Prefix
83 ___ monde
84 Like the GE Building

by Patrick Berry

85 Locomotive furnace
86 Lost Colony's Island
92 Companion of Rex and Rover
93 Bird that may nest on volcanic ash

94 Unable to agree
95 Pack leaders
97 R&B's ___ Brothers
98 Car dealer's offering
99 Farmland rolls
100 Bungling fool
101 Fishing accoutrement

102 1980s–'90s Chrysler offerings
103 Iota
106 Woes
110 Mugger on stage
111 Not straight
112 Novelist McEwan
113 Station for cinephiles

21 CHICK LIT

ACROSS

1 Dinner party
8 Accompanied on a ticket
15 ___ Works
20 Biofuel option
21 Size of a football field, roughly
22 "Wyoming Outlaw," e.g.
23 Chick lit book #1 (1992)
25 Italy's longest river
26 ___ Pie Island (artist commune on the Thames)
27 Turned right
28 The Browns, on sports tickers
29 Headline
30 A nut might go on one
33 Chick lit book #2, with "The" (1843)
36 Bear witness
37 ___ Franco (watch brand)
38 "Down with thee!"
39 Chick lit book #3 (1965)
44 ___ D. Young (Time's Man of the Year in 1929)
48 Two-time N.B.A. M.V.P. Steve
49 Kerfuffles
50 Emphatic acceptance
51 Italian city where pizza was invented
53 Mich. neighbor
54 Clumsy handler
56 P.R. locale
58 Brand introduced by Philip Morris in 1975
59 Chick lit book #4 (1974)
64 Iron Man co-creator
67 Where 76-Across may be worn
68 Affixes on
69 Chick lit book #5 (1960)
74 "A Dog of Flanders" writer
75 Pip of "Great Expectations," e.g.
76 67-Across jewelry
77 Fold member
80 Says
82 Theater with fans
84 Political commentator Colmes
85 Nerve cell projection
86 Opponent of Napoleon
87 Chick lit book #6 (1930)
92 Start to production?
93 Tel Aviv's ___ Park
94 Refer (to)
95 Chick lit book #7 (1985)
101 Group in "Sex and the City," e.g.
103 Some washers and dryers
104 Wine container
105 Philadelphia's ___ Whitman Bridge
106 Environmental pollutant, for short
108 Snarl
109 Chick lit book #8 (1967)
114 Bracelet attachment
115 Christmas or Yom Kippur
116 Spread, as rumors
117 Some church overhead?
118 Bony
119 Game highlights shower

DOWN

1 Rose high in some people's estimation
2 Besides
3 Gossip fodder
4 Down, with "up"?
5 Mille & ___ Roses (Lancôme perfume)
6 School in the Patriot League
7 Stage light
8 Artery
9 True-crime writer Rule
10 Home of Agate Fossil Beds Natl. Monument
11 First horse to compete in all three Triple Crown races
12 With cold feeling
13 Stuck
14 Famous bathrobe wearer, informally
15 Folk guitarist Leo
16 1986 Indy 500 winner
17 Wombs
18 ___ the Short, early king of the Franks
19 Power cord feature
24 Chess opening?
29 "What moves you" sloganeer
31 Mosquito protection
32 Reno setting: Abbr.
33 180s
34 Vitamin and supplement chain
35 Night light?
36 ___ time (never)
37 Old or morning follower
40 Harsh treatment
41 "If at first, the ___ is not absurd, then there is no hope for it": Einstein
42 Ulster or Norfolk
43 Friends and neighbors
44 Broached
45 A quarrel
46 "A Cooking Egg" poet
47 Dodge S.U.V.
52 Affairs
54 Part of a support group
55 Skating maneuver
57 Femur or tibia
59 Rock singer Dee
60 "Just a ___"
61 Bookcase material
62 When most movies open: Abbr.
63 YouTube selection
64 Bar selection
65 Hypes
66 Dog named after a Japanese prefecture
70 Werewolf feature
71 Lakers star Lamar
72 Flame, e.g.
73 Impersonate, in a way
77 Clear of charges
78 Carpentry fastener
79 -ess alternative
81 2005 World Series team, for short
83 Classic sandwich
84 End in ___
85 Part of many ristorante dish names
88 Shift's end?
89 Book before Num.
90 Hesitates
91 Locale for many a gondola
92 Whence the phrase "I will both lay me down in peace, and sleep"
95 Conifer with durable wood
96 Home of ConAgra

by Brendan Emmett Quigley

97 Seagoing
98 Dia de los Reyes month
99 Group think?
100 Pacers' contests?
101 [blech!]
102 "Let's ___ There" (old NBC slogan)
105 Maze choices

107 Tanning salon fixtures
109 Doctor ___ from the planet Gallifrey
110 Samurai's home
111 Évian, e.g.
112 "Yo!"
113 Hue and cry

ACROSS

1 Ornate
5 Spreads
12 Old pol. entity
15 Like some skiing
16 Dark patch on a distant sun
17 Niña accompanier
18 Roams
19 Century in Amer. politics
20 Pony
21 Yenta's habit
23 River to the North Sea
24 Bally enthusiasts
26 Off-white pottery
28 Sharp-tongued
29 Land in a stream
31 Thin as ___
32 Temper
34 Galumph
36 They may get people talking
38 Jazz style
42 General Assembly figure, for short
43 Mine, to Marie
45 Sun Devils' sch.
46 Underlying
47 Dutch brews
50 Ticket presenter
51 Shred
53 Period of the Cenozoic Era
55 Meditate (on)
58 Like much of New Orleans's French Quarter
60 Beaver's home
61 Shankar piece
62 ___ acid
63 Hoedown seating
64 Pooh's pal
66 What you used to be?
68 Bickering
72 "I like your thinking"
76 "Cat ___," 1965 film

77 Red-haired film princess
79 Olds sedan
80 Shot source
82 Exchange fig.
83 Citrusy cocktail mixer
86 Focus of a class action?
88 Novelist Hoag
89 Cancún, e.g.
92 Flap
94 Drink with tempura, maybe
97 "Howards End" role
98 Centipede maker
101 Singular
102 Balancing acts?
103 Kaplan course, briefly
105 Waited longer than
107 Drillmaster's call
108 Called
110 Rhodes of the Rhodes scholarships
114 M.P.G. watcher
115 "make.believe" sloganeer
116 ___ guisada, Tex-Mex stew
117 Kind of gun
119 Continue
123 Twin Cities sch.
124 Waikiki wear
126 Yellow pool items
128 That, in Toledo
129 Sophocles title hero
131 Station line
134 ___ del Carmen, Mexico
135 Told stories
136 Norwegian king called "the 77-Down"
139 Clear
140 Station identification

143 Tie up
144 Pixar robot with a female voice
145 London daily
146 Rot
147 Letter in 145-Across
148 Cheat
149 Cheers

DOWN

1 Luggage
2 Asian capital name starter
3 P.R. people
4 ___ no
5 Some N.F.L.'ers
6 Runaway
7 Make ready for a winter storm, as a highway
8 Ed heard in "Up"
9 Bit of free time
10 Onesie wearer
11 Enter
12 Game piece
13 "Go" square in Monopoly, e.g.
14 Cinderella's wear, at home
16 Darling
22 Hawaiian pizza topping
25 Minstrel songs
27 Month before juin
29 Swift's "A Tale of ___"
30 Soap opera creator Phillips
33 "___ Mio"
35 Ambulance, slangily
37 One in a maze
39 Schemed together
40 For ___ (cheaply)
41 Alexander, to Aristotle
44 Sardegna, e.g.

47 Asia's ___ Sea
48 What writer's block may block
49 5-4 ruling, e.g.
52 Assembly area
54 Spanish food brand
55 Old PC part
56 O.K., in Osaka
57 Ones with the Christmas spirit?
59 Mariner of note
63 Steel or bronze
65 Card catalog abbr.
67 Tracker's aid
69 Child-sized mitt
70 Promise to pay
71 Large cask
73 The Crimson Tide, for short
74 Bass lover?
75 Irish Rose's beau
77 See 136-Across
78 "___ had it!"
81 Nine
84 Skater Midori
85 Exsiccates
87 Campsite sight
90 Slowing, in mus.
91 French possessive
93 Highlands daggers
95 Water color
96 "Survivor" homes
98 More than pale
99 Hosiery color
100 How some shares are sold
101 Suited to a person's strengths
104 Edible mushroom
106 Charge
109 Fork
111 Said "No fair!"
112 They have rates and ratings
113 Jay who jests

by Kevin G. Der

TRIPLE BONDS

ACROSS

1 Henry II player in "Becket"
7 Something that might get a rise out of people?
13 Clinch
16 Clinch, with "up"
19 Arrange again
20 Suburb of San Diego
21 "Livin' on a Prayer" band
23 Chinese restaurant offering / Wonderland affair / Group on the left?
25 Indigenous
26 Neo, for one
27 Baltimore specialty / Effortless task / Move on all fours with the belly up
29 Admit
31 Skins, e.g.
32 Ancient city NW of Carthage
36 Most red, maybe
39 Firmly fixed
43 Plunging / Play hooky / Vulgar
47 Scrunchies
51 Tip reducer?
52 Northern flier / Mixer maker / Put on the line
55 Buffoon
56 Lure
58 Idiots
59 "Up to ___," 1952 game show
60 ___ Hunt, Tom Cruise's character in "Mission: Impossible"
63 Sénat vote
64 God of shepherds
65 Dials

67 Yellowish brown / Bit of "dumb" humor / Many a forwarded e-mail
72 Hot cider server
74 Seat for toddlers
75 Time, in Torino
76 Indo-___
80 Item for a mason
81 Previous
84 Idiotic
86 Wonderment
87 Cause of congestion / Detective's challenge / Loony
90 Style of chicken
93 "Naturally!"
94 Winnie-the-Pooh possession / Baked entrée / Sweetie
96 Grow together
97 Best to follow, as advice
100 Attention getters
101 It's no good when it's flat
102 Hero
106 Fancy Feast product / Cafeteria outburst / "Mean Girls" event
114 Hooded jackets
118 ___ sunglasses
119 Democratic territory / Cardinal, e.g. / "Over the Rainbow" flier
122 Biracial Latin American
123 "Ditto!"
124 1966 best seller set in Hong Kong
125 See 126-Across
126 Half a 125-Across year: Abbr.

127 They might be crossed
128 "The Battleship Potemkin" setting

DOWN

1 Alternative to gov
2 Trillion: Prefix
3 Word with French or U.S.
4 Olive genus
5 Cross-country skiing
6 ___ deux âges (middle-aged: Fr.)
7 John Wayne western, with "The"
8 Toddler's need
9 Nickname for a seven-time N.B.A. All-Star
10 Frau's partner
11 Billionaire's home, maybe
12 Halfhearted R.S.V.P.'s
13 Letter-shaped support
14 Bean
15 German finale
16 "Brave New World" drug
17 ___ eye
18 Lit part
22 Ashkenazi, for one
24 Take in
28 Polo locale
30 New Deal inits.
32 They turn on hinges
33 A goner
34 "If only!"
35 Third-century year
37 "This ___ outrage!"
38 Reciprocal Fibonacci constant
39 Bomb

40 Suffix with drunk
41 Desk item
42 Kind of wave
44 "___ the season . . ."
45 Black in a cowboy hat
46 "Sleigh Ride" composer Anderson
48 Enero starts it
49 Times to remember
50 Med. land
53 Cornelius who wrote "A Bridge Too Far"
54 Creature worshiped by the Incas
57 As one
61 Appended
62 Zip
64 101-Across, e.g.
66 Alias initials
68 Bit of homework
69 Actress ___ Flynn Boyle
70 Rub out
71 Stimulating
72 Gladly
73 Old cry of dismay
77 Barks
78 Anticipate
79 Yucatán youth
80 Howe'er
82 "Treasure Island" inits.
83 Words before any month's name
84 Fortune profilees, for short
85 "Uh-huh"
88 ___ bono (for whose benefit?: Lat.)
89 "___ Bangs" (Ricky Martin hit)
91 Check, as text
92 Bklyn. ___

by Oliver Hill and Eliza Bagg

95 Kind of power, in math
98 Outs
99 Speech blocker
101 One going into a drive
103 Hall's partner
104 Santa ___
105 Bugged

106 They take vids
107 ___ plaisir
108 "Oh, pooh!"
109 Butcher's trimmings
110 Soulful Redding
111 Slime
112 Venezuela's Chávez

113 Colonial land: Abbr.
115 Rose's beau
116 ___ Bay (Manhattan area)
117 Sp. titles
120 But: Lat.
121 Some evidence

ALL-PRO

ACROSS

1 Reduces to pulp
7 Betray, in a way
15 They're unoriginal
20 Haitian ___
21 Haiti's first democratically elected president
22 Iconoclast
23 Skip Thanksgiving leftovers?
25 Early spring bloomers
26 Operagoer's accessory
27 Broke bread
28 Longfellow's words before "O Ship of State!"
29 Singer Sumac
30 Say "No," "Never" and "Uh-uh"?
34 Mrs. Robert ___ (Mary Custis)
36 Make a big stink
37 Chacon of the 1960s Mets
38 Put up with
41 One may be original
43 Hopelessly lost
47 Plea for immediate absolution?
52 Abbr. on a cover letter
53 Wind in front of a stage
54 Kin of fairies
55 Not
56 Crested ___, Colo.
58 Chairlift alternative
60 Shake
62 Blot with a paper towel, maybe
63 Like food that's acceptable to cattle?
67 Inuit relatives
69 Checked, say
70 Italian sportswear name
73 They come with turndown service
74 Soviet ___
75 Burial site of early Scottish kings
77 Rents
78 Pipe material, for short
79 Memorable theatrical performance?
83 Shell, e.g.
86 Warning from a driver
87 Extremely, in 1970s slang
88 Joyce's land
89 Bottom-line bigwigs, in brief
91 Head-turning sound
93 Abstain happily?
99 Fairy
102 Steven who co-wrote "Freakonomics"
103 New Guinea port
104 Life-threatening
107 Blow away
108 Is well-endowed?
111 One giving an order
112 Declared
113 Dammed river in North Carolina
114 Maurice of Nixon's cabinet
115 Region conquered by Philip II of Macedon
116 Mounts

DOWN

1 "Back to the Future" family name
2 "Get ___!"
3 California missions founder Junípero ___
4 Scottish poet James known as "The Ettrick Shepherd"
5 Southern university that shares its name with a biblical judge
6 Form a splinter group
7 Sled dog with a statue in New York's Central Park
8 Elizabeth in the cosmetics department
9 Abbr. following op. and loc.
10 The Wildcats of the Big 12 Conf.
11 Attack from the air
12 2010 chart-topper for Ke$ha
13 Like ___ in the headlights
14 Old Ottoman governor
15 Rural setting, in poetry
16 Green gemstone
17 Place in a Carlo Levi memoir
18 Scout's mission
19 David's weapon
24 Western tribe
28 Preposterous
31 Once, a long time ago
32 "Family Guy" creator MacFarlane
33 Ignore, imperatively
34 Barely beat
35 Oahu offering
38 In ___ (confused)
39 Mr. Burns's teddy bear on "The Simpsons"
40 Typical cemetery enclosure
41 Driver's target
42 Balloonhead
43 Seller of space or time, for short
44 Showy craft?
45 ___'acte
46 ___-deucy
48 Tennis's 1977 U.S. Open champ
49 Salon, e.g., informally
50 Accustom
51 ___-masochism
56 False deity
57 Baloney and then some
59 Dinner scraps
60 Memorable time
61 Vintage platters
62 Kebab go-with
64 Bravura
65 Cry to a mate
66 City east of the Sierra Nevada
67 Concert stack
68 Unexploded
71 Made haste
72 "___ dignus" (Latin motto)
74 Sans pizazz
75 Chapel line
76 Giant of old
79 Gist
80 Basic first step
81 Mateus ___
82 Chant syllables
84 Bear vis-à-vis the woods, e.g.
85 Fails miserably
89 Like a hair shirt

by Paula Gamache

90 Bordeaux brothers
91 La Môme ___ (The Little Sparrow)
92 Sharpening devices
93 Sword lilies, for short
94 Send, as a check
95 Trump who wrote "The Best Is Yet to Come"
96 Instant
97 Lensman Adams
98 Good to go
99 Dexterity exercise
100 Like an Interstate
101 Jumps bail, say
105 Say "What to do? What to do?," e.g.
106 To ___ (precisely)
108 Siamese, e.g.
109 Filing org.
110 H

ACROSS

1 Screen grp.?
4 Solzhenitsyn subject
9 Dives (into)
14 Song accompanied by a harp
19 Huffington Post buyer in 2011
20 Lyric muse
21 Wear down
22 Tree-lined path in une forêt
23 "I used to do drugs. ___": Mitch Hedberg
27 Invent
28 Ignores
29 Dam result, often
30 Sends one out of the park
33 Alone, in Paris
35 Lady of Lammermoor
36 "The car stopped on a dime. Unfortunately, the dime was ___": Anonymous
42 Mexican Valentine's greeting
43 Madre's hermano
44 Recuperate
46 Kind of diet
49 "Never mind"
52 Asian flatbread
55 Mystifying Geller
56 Biblical name meaning "hairy"
58 "I don't want to achieve immortality through my work. I want to achieve it ___": Woody Allen
63 Like Jack, it's said
66 Some doors
67 Exploding stars
68 "Whoever named it necking was ___": Groucho Marx
75 Sci-fi film with a hatching egg on its poster
76 Cork's place: Abbr.
77 More moist
79 "You know what I hate? Indian givers. ___": Emo Philips
86 Affix carelessly, with "on"
87 Crush, sportswise
88 Whisked mixture
89 Send continuously, as video
92 Physicist Georg
93 Cut off
97 Dinner table command, with "up"
99 Above
101 "I don't mean to sound bitter, cold or cruel, but I am ___": Bill Hicks
109 Fool's deck
110 Fashionable '70s dress
111 Breastbones
112 Saint's place
116 Essentials
119 Con Ed, e.g.: Abbr.
120 "I have the heart of a small boy. It ___": Stephen King
124 Classic role-playing game, for short
125 Dairy mascot
126 Slate, for one
127 Fooled
128 Out-line?
129 Perform à la Shakespeare
130 Place for military supplies
131 Mayo container?

DOWN

1 Feature of many a Jet Li film
2 "Already?"
3 Stanza successor
4 Get fixed?
5 19-Across has a much-used one
6 The Beatles during Beatlemania, e.g.
7 Heaps
8 Totally fail
9 Diving duds
10 J.F.K.'s successor
11 Forbidding
12 1960s doo-wop group with an automotive name, with "the"
13 Escorts to a second-floor apartment, say
14 First Congolese P.M. Lumumba
15 Czech neighbors
16 Liza Minnelli, for one
17 First pope to be called "the Great"
18 "Love ___ leave . . ."
24 Like Inspector Clouseau
25 Superlative prefix
26 Inside look?
31 Roger of "Cheers"
32 Pierre is there: Abbr.
34 Scottish psychiatrist R. D.
37 Squirt, e.g.
38 '13 grad in '11, e.g.
39 Biblical patriarch "righteous in this generation"
40 Decorative kit
41 Become a traitor
45 Glutton
46 Wet lowland
47 ___ Minor
48 Wettish
50 Crocus or freesia, botanically
51 Chinese gang
53 Eugene O'Neill's "___ Christie"
54 Palindromic time
57 Battle of the Atlantic vessel
59 Start of a fitness motto
60 Spot
61 Fruit that grows in a cluster
62 Cries of pain
64 Bugs Bunny's girlfriend
65 The Phantom of the Opera
69 Taunt
70 A law ___ itself
71 Venus and others
72 Grand slam, e.g.
73 Whence Venus?
74 When said three times, "Of course, obviously!"
78 Record stat
79 Sleep precursor
80 Gets charged up?
81 Really liking
82 "Quit your crying"
83 It's assumed
84 Nile menace, informally
85 Vegas attraction
90 Cashpoints
91 Vintner Claude
94 Doesn't cut
95 Empty pretense
96 Garage opener?
98 F-15, e.g.
100 Ann Landers or Ayn Rand: Abbr.

by Matt Ginsberg

102 Drove (along)
103 French walled city on the English Channel
104 Something that can't be patented
105 Like stadium seating
106 Daniel of Nicaragua
107 Simultaneity
108 Admonish, as a child
112 Aspect
113 Org. for part-time soldiers
114 Colada fruit
115 Latin 101 verb
117 What you might do after retiring
118 Fabric scrap, say
121 Family girl
122 6 letters
123 Thus far

USE IT OR LOSE IT

ACROSS

1 Fix, as a program
6 Water skimmers
10 Nickname for Baryshnikov
15 Gds.
19 Steve McQueen's ex-wife and co-star in "The Getaway"
21 Vogue's Wintour and others
22 Kind of torch
23 Electrical paths in New York City?
25 They're always charged
26 Flap
27 Poet's "before"
28 D preceder
29 Divert
31 Deux of these are better than un
33 Spill a Cuban drink?
36 Shelter that's often octagonal
39 Housing for the homeless: Abbr.
40 Pit crew's supply
41 One who says "Beg your pardon" after stepping on your toes?
47 Mordant Mort
49 "Exodus" hero
50 Father of Deimos and Phobos, in myth
51 Seedcase that inspired Velcro
52 Scot's "own"
53 Noblewoman
55 Dorm heads, for short
56 Mmes., in Iberia
57 Speak on C-Span, say
60 Burn cause
61 Gentleman's partner
63 Preachers' lies?

68 Get up?
69 Subj. of modern mapping
71 Bust planner, in brief
72 Sly sort?
73 What a mashed potato serving may have?
78 "Sock it to me!" show
80 Unbar, to the Bard
81 High-end camera
82 Superior body?
83 Abbr. unlikely to start a sentence
84 Revolutionary?
88 Continuing plot in a TV series
89 "___ Did It" (2007 memoir)
90 Cookie first baked in Manhattan's Chelsea district
91 "Confiteor ___ omnipotenti" (Latin prayer starter)
92 "Understood, man"
94 Hairdresser's first do?
97 Luggage attachment
99 Cartoon exclamation
101 One way to serve café
102 Author Amy's family squabble?
107 Our sun's type
111 Baker or Loos
112 Pizza topping
113 FICA fig.
115 Prefix with metric
116 "It won't hurt ___"
117 The Miracles?
121 Ball boy?
122 Like a bagel
123 Homey's rep
124 Mtn. stats

125 Shakespeare's "spot"
126 Tofu sources
127 Spine-tingling

DOWN

1 Blot with gauze, say
2 Pass over
3 One who sees everything in black and white?
4 Actress Thurman
5 Regards in wonderment
6 Rubberneck
7 Art, nowadays
8 Rocky of song
9 Tell, e.g.
10 Asian gambling mecca
11 Stores after cremation
12 Long-range shooters
13 Word after high or top
14 Source of Indian tea
15 Volcano near Aokigahara forest
16 Mass part
17 Bitin' things
18 ___ for elephant
20 Red Cross course, briefly
24 Line score inits.
30 Group with the 6x platinum album "Dr. Feelgood"
32 Backing: Var.
33 Bent beams
34 Some flakes
35 Suffix with psych-
37 Whistle-blower, in slang
38 Facebook co-founder Saverin
41 3.26 light-years
42 Sibyl, for one
43 Writer Eda

44 Chinese dynasty during the time of Confucius
45 Marquess's subordinate
46 Sow's counterpart
48 Prefix with port
54 Change the price on
56 Bedtime comment
58 Neaten
59 Season in le soleil?
62 First German emperor of Italy
63 Runner
64 Mideast nosh
65 Announcement upon arriving
66 ___ dictum (incidental remark)
67 Sarge, e.g.
70 CBS's "The ___ Today"
74 Audition (for)
75 100 Iranian dinars
76 Israeli seaport
77 Cow, in Cádiz
79 Director Kurosawa
82 Comics character who said "Big sisters are the crab grass in the lawn of life"
84 Keatsian, e.g.
85 Johnnie Walker variety
86 Plant manager?
87 Willingly
90 Chooses
93 Start to boil over?
95 Met by chance
96 Intaglio seals
98 If nothing changes
100 Base wear?
103 They have hops
104 Choose
105 Scotland's Firth of ___

by Caleb Madison and J.A.S.A. Crossword Class

106 Rake in
108 Sash go-with
109 "Rich Man, Poor Man" Emmy winner
110 Actor McDowall
113 Jeanne et Julie, e.g.: Abbr.
114 Any boat
116 ___ Lovelace, computer programming pioneer
118 ___ Szyslak of "The Simpsons"
119 Dull
120 E-mail add-on

ACROSS

1 One keeping a watch on someone?
6 Steal
13 Swine swill
17 One who may be removed
19 21, at a casino, say
21 Home for clover lovers
22 *Most awful thing you could imagine
25 One with a deadly tongue
26 Rapscallion
27 Founder of an eponymous berry farm
28 Some pipe joints
29 Dogie, e.g.
32 Declaration upon checking oneself into rehab
36 *Destination of 1911
40 "Does not compute"
41 Where lavalava skirts are worn
44 Davy Jones's locker
45 Graduates
46 *First rung on a ladder
49 Times in classifieds
51 Wood shaper
52 Hits and runs?
53 ___ Lingus
54 Hits or runs
55 Stub ___
56 "2001: A Space Odyssey" studio
57 Dost possess
59 A laser might read it
62 Brain-racked state
64 *Dunce's place
67 It may have a cross to bear

70 Minute, informally
71 Skin-and-bones
72 Pluto, to Saturn
75 ___ Stix (powdered candy brand)
76 Big boats
78 Doctor whose patients never pay the bills
79 Holdup
81 52 semanas
82 She, in Rome
83 *Destitution
87 Color again, as hair
89 Director's cry
91 Ones running shoulder to shoulder?
92 Corrupt
93 *Coldest point
96 Burger King vis-à-vis McDonald's, fittingly
98 Town House alternative
99 Russian legislature
103 "The Old Wives' Tale" playwright George
104 Years on end
107 Above all others
110 Optimist's phrase under adverse circumstances . . . or a hint to completing the answers to the six starred clues
115 Introductory drawing class
116 Like stars on a clear night
117 Luxury hotel along Manhattan's Central Park, with "the"
118 Unwelcome guest
119 Real softball
120 Baroque painter Hals

DOWN

1 Teatime biscuit
2 Rich cake
3 Surprise birthday parties often involve them
4 Wirehair of the silver screen
5 Pub order
6 "Ugh!"
7 Go-between: Abbr.
8 Do followers
9 1970s rock genre
10 Scuba mouthpiece attachment
11 "___ Mine" (George Harrison book)
12 Over three-quarters of bunsenite
13 Sheer, informally
14 Almost every puppy has one
15 Bobby on the ice
16 Little, in Lyon
18 Many a flower girl
20 Pitch
22 Buddhist temple
23 Foie ___
24 Some miniatures
30 #2 or #3, say
31 Coal, e.g.
33 Tacitly agree with
34 2012 Olympics site
35 Close to one's heart
36 Place to get a yo-yo or choo-choo
37 Shakespearean prince
38 ___ Mahal
39 Cable inits.
41 Kiss, in 34-Down
42 One of three for H20
43 Mohawked muscleman
45 Fifth-century invader

46 Slippery ___
47 Dates determined by the lunisolar calendar
48 Ixnay
50 Actress Farrah
54 Principal's charge: Abbr.
55 Hinny's mother
58 "It's about time!"
59 Freckle
60 They're hypothetical
61 Quarters that haven't been picked up?
63 Naan cooker
64 Ottoman bigwig
65 Prefix with information
66 Monopoly util.
67 Leonidas' kingdom
68 Noted weakness?
69 Tamed tigers, say
72 Bob, e.g.
73 Things in locks
74 Big Apple media inits.
77 Most sacred building in Islam
78 20-ounce Starbucks order
80 Mendes of "Hitch"
82 Something with one or more sides
83 From ___ Z
84 "The Family Circus" cartoonist Keane
85 Plat du ___
86 Start to fix?
88 Come into
90 Creator of Aslan and the White Witch
93 Settle a score
94 Pennsylvanie, e.g.
95 "Legs" band, 1984
97 "Casablanca" role

by Xan Vongsathorn

99 Messing of "Will & Grace"
100 Reversal
101 Specks of dust
102 Kwik-E-Mart operator
105 "Goodness gracious!"
106 Verne captain
108 Late-week cry
109 Gardener, at times
110 Pick
111 Charlemagne's realm: Abbr.
112 Pay ending
113 Nickelodeon dog
114 Poet's "before"

WORKING IN OPPOSITION

ACROSS

1 Rides
5 Nickname for Joseph Haydn
9 Part of a girl scout's uniform
14 Home for 22-Across
19 Needle case
20 Tender areas
21 Fix, as a hem
22 Pitcher Hideki ___
23 Capris?
25 Dweller along the Tigris
26 Ending with sea
27 See 66-Across
28 Kind of intake
30 Domes to let in London?
32 Southern city known as the Horse Capital of the World
34 It may bring a tear to your eye
36 Squeezes (out)
37 Verizon forerunner
38 Pre-2004 purchase from G.M.?
41 "___ Only Had a Brain"
42 Cruise stops: Abbr.
43 Convention conclusion?
44 "Spaceballs" and the like
47 Sour notes?
50 "___ Poetica"
53 Accustom
54 Toy rocket company since 1958
55 Verdi aria "___ tu"
56 Fractions of acres?
59 Boston Tea Party issue
60 He wrote "None but the brave deserves the fair"

63 Towers in the high country?
64 "Flashdance" actor Michael
66 "King ___," song premiered on 27-Across on 4/22/78
67 Month before Tishri
69 "___ Do Is Dream of You"
70 Shabby wares sold at an expo?
74 Featured singer on Eminem's "Stan"
75 Shipwreck site
76 Org. whose functions follow forms?
77 "___ evil . . ."
78 Lead singer of the fictional Pussycats
79 Famous answer giver
81 HBO's ___ G
83 What socialists campaign for?
86 Pokey
87 Unkempt types
89 First player listed in "Total Baseball"
90 Shakespearean assents
91 B and O, for presidents #43 and #44?
95 Battlefield sorting system
97 Spanish pot
98 Crucifix letters
99 Batter's need
101 Career criminals?
105 Eastern wrap
106 Actor Robert who played the villain in "Licence to Kill"
107 Rick who sang "Never Gonna Give You Up"

110 Overly air-conditioned room, facetiously
111 Material for a biographer with a recorder?
114 Monkeys
117 Disco ___
118 ___ Gay
119 Church gift
121 Best-looking rear ends?
123 ___-dink
124 Key key
125 Sub-sub-players
126 Blind piece
127 Some encls.
128 "Great Scott!"
129 Pianist Myra
130 Numbers game

DOWN

1 Hold on a mat
2 Chop-chop
3 N.R.A. concern
4 Mr., in Milano
5 March Madness activity
6 Lane marking
7 Millennia-old Jordanian city that's a World Heritage Site
8 St. Clare's home
9 Asian title
10 Walsh with 2004 and 2008 gold medals in beach volleyball
11 Golf's Aoki
12 D.J.'s considerations
13 Like stars at night
14 Secs
15 Asia's ___ Sea
16 Ideal
17 Covered for, maybe
18 Baby bottles
20 Doo-wop syllable

24 Masked people wield them
29 ___ latte
31 Courses people look forward to?
33 Part of L.A.
35 Radial alternative
39 Through
40 "O my prophetic ___!": Hamlet
42 Genus of holly
43 One in a harness
45 Palm features
46 ___ circumstances
48 Actress Hagen
49 Suffix with audit
50 Union locale
51 Barbecued bit
52 More clichéd
57 Ambitious track bet
58 ___ sponte (legal term)
60 Fizzler
61 Actress Cuthbert of "24"
62 Reason for a TV-MA rating
65 Sense of humor
66 How some practical jokes go
68 Windblown soil
70 Like House elections
71 Animal shelter?
72 Pomade alternative
73 ___ a time
78 International bully
80 Actress ___ Ling of "The Crow"
81 Et ___
82 "Long," in Hawaii
84 Lead-in to -meter
85 Jet's noise
87 Giving it 110%, so to speak
88 Certain N.C.O.'s
91 Targets of martial law
92 Modern locale of ancient Illyria

by Daniel A. Finan

93 Loafers, e.g.
94 One asked to R.S.V.P.
96 Heart meas.
100 Snag
102 Fútbol cheer
103 Oklahoma city
104 In order that one might
106 Pivotal times
107 Incinerated
108 Express shock or happiness, say
109 "Great Scott!"
112 Sommer in Southern California
113 Jazzy James or Jones
115 "___ le roi!"
116 Athos, Porthos or Aramis
120 Signs of ineloquence
122 Utterance of a finger wagger

INCLUDED HEREWIT

ACROSS

1 Jewish grandma
6 Crooked
10 "Laugh-In" airer
13 Barney Gumble of "The Simpsons," e.g.
17 Woody and Steve
19 Attire for an Indian bride
20 Suffix with buck
22 Rain cats and dogs
23 Close by
24 Salt Lake City athlete's dear hawk mascot?
27 Possible result of a costly Italian vacation?
29 Leave the outdoors
30 First Nations group
31 Place for Wii play, say
32 Frank writing in a diary
33 Turf
34 Sierra Nevada lake
37 Comparable to a March hare
39 Slowly, on scores
41 Elvis ___ Presley
42 Hit show with New Directions singers
43 Some whiskeys
44 Gymnastics great Comaneci
48 Flurry of activity
50 Tribal healer
53 In pain
54 Shakespearean fairy king
55 Jokes in a campy 1960s TV locale?
58 Hazardous household gas
59 Marisa who played 75-Down's girlfriend
62 Kyrgyzstan range
63 ___-Caps
64 Akin to milking a cow?
69 Car safely feature, for short
72 Singer India. ___
73 Musical endings
74 Baseball : Oriole :: football : ___
78 Bless butter with a gesture?
82 Apt to fluctuate
83 Bullying words
84 Former SoCal N.F.L. team
87 Never-before-seen
88 Damascene's homeland
89 Saharan
91 Gross
93 Equivalent of -trix
94 Wordy
96 Video game pioneer
98 What we may be?
99 Like some baseball teams
102 Leak sound
103 Slip up
104 "A momentary madness," per Horace
106 Misers
108 Vessel for just the two of us?
113 Role of a boxer's physician?
115 Tennis's Goolagong
116 Yank or Ray
117 Politico Gingrich
118 Concerning
119 Many a Bush military adviser
120 Org. in a big race of years past
121 That, in a bodega
122 Saxophonist Getz
123 Surgical tube

DOWN

1 Word after string or rubber
2 Peter Fonda title role
3 Tattle
4 What Ernie may wish he had vis-à-vis his roommate?
5 Complete
6 Evaluates
7 It may be manicured
8 Frozen tater brand
9 Like quilts
10 Catch
11 Quartermaster's group
12 Alternatives to Dos Equis
13 UV blockage nos.
14 Automaker Chevrolet
15 Surpass
16 Shetland, e.g.
18 Loudness unit
21 Taking way too many meds
25 X
26 Margin size, maybe
28 Calf product
34 Small drum
35 One of the Leeward Antilles
36 Scammed
38 Interjection of disinterest
39 "The Fountainhead" author
40 Home of Punchbowl Crater
42 See 51-Down: Abbr.
43 Teller
45 Darkens
46 Hip to
47 Soil: Prefix
49 Actress Anderson
51 First name alphabetically in 42-Down
52 Train part where sorting was once done
53 Gallic gal pal
56 One of Chekhov's "three sisters"
57 Feel one's ___ (be confident)
59 Cousin of a gull
60 Mayberry boy
61 Kellogg's cereal
65 Villainous group in "Get Smart"
66 Minute bit
67 Asia's ___ Sea
68 Non-choice for restaurant seating?
69 New Testament book
70 Donkey's cry
71 Go bad
75 Film cousin whose accent this puzzle spoofs
76 Justice Kagan
77 Stairway post
79 Short cut
80 Fame
81 Tablet
82 Was supine
85 War stat
86 Setting for "The Office"
89 Property recipient, in law
90 They cut wood with the grain
92 Humane
95 Pipe holder
96 Restaurant lures
97 Most faithful

by Cathy Allis

98 Actor Keanu
99 City on the Nile
100 Fleet Amtrak train
101 "Bedroom at ___" (classic painting)
103 Image on the back of a $1 bill
105 Feds
107 Other: Sp.
109 Architectural pier
110 Formerly
111 Soon, poetically
112 Big top, e.g.
114 G.M. debut of 1964

Happy Birthday, New York Public Library!

ACROSS

1 Be bratty
6 Chaplin chapeau
11 Center of emotions
16 Long-range weapon, for short
20 Spa spot
21 It's got game, often
22 At just the right time
23 Pants, in brief
24 The Library's rare first-edition printing of "The Star-Spangled Banner" is, to its publisher's chagrin, ___
28 Pont Neuf's locale
29 Tractor-trailer
30 Betty of "Dizzy Dishes"
31 King at Karnak
32 Wingding
33 Unmanned vehicle that found the Titanic
35 "Yankee Doodle Dandy" Oscar winner
37 Piggish
38 Spanish treasure
39 Heavy cart
40 Very
41 Go out
43 Norbert Pearlroth spent 52 years of 60-hour weeks in the Library's Reading Room collecting material for ___
51 Fabulous writer?
52 "The Creation" composer
53 Ring site
54 Jagged chain
56 Lee, e.g.: Abbr.
58 Big name in country
59 This is not going anywhere
61 Cry of praise
65 Do some grilling
67 Rail org.
68 Amigo
69 The Library's Special Collections include one of George Washington's creations, ___
76 Uganda's Amin
77 Some chest-pounding, briefly
78 Have something
79 Boxes
80 Progresso offering
85 Take to a higher power
88 Plot thickener
89 Smooth as silk
90 Article used by Einstein
91 Grace in film
93 Fashionable beach resorts
97 The Library's Periodicals Room was the source of most of the excerpted material in the first issue of ___
101 Thermal opening?
102 A Lincoln
103 KFC side dish
104 Dye container
105 Hines of jazz
109 Pull-up pullers
112 Fret
113 Tease
114 Pinafores
116 Spot on the staff?
117 Neighbor of Swe.
118 Button ridge
120 The handle of Charles Dickens's ivory letter opener, in the Library's collection, is ___
125 Reddish purple
126 Without digressing
127 John who wrote "The Bastard"
128 Go-between
129 Goes on to say
130 Cartoonist Bil
131 Indolence
132 Irascible

DOWN

1 Bozo
2 Informal talk
3 Stretchy garments
4 Disconnect
5 Hassle
6 Internet option, briefly
7 Vitamin-rich snack
8 Kind of wave
9 Crow
10 Short agreement
11 "Jabberwocky" birds
12 Lyonnaise sauce ingredient
13 With 14-Down, visually investigate
14 See 13-Down
15 Predecessor of Rabin
16 Caller ID?
17 Sign of the times?
18 Ulna and fibula
19 Cartoon criminal
25 Lachrymose
26 Humble
27 Wales, in medieval times
32 Roman squares
34 Torrent
35 Borneo borderer
36 Besides
39 Bank (on)
40 Hag
42 Pear variety
44 The Hub hub
45 Look on
46 Wonderland cake message
47 Inflamed
48 Hockey goal part
49 Small African antelopes
50 Barnstormers
55 Llullaillaco's locale
57 Shanghai-to-Beijing dir.
60 Easily handled, as a ship
61 Huzzahs
62 Words of worry
63 Hélène or Geneviève
64 Missile paths
66 You may get them in a bunch
70 Products with earbuds
71 Set straight
72 Melancholy, musically
73 Chart checkers, for short
74 Mandatory recycling, e.g.
75 Andalusian port
81 Andalusian aunt
82 Where "Parks and Recreation" is set
83 High-pH solutions
84 Heyday
86 Alphabetical order?
87 Setting of Johnny Depp's feature film debut
92 Noah Webster's alma mater
94 Splits
95 Tilted
96 Dickens's Mr. Pecksniff
98 Good name for a thief
99 Goggles
100 Goggles
105 Mullah's edict

by Bob Klahn

106 Honeydew producer
107 Drift
108 They may be high
110 ___ dignitatem
111 Folkie Leonard
112 Show-stopping
113 Bench warmer?
115 Love letters
117 Actress Patricia
119 Spruce
121 Words of praise
122 Spinmeisters?
123 Can opener?
124 Communication syst. for the deaf

YOU'LL GET THROUGH THIS

ACROSS

1 Herbert Hoover and Richard Nixon, e.g.
8 Go canvassing, say
12 Partner of whistles
17 Cop squad in "Monk": Abbr.
21 Surround
22 "Dies ___"
23 How olives may be packed
24 "Can't argue there"
25 Done for, finito, kaput
26 Execute perfectly
27 Auto security feature
28 Canal part
29 Knock off
30 Demander of special treatment
31 Suffix with exist
32 Univ., e.g.
35 Firmed up
36 Course after trig
40 Singer Redding
41 Is for you?
42 Pull in
46 Back on the ranch?
47 Backwoods
48 Drag wrap
49 Elands, to lions
50 Muse for Whitman
51 Sen. McCain's alma mater
55 Superlative suffix
56 "Hells Bells" band
57 Some fun in the sun
60 Petty manipulations
61 Spring (from)
62 Parade paths: Abbr.
64 W.W. II beach craft
65 ___-Magnon
66 Author R. L. ___
67 Hot
68 Mashed, e.g.
69 Dazed and confused
71 Cornerstone abbr.
72 What sgts. turn in at HQ's

73 Shrub used in dyeing
74 Some Nissan cars
75 Teaser on party fliers
76 Cherish
77 Light reflector
82 Diminish
86 Show a bit of courtesy (for)
88 Unwrap
89 Runs (around), informally
93 Nothin'
97 Under debate
98 Quite a tale
99 Bajillions
100 Turn away
102 Java
103 Mine blower
104 Creator of Genesis
105 Surfeit
106 Secretary of state under Carter
107 One of TV's Clampetts
108 Suffix with senior
110 Pre-sneeze sounds
111 Moolah
112 Parting of the Pacific?
113 It may be touch-screen
114 Diamond stat
115 Hilton or Westin welcomer
116 "Holy mackerel!"
119 Cusp
120 Bajillion
121 Rice pad
125 Linear, for short
126 I love, to Luis
127 Assn.
128 Funny Caroline
129 Sticks up
131 Off the shore
135 Opening letters
136 Conductor in a white turtleneck
141 Burrowing arthropods

142 Classic Alfa Romeo roadsters
146 Chrysler 300, e.g.
147 Chair toted on poles
148 It rarely has more than one part
149 Walloped
150 It rolls on a Rolls
151 "I'm outta here!"
152 Compatriot
153 [See blurb]

DOWN

1 Argument ender
2 A, in Amiens
3 Actress Gardner
4 "The original sneaker" sloganeer
5 Carrier to Ben-Gurion
6 Parks in a bus
7 Neuter
8 Brie exterior
9 Hold 'em declaration
10 Less sophisticated
11 Treat in Torino
12 Repeating heart monitor sound
13 Musician Brian
14 Fan setting
15 Rewrite history, in a way
16 Photog's choice
17 Fifth-century pope
18 UPS drop-off site, often
19 Emilio of fashion
20 Hockey fake-outs
32 Portable cutter
33 Italian appetizer, literally "little toasts"
34 All-weather resort amenity
36 Run, as an exhibit
37 Literary duelist
38 Unexpressed
39 Hush-hush powwow
42 UV index monitor
43 Light in a floodlight

44 Macy's logo feature
45 One in a line at J.F.K. or La Guardia
47 Rules, quickly
51 Country that disappeared in '91
52 How-to unit
53 Seinfeld vis-à-vis Kramer
54 Author Tan and others
57 Noel starter
58 ___ Minor
59 Cast
63 Actress Ward
70 Gossipy Smith
77 Practiced actively
78 Some of them are turnoffs: Abbr.
79 "We've waited long enough!"
80 Pushed (aside)
81 Satisfying
82 Headaches
83 Do, by all accounts
84 Touch
85 Keeping under glass, e.g.
86 Muslim trek
87 Missouri River native
89 Involuntary extension of troop tours
90 Pueblo vessel
91 Its winner beats the loser with a stick
92 Lid problem
93 Bygone missile with a tribal name
94 Literary paradise
95 Mark
96 Colosseum entrance, e.g.
101 Blue-green
109 Go after

by Jeremy Newton and Tony Orbach

116 Daily talk show beginning in 2005
117 Unprincipled
118 Harsh pronouncement from a judge
121 Pub order
122 "Whoopee!"
123 Happen again
124 Niño producer
130 Nimble
131 Tennis's Arthur
132 Filtered stuff
133 Home to the sport of hurling
134 P.O. box, e.g.
136 Pre-C.I.A. grp.
137 Capital of Zaire?
138 Suffix on fruit names
139 Exceptionally
140 Santa ___
143 Apathetic reactions
144 Hit 2011 animated film
145 Place to buy tkts.

ACROSS

1 Punch
4 Birthstones whose name starts with the same letter as their month
9 Senescence
15 Puzzle
20 Advantage
21 "Chasing Pirates" singer Jones
22 "Stop that!"
23 Matt in the morning
24 It means nothing
25 Parting words from the busy type
28 Whom a guy might hang with when he's not with the guys
30 Isn't shy with an opinion
31 Area in a 1969 Elvis Presley hit
32 "The Chosen" author Chaim
34 Cabinet dept. since 1965
35 Pottery base
36 Hans Christian Andersen story
43 Kind of shot
46 Critter with foot-long teeth
47 Dipped sticks?
48 Island known for having "the wettest spot on Earth" (450+" of rain per year)
49 French Revolution figure
51 Adrien of cosmetics
52 Iraq war subj.
53 Hardly breaking a sweat
55 Goldenrod, e.g.
56 Article for Lil Wayne
57 Eastern sect
58 Appears gradually on the screen
59 One of 15, once: Abbr.
60 Major upset, say
62 See 72-Across
65 Monster of Norse myth
66 End of a command at the Battle of Bunker Hill
69 Symbol of strength, to the Maya
72 With 62-Across, Whoopi's "Ghost" role
73 Granter of an honorary degree to George Washington in 1776
74 Farmer's ___
77 Where K-I-S-S-I-N-G happens
79 Hydroxide, e.g.
80 C.I.A. forerunner
81 Palm variety
82 "Godspeed!"
86 Water ___ (dental product company)
87 How some stock is purchased
88 City on the Ruhr
89 Pianist Albéniz
90 TV part
91 Gymnast Comaneci
92 Place with snorts
93 End of a Benjamin Franklin aphorism
96 Bring to a ___
98 9/
99 Pacifist's protest
100 The Jackson 5's first major label
103 Most clueless
108 Papal legate
111 2009 fantasy film based on a best-selling book
114 Goof
115 Former U.N. leader Kofi
116 Key of the "Odense" Symphony
117 "Swan Lake" maiden
118 Arm of a starfish
119 Has over
120 Tree with fan-shaped leaves
121 Grill brand
122 Cause for a TV-MA rating

DOWN

1 Contemporary of Freud
2 See 96-Down
3 Vegetable on a vine
4 Cruising the beat
5 Hoi ___
6 Coach Parseghian
7 Varnish resins
8 Jesus, to Christians
9 Quarterfinal groups, e.g.
10 "The way I see it . . ."
11 See 15-Down
12 Jesús, for one
13 Notre Dame football legend
14 Time to enjoy le soleil
15 With 11-Down, leaders
16 Chicago mayor before Emanuel
17 Number with two
18 Riga resident
19 Switch ending
26 Creator of Thidwick the Big-Hearted Moose
27 Watch on the beach, maybe
29 Like bubble gum and questions
33 Skills
35 Main
36 Détentes
37 Classic root beer brand
38 1980s lightweight boxing champ
39 Of the same sort
40 D.C. baseballer
41 "Ya think?!"
42 Stuff in a pit
43 Give a body check
44 "C'est ___"
45 Vols' school
49 Where Julio Iglesias was born
50 Rampaging, after "on"
53 Had been
54 They moved from Minnesota to Los Angeles in 1960
56 1994 Denis Leary/Kevin Spacey flick
57 Sorority letter
60 Stone in Hollywood
61 Word repeated in "I ___! I ___!"
62 Bellyache
63 Home of the 46-Across: Abbr.
64 "Ta-da!"
66 "Così fan ___"
67 "Buzz off!"
68 Eddie on "Leave It to Beaver"
69 Dovetails
70 Emily Dickinson poem "For Every Bird ___"
71 Bombastic
74 Some clickers
75 Over
76 Military group headquartered in Colo. Spgs.

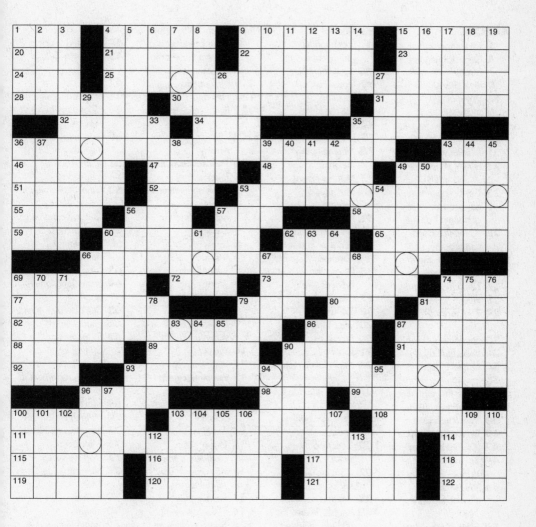

by Daniel A. Finan

78 Architect Saarinen
79 Hankering
81 "___ Alive"
83 Today preceder
84 "Silent" one
85 Krazy ___
86 Something to
   watch when there's
   nothing on?

87 Big name in
   brewing
90 Modern update
93 Clue
94 San ___, Calif.
95 Little thrill
96 2006 comedy title
   character from
   western 2-Down

97 Buck in the
   Country Music Hall
   of Fame
100 [Kiss]
101 "Yikes!"
102 Perfect specimens
103 Half: Prefix
104 Cry after hitting a
   jackpot

105 "Peter Pan" fairy,
   for short
106 Struggle (through)
107 Surfer's concern
109 "Dies ___"
110 Serengeti
   antelope
112 Witch
113 Point of writing?

ACROSS

1 Crackerjack
4 Org. fighting pirates?
9 Pink shade
14 Wyle and Webster
19 Man of mystery
20 Stylish
21 Mountain ridge
22 Hit TV show that ended in 2011
23 Cuts in a cardboard container?
25 American-born Japanese
26 Prefix with meter or methylene
27 Tax lawyer's find
28 Heel
29 7'1" former N.B.A. star
30 Feminine suffix
31 Yelled initially?
34 Nursery noise
36 Empty
37 26 of the 44 U.S. presidents: Abbr.
38 Instruction part
40 Beach site, maybe
42 It might be skipped
44 So-so formal dance?
46 Went far too slowly during the 10K?
54 State symbols of North Dakota and Massachusetts
55 Leader who said "All reactionaries are paper tigers"
56 Slight
57 "Use the Force, ___"
58 Arizona is the only state to have one
59 Attach to
61 "Rocks"
62 Certain helicopter
63 Piece of black-market playground equipment?
69 Cousin of kerplunk
71 ___ for life
72 Purple shade
73 Press
76 It comes out in the wash
77 Northernmost borough of London
81 Freud's one
82 Antlered animal
83 Wool or cotton purchase request?
85 Disgusting advice?
87 Way out
88 24 hrs. ago
90 Isle of the Inner Hebrides
91 Brown-___
94 New York's historic ___ Library
97 Top of a ladder?: Abbr.
98 Whiskey bottle dregs?
103 Courtroom entry
107 Corporate shakeup, for short
108 Beyond ___
109 People whose jobs include giving tours
111 To have, in Le Havre
112 "I don't give ___!"
113 Nobleman after a banquet?
114 Rita Hayworth's femme fatale title role of 1946
115 Effects of many waterfalls
116 Felt bad
117 Bind
118 Toothpaste brand once advertised as having the secret ingredient GL-70
119 Not settled
120 Hits and runs
121 Rev.'s address

DOWN

1 Mosey
2 Perform Hawaiian music, say
3 Shell alternative
4 "Uncle Moses" novelist Sholem
5 Smack
6 former French first lady ___ Bruni-Sarkozy
7 Staggering
8 Game tally: Abbr.
9 It was invaded in the War of 1812
10 Prayer
11 Airlift, maybe
12 Really bugged
13 Orphan girl in Byron's "Don Juan"
14 Seldom
15 Urging at a birthday party
16 I-5 through Los Angeles, e.g.
17 Heckle, e.g.
18 Thou follower?
24 Some volcanoes
28 Doesn't stop, in a way
32 Pitcher part
33 Animal with a snout
35 Urgent transmission, for short
38 Result of a pitch, perhaps
39 Schedule opening
40 Trolley sound
41 Distant
42 Side in checkers
43 Metered praise
44 Tasseled topper
45 Leader exiled in 1979
47 Not much
48 Nobelist Walesa
49 Queen's request, maybe
50 Skin cream ingredient
51 Adds insult to injury, say
52 Land on the Sea of Azov: Abbr.
53 Cultural org.
59 Stomach area
60 Deferential denial
62 Junk bond rating
64 Something on a hog?
65 Stalk by a stream
66 Feudal lands
67 Ex-governor Spitzer of New York
68 When repeated, a TV sign-off
69 Kind of story
70 Hi-tech organizer
74 Sonoma neighbor
75 Metric wts.
77 Vast, in verse
78 Vietnam's ___ Dinh Diem
79 "What ___?"
80 Towel
82 Reach at a lower level
84 Emoticon, e.g.
86 See 102-Down
89 "___ tu" (Verdi aria)
91 Words following see, hear and speak
92 1972 Best Actor nominee for "The Ruling Class"
93 Winning length in a horse race

by Kurt Mueller

94 Finally
95 Side in a pickup game
96 Minute
97 Swiss quarters?
98 Confederate general who won at Chickamauga
99 Noted 1991 Harvard Law grad
100 Supplied, as data
101 Slot machine symbols, often
102 With 86-Down, what Washington purportedly could not do
104 Boors
105 Banks who was known as Mr. Cub
106 Late bloomer
110 Some notebook screens, for short
113 Fourth notes

SEPARATE CHECKS

ACROSS

1 When repeated, advantageous to both sides
4 71 answers in this puzzle
9 Get used to it
14 Several CBS dramas
18 "___ Story: A Journey of Hope" (Jenna Bush best seller)
20 Expect
21 French toast piece?
22 It might be pulled
23 Pompeii, e.g.
24 Bride in "The Gondoliers"
25 "What the Butler Saw" playwright, 1969
26 Noted diamond family name
27 See circled letters in 76-/109-Down
30 Restless walker
32 Title character in a 2009 Sandra Bullock crossword film
33 "Well, I'll be!"
34 "Told ya so!" looks
36 "Fear is pain rising from the anticipation of ___": Aristotle
39 Wampum, e.g.
41 Endangered
44 . . . in 119-/120-Across
48 Sweetheart
50 Sweetheart
51 Part of a pack?
52 Panamanians and Peruvians
53 1960 Olympics host
54 Duel tool
55 Radii, e.g.
57 Cut
58 Some drink garnishes
59 Place for some animal baiting
60 Sharpness
62 Bit of physics
63 Hostess's ___ Balls
64 . . . in 116-/117-Across
67 Summer letters
70 Enter, for one
72 Give a hard time
73 Check, as one's numbers
76 Huntee in a game
79 Mounted
80 Authorizes
81 "Of thee" follower
82 Michael Jordan, e.g.
83 Conservative side
85 Comparison's middle
86 T. S. of literature
87 Neither more nor less, in France
88 . . . in 39-/60-Down
90 Item in a restaurant basket
92 Virus named for a river
94 French CD holder
95 Enemy of a Medici
97 Composition of many a cask
98 Techie's hangout
102 It may have sand in it
103 . . . in 17-/43-Down
109 User-edited Web site
110 Words on a sandwich board
112 Emerson's "___ Beauty"
113 "The Neverending Story" writer
114 Upper class?
115 First woman to teach at the Sorbonne
116 "Think" or "Think different"
117 They're stranded, briefly
118 Times past
119 Best ___
120 Rear's rear?
121 Radiator sound

DOWN

1 Hospital wings
2 Language akin to Kalaallisut
3 Like Gomer Pyle
4 See
5 Had a balance
6 Dry's partner
7 Not yet final, at law
8 Leaves a crooked trail
9 Owned up to
10 ___ Marquez, Nickelodeon cartoon girl
11 ___-at-law: Abbr.
12 Master
13 Game with a setter
14 . . . in 1-/4-Across
15 Pitcher's place
16 "___ out?" (poker query)
17 Merchandise ID
19 Cowardly sound
28 Unfold
29 Miami squad
31 Dada figure
35 Tightfisted sort
37 Silliness
38 Missing, as the start of a party
39 The U.N.'s ___ Ki-moon
40 Definitely not Felix Unger types
42 "___ Pastore" (Mozart opera)
43 Honorary law degs.
44 Inches for pinches
45 Buenos ___
46 Lake ___, Switzerland/France separator
47 Some tails, for short
49 Add to, perhaps
53 Uncle ___
54 Brief word of caution
56 . . . in 12-/35-Down
57 Pulitzer-winning Sheehan
60 France from France
61 "Do You Hear What I Hear?," e.g.
62 "In case you didn't hear me . . ."
65 1970s TV spinoff
66 Wrap for a queen
68 Big bargain
69 Ankle supports
71 Piece of work?
74 Even chances
75 A perfect score on it is 180: Abbr.
76 Daily weather datum
77 Aoki of the World Golf Hall of Fame
78 Off-road specialist
79 2003 Affleck/Lopez flick
80 Century 21 competitor
83 "I'm listening"
84 ___ leash
87 "View of Toledo" artist
88 U.K. carrier, once
89 Word with cherry or cotton
91 Rush igniter

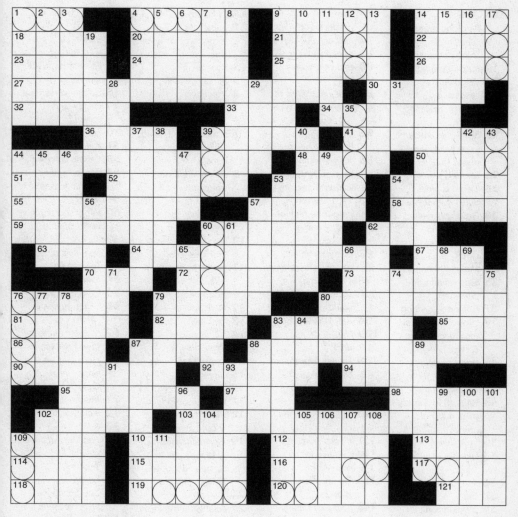

by Pamela Klawitter

ACROSS

1 Airplane amenities
9 "The Dublin Trilogy" dramatist
15 Kind of attraction
20 Windward
21 Fashion frill
22 Add-on meaning "galore"
23 Start-press order for a New York daily?
25 Shaded shelter
26 Sleuth Lupin
27 Suffix with form
28 Dresden's river
30 St. Pete-to-Savannah dir.
31 Flaps
32 Make out
35 Big name in potatoes
37 Explorer's writing
39 Flippered animal that runs a maid service?
43 Legal assistants
46 Mart start
47 Sparks
48 Request for candy from a kid at camp?
52 Nutritional abbr.
53 Like the yin side: Abbr.
56 Author Sinclair
57 Start
59 Dewlapped creature
62 When to call, in some ads
64 "Rocky III" co-star
65 Gnarly
67 Ohio university
68 Congratulatory phrase at a "Peanuts" bar mitzvah?
74 "Sounds like ___!"
75 Western Indian
76 High lines
77 Romeo's predecessor?
78 Keir of "2001: A Space Odyssey"
80 End of a Greek run
82 Ones gathered for a reading, maybe
85 ___ result
86 One of the Bobbsey twins
88 Jaded comment from a constantly updated person?
93 1981 German-language hit film
96 Part of some itineraries?
97 Leisurely time to arrive at the office
98 1970s, to a schmaltzy wedding band?
104 See 106-Across
105 Musée d'Orsay artist
106 Things determined by 104-Across
107 Everybody, to Erich
110 "___ me" (phone comment)
111 Match part
114 Geneviève, for one: Abbr.
115 Denmark's ___ Islands
118 "Scooby-Doo" girl
120 Amnesiac's vague recollection of having a hobby?
125 Construct
126 Environment
127 TV character who worked for Steinbrenner
128 Six-pack holder?
129 Certain newspaper advertisement
130 Washed

DOWN

1 Substitute for forgotten words in a song
2 Pour thing?
3 Stops panicking
4 Valued
5 Prefix with -centric
6 "I can't believe it!"
7 Holiday celebrated with bánh chung cakes
8 Asian title that's an anagram of an English one
9 Unsettling last words
10 Two-time Oscar nominee Joan
11 Home to about 15% of the world's population: Abbr.
12 W. Coast air hub
13 Fashion magazine
14 "2, 4, 6, 8 - Who do we appreciate?," e.g.
15 ___ egg
16 Back
17 College-area local
18 What a chair should cover?
19 Cosmetics brand with the classic slogan "Because I'm worth it"
24 Swiss mix
29 Often-trimmed tree
32 Designed for two
33 Takes in
34 "___ out!"
36 Serpentine shape
37 "Beatles '65" and others
38 Hanauma Bay locale
40 Antipollution mascot Woodsy ___
41 AOL's Web site, e.g.
42 Birth control option, briefly
44 Lacking a surrounding colonnade, as a temple
45 Ljubljana resident
49 Ready to be called
50 French meat
51 Active
53 Casino offering
54 Poetic "plenty"
55 Singer Aimee
58 Muffs
60 What a pajama party often is
61 It's NW of Georgia
63 Sch. that plays Texas A&M
64 Memory: Prefix
66 Calendario unit
68 When tripled, et cetera
69 Musical number
70 "The Producers" character who sings "When You Got It, Flaunt It"
71 Mucho
72 Actor Rickman
73 K-12
79 "Broken Arrow" co-star Michael
81 Type in
83 Portrayal
84 Zeus' disguise when fathering Helen of Troy
87 Blood-typing system
89 Modern party planning aids
90 Sports column
91 Go south, as sales
92 Scot's "wee"
93 In excelsis ___
94 Japanese "thanks"
95 Frequent, in verse

by Tony Orbach and Janie Smulyan

98 Stand on short feet
99 Straight
100 Eve who wrote "The Vagina Monologues"
101 — egg
102 Beat it
103 Best in crash-test ratings
108 Order to a barista
109 "Zigeunerliebe" composer
112 "La Bohème" soprano
113 Key of Brahms's Symphony No. 4: Abbr.
116 Eleven, to Héloïse
117 Edwardian expletive
119 Ones putting on a show, for short
121 They: Fr.
122 German rejection
123 Cause of some repetitive behavior, in brief
124 A Stooge

Note: When this puzzle is completed, connect the circled letters in alphabetical order from A to R to show the outline of an 84-Across.

ACROSS

1 Animal with a huge yawn
6 Garden support
10 ___ of roses
15 "Swans Reflecting Elephants" artist
19 Formula One driver Prost
20 Bandleader Puente
21 Religion founded in Iran
22 Dash
23 Reduces significantly
25 "Your Movie Sucks" writer
26 Billion: Prefix
27 "A penny saved is . . ."
30 "___ me anything"
32 Winery wood
33 Needle case
34 Like a black hole
35 "Where there's a will, there's . . ."
42 Mama Cass
43 Partner of 74-Across
44 Spread out
45 E-mail alternative
48 Effrontery
49 Entertainment providers at a sports bar
52 Pop's ___ Tuesday
53 Fill
54 Perfect service
55 Certain commando
56 "Where there's smoke, there's . . ."
60 Founder of United We Stand America
62 Despicable
64 John who searched for the Northwest Passage
65 Buddhist teaching
66 "People who live in glass houses . . ."
71 Rhododendron cousin
74 Partner of 43-Across
75 Chinese "path"
76 Stinks to high heaven
80 "He who laughs last . . ."
84 Russian council
86 Land in a river
87 Some are queens
88 Part of a cul-de-sac address, maybe: Abbr.
89 Neighborhood east of SoHo
91 "This ___ You're Talking To" (Trisha Yearwood song)
92 "Riddle me, riddle me ___"
93 Public respect
96 Managed
97 2, 3, 4 or 6, for 12
99 "If at first you don't succeed . . ."
102 Revenue line
105 It can make a 10 a 9
106 Alley ___
107 Sante Fe-to-Denver dir.
108 "Don't bite the hand . . ."
115 Legend of the Himalayas
116 Oldest von Trapp child in "The Sound of Music"
117 Protein building blocks
120 Reposed
121 Looped handles
122 Bone-dry
123 Sacred city of Lamaism
124 Mrs. Garrett on "The Facts of Life"
125 Places to live in the sticks?
126 Struck out
127 Stupid, in Sonora

DOWN

1 Is sick with
2 Sick
3 Analgesic
4 Boulevard where Fox Studios and the Los Angeles Convention Center are located
5 "Almost finished!"
6 Wasted
7 Former Yankee Martinez
8 Departing words?
9 Synthesizer designer Robert
10 Helped in a job
11 Middle Eastern salad
12 Area of Venice with a famous bridge
13 It has banks in Switzerland
14 Director Martin
15 Step
16 It's out of this world
17 Port on the Gulf of Guinea
18 Silly
24 Western terminus of I-90
28 ___ Majesty
29 Contraction with two apostrophes
30 Relationship disparity, perhaps
31 Console
36 Naught
37 Rapscallion
38 New newt
39 Part of T.A.E.
40 Comet part
41 "That's good enough"
45 C-worthy
46 Scintilla
47 TV warrior for good
50 It's north of Baja, informally
51 Prime cut
53 A star may represent it
55 ___ blue
57 College cheer
58 Bog buildup
59 "Star Trek" role
61 Cooking pots
63 Baylor's city
67 Applied some powder to
68 Wasted
69 Title girl in a 1964 Chuck Berry hit
70 Toe woe
71 Come from ___
72 Fanboy's reading
73 Stud money
77 Javanese or Malay
78 Ban ___ (Kofi Annan's successor)
79 Laurence who wrote "Tristram Shandy"
81 "Good grief!"
82 Surly manner
83 Material for a suit?
85 Party of the underworld
90 ___-di-dah
91 Suffix with robot
93 Hebrew letter after koph
94 Fights with
95 Permits
98 It might be on the road
99 One behind the lens
100 Farm mate
101 Didn't suffer in silence

by Paula Gamache

102 Flair
103 Forward
104 Exempli gratia, e.g.
109 Economist Greenspan
110 It has a period of 2(pi)
111 No pressure
112 Its highest point is Wheeler Peak: Abbr.
113 Current carrier
114 Nymph spurned by Narcissus
118 August hrs.
119 ___ Tomé

ACROSS

1 One going into an outlet
6 Sonata movement
11 Org. for Lt. Columbo
15 33 ⅓ and others
19 Buzz
20 Huge quantity
21 Cross letters
22 "___ la Douce"
23 Again
25 "I before E except after C" and others
27 Tampa-to-Orlando dir.
28 Swelling of the head
30 Carry illicitly
31 Modern: Ger.
33 Old Turkish V.I.P.'s
34 "Now you ___ . . ."
35 Skippy alternative
38 Attachment points under the hood
42 Finnish city near the Arctic Circle
46 Oodles
48 Street on old TV
49 Racketeer's activity?
51 "Ideas for life" sloganeer
53 Skips on water
55 "The Canterbury Tales" pilgrim
56 Sight near a drain
57 Also
61 Dues payer: Abbr.
62 Mark Twain, e.g., religiously speaking
64 Sp. miss
65 Human, e.g., foodwise

67 Salad orderer's request
70 Mercedes competitor
73 Bothered
74 Attractive
77 Mother of Horus, in Egyptian myth
79 "Mona Lisa" feature
82 Prince Valiant's son
83 Part of the Hindu Godhead
88 Summer hangout
89 Italian 10
91 Organic compound
92 Rights of passage
94 1936 Loretta Young title role
96 Pioneering computer
99 Back end of a time estimate
100 Carolina university
101 Terminology
104 ___ Banos, Calif.
105 Skipping syllables
107 Edible Andean tubers
108 Cousin on "The Addams Family"
110 Prepared for YouTube, say
113 Tyson nickname
116 Suffix with planet
119 "Just a sec"
121 Hillary Clinton and Nancy Pelosi
124 "Fargo" director
125 "This ___!"
126 Inner tube-shaped
127 Perplexed
128 Objectives
129 Firm part: Abbr.
130 Bag of chips, maybe
131 Unlocked?

DOWN

1 Maven
2 Bit of Viking writing
3 Sign
4 Ladies' club restriction
5 Miracle-___
6 Nicolas who directed "The Man Who Fell to Earth"
7 Twice tetra-
8 Big name in upscale retail
9 Cracked or torn
10 What Rihanna or Prince uses
11 City of the Kings
12 Former Texas governor Richards
13 Like the alarm on many alarm clocks
14 Least hopeful
15 Notes to pick up on?
16 Self-righteous sort
17 Mid 22nd-century year
18 Ed.'s convenience
24 French island WSW of Mauritius
26 Non's opposite
29 Tryster with Tristan
32 Slippery ones
34 Awake suddenly
35 Teased
36 "Have ___ myself clear?"
37 2003 Pixar film
39 "___ further . . ."
40 U.S.A. or U.K.
41 ___ Bator, Mongolia
43 Stoic
44 Occasional ingredient in turkey dressing

45 1972 Bill Withers hit
47 Applies, as paint
50 Banks and Pyle
52 PC key
54 Lower layer of the earth's crust
58 Suffix with Capri
59 Magazine with an annual Hot 100
60 Neighbor of Que.
63 Stood like a pigeon
66 Improvised musically
68 "Lord, is ___?"
69 In concert
71 Hope grp.
72 Spot
74 One concerned with el niño
75 Sans-serif typeface
76 Field of stars?
78 Will of the Bible
80 Pick 6, e.g.
81 Someone ___
84 Zero
85 "Sense and Sensibility" sister
86 "___ Wood sawed wood" (old tongue-twister)
87 Hears again, as a case
90 Treats with scorn
93 It often has dashes
95 Fatigue may be a symptom of it: Var.
97 Approaches boldly
98 O.K. Corral gunfighter
102 Senior
103 Capital of Eritrea
106 Little hopper?
109 Crown holder

by Alan Arbesfeld

110 Viva __
111 Home __
112 One may be good or dirty
113 Wee, informally
114 Suffix with arthr-
115 Sergeant in "The Thin Red Line"
117 "__ sorry!"
118 One of them does?
120 Annual b-ball event
122 Has been
123 Palindromic girl's name

ACROSS

1 Director
6 Stereo syst. component
10 Recipe abbr.
14 Number crunchers, for short
18 State capital whose name comes from the French for "wooded area"
19 Mississippi River's largest tributary
20 The Hermit Kingdom, once
21 Lie a lot
22 Island from which Tiberius ruled
23 Lively dance performed as a six-pack is being laid to rest?
26 Canine king's regime?
28 Small chain component
29 Baker of jazz
30 Dominant theme
31 West African monetary unit
32 Ones crunched during crunch time?
35 Tanned skin
38 Hostile feelings
41 Eco-warriors?
48 Grammatical topic
49 Earth tone
50 Smoke
51 Web address component
54 Beat soundly
56 Encounter with an Alaskan bear?
59 Beneficiary of a 2008 bailout
63 Expected
64 Very unpleasant
65 Red Scare prosecutor Roy
67 Mr. of old cartoons
68 1813–14 vice president
70 Fan club focus
71 Stockpile
73 Hundred Acre Wood young 'un
74 Not permanent
76 Set of shot glasses for Christmas?
80 A man or a mouse
83 ___ equivalent (measure of explosive strength)
84 Eggs served raw
85 W.W. II title
88 Native New Zealander
89 Sharpshooter Oakley when she was a charming young musician?
93 Have an emotional impact
96 "Or ___ what?"
97 Interject
98 Canning seal
99 Paterson's successor as New York governor
104 Newborn on a ranch
107 Sneaky trick
108 Interstellar valet's job?
113 Ship info kept for the Spanish Armada?
115 Foo Fighters frontman Dave
117 Golf rarities
118 Drew on a screen
119 A.L. M.V.P. in 2005 and 2007, informally
120 House that won't catch fire
121 Old Harper's Weekly cartoonist
122 Wheelless vehicle
123 Desires
124 Bygone communication

DOWN

1 1970 # 1 hit for the Jackson 5
2 Waterfall sound
3 Sufficiently aged
4 "Hamlet" courtier
5 Consider carefully
6 Stiffly awkward, as movement
7 One doing course work
8 ___ Minh (1940s independence movement)
9 "Miss Julie" composer Ned
10 Shinto shrine entrance
11 Filled in
12 Cook so as to lock in the flavor, say
13 Comrade
14 Bogeymen's hiding places
15 Hoi ___
16 Compound also called an olefin
17 Puts on the ballot
20 Mathematician Gödel
24 Comrade
25 Continuing to criticize unnecessarily
27 Pop name
32 Border
33 "What nonsense!"
34 Plan for the evening?
36 Start of a Wagner title
37 Biblical priest at Shiloh
39 Stable sounds
40 Hurt badly
42 Opposing
43 Snug retreat
44 "Wall Street" character Gordon ___
45 ___ Chicago Grill
46 Far-away connector
47 Notorious investor
51 Brabantio's fair daughter
52 Not deceived by
53 "Gotta go," in chat rooms
55 "Last Time I Saw ___" (Diana Ross song)
57 Seer's perception
58 Blue uniform wearer
60 All-Star Dick of the 1960s–'70s Knicks
61 Dumbfounded
62 Knuckle-headed action?
65 U.S.N. rank
66 It's due south of Iran
68 "C'mon, sleepyhead!"
69 Starchy staple of Africa
72 Bloodmobile supply
75 Tuscaloosa university, for short
77 Smidgen
78 Workers' rights agcy.
79 W.P.A. initiator
81 Like the climate of 66-Down
82 "So I ___"
86 "Evita" narrator
87 Predatory fish
89 Like the day of the summer solstice

by Patrick Berry

90 Smiley's creator
91 Is caught up in the Rapture, e.g.
92 "Cool"
93 Dennis of the court
94 Orchestral work premiered in 1805
95 Moves laterally
100 Tried to convince
101 "That's fine"
102 Thousand thou
103 Certain dental repair
105 Aboveboard
106 Valley ___
108 Ring
109 Richard of "Bee Season"
110 Outhouse door symbol
111 Take turns?
112 One going on foot?
114 HP products
116 Salty fillet

THAT'S DISGUSTING!

ACROSS

1 Word with liberal or visual
5 Foliose
13 Hero of a John Irving best seller
19 Beverage whose logo was once the bottom half of a woman's legs
20 Actress who co-starred in "Havana," 1990
21 Protect
22 Heads-up in Ireland?
24 Danish cheese
25 "Gerontion" poet
26 "Yikes!"
27 Australia's Great ___ Basin
28 Dorm police, for short
29 Superman's attire, e.g.?
34 Head of London?
35 Venezuela's Chávez
36 Security interest
37 Metric liquid meas.
38 Achievement
40 Farm pails?
47 City raided in "Godzilla Raids Again"
49 Cloud producer, informally
50 ___ Highway (route from Dawson Creek)
54 Willing to do
56 Fluid
57 Boxer on season four of "Dancing With the Stars"
60 Aggregate
61 Like items at a supermarket checkout

64 "I feel the earth move under my feet," e.g.?
65 Q.E.D. part
67 Paris's Musée ___
68 Benjamin
69 W.W. I German admiral
70 Fancy garb for Caesar?
72 Characterized by
74 Suffix with absorb
75 Exploited
76 Sugar providers
77 Flower also known as love-in-idleness
79 French school
80 "___ my case!"
81 "Button your lip!"
83 Antisthenes, notably?
88 Veronese masterpiece "The Feast in the House of ___"
91 ___ Canals
94 Birthplace of the Rep. Party
95 First tribe met by Lewis and Clark
97 Hard butter
98 Something talked about on "Today"?
105 Surrealist who avoided the draft by writing the day's date in every space on his induction paperwork
106 Victuals
107 Michael of "Juno"
108 "Who ya ___ call?"
110 Unnatural
111 Extremely occult?
115 Happy
116 Set sail
117 Tick off
118 Deeper blue?

119 O.K.
120 "The War Is Over" writer/singer

DOWN

1 Ticked off
2 Beer served without artificial carbonation
3 Vacation spot that's crazily busy?
4 Round storehouse
5 Cousin of Inc.
6 "Ick!"
7 Tennis's Ivanovic
8 Cabbies' clients
9 End of July by the sound?
10 Pelvis-related
11 Somewhat informal?
12 Grade school subj.
13 Pointer's words
14 Start of all Oklahoma ZIP codes
15 Tumbler
16 Architectural space
17 Regular price
18 Set for a detective, maybe
21 "Eek!," e.g.
23 Yearn (for)
27 Suffix with problem
30 Watch from the sidelines
31 Río makeup
32 Kind of pad
33 Certain triple-decker
39 U.K. decoration: Abbr.
41 Bitter, in a way
42 "Ghosts" playwright
43 What Bryn Mawr College is not
44 N.Y.C. subway inits.
45 Skyscraping

46 Wows
48 Married couple?
51 Prank involving a hammer and nails?
52 1986 film shot partly in a decommissioned power plant
53 Mint on a hotel pillow, e.g.
54 Good for something
55 What karats measure
56 Reversed
57 Columbia athletes
58 Bread on the table, maybe
59 "___ that a lot"
62 Salsa singer Celia
63 U.S. visa type issued to visiting diplomats
64 Labyrinthine
66 Complete: Prefix
68 Gradual increase in vol.
71 Row
72 Strip
73 Yes, to no: Abbr.
76 Woman's support
78 Bother
80 Word derived from the Latin "uncia," meaning "one-twelfth"
81 Baked ___
82 Uncle Sam, for one
84 "Hmmm . . ."
85 Quick
86 Followers: Suffix
87 French vote
89 Nail polish, e.g.
90 Collisions
91 Sticky roll?
92 "C'est si bon!"
93 Put in one's two cents' worth
96 Like custard

by Dana Delany and Matt Ginsberg

99 "This has got me fuming!"
100 Die out
101 Creamy shades
102 Dashes may be part of them
103 Speak to the masses
104 Betray
109 Capital near the 60th parallel
111 No. typically between 2.0 and 4.0
112 Omaha Beach craft, for short
113 One of these days
114 Kind of jacket

ACROSS

1 *Nitty-gritty, as of negotiations
6 *Boater
11 Sponge (up)
14 *Title figure in an Aesop fable
19 Royal African capital
20 Something plighted
21 Co. once owned by Howard Hughes
22 "L'shanah ___!" (Rosh Hashana greeting)
23 Amtrak train
24 Emulated the phoenix
26 New Mexico county
27 Roughly plan
29 Effects
31 Losing casino roll
32 Not included
34 James ___, duettist on the 1982 #1 hit "Baby, Come to Me"
36 It might be French, Swiss or Italian
37 Insipid writing
40 Globular
42 Fight (off)
43 "Well, that's odd"
44 Go ___ great length
46 More placid
48 Boss
50 Corporate owner
52 Passé
54 Term of address in Dixie
55 Susan of NPR
58 *Work on at a desk, say
60 Shot up
64 Death, in Dresden
65 Thief
67 Take no action regarding
69 Bale binder
70 Settled down
72 Grunts may come out of them
74 Author Shute of "On the Beach"
76 Throw out
77 *Bracket shape
79 Mini-tantrums
81 Barrio babies
83 Eavesdrop, maybe
84 Exactly like
86 Log holder
88 What Chesapeake dogs are trained to do
90 Golden rule word
92 Leader of Abraham?
94 Time of lament
95 Ayn Rand protagonist
99 "I have been half in love with ___ Death": "Ode to a Nightingale"
102 Locus
103 "Il était ___ fois . . ." (French fairy-tale starter)
104 Ancient kingdom in Asia Minor
106 Incredibly stupid
108 Newsman Baxter on "The Mary Tyler Moore Show"
109 Kitten's cry
110 Fishermen with pots
112 Onetime weight-loss drug
114 Exclamation after a workout
116 Convertible
118 The dot on the "i" in the Culligan logo
122 ___ acid
124 Alabama speedway locale
126 2011 revolution locale
127 Crazy
128 Britney Spears's "___ Slave 4 U"
129 More judicious
130 Stimulant
131 Really feel for?
132 Ia. neighbor
133 Stellate : star :: xiphoid : ___
134 Artery opener

DOWN

1 Some intimates
2 Billiards need
3 Have ___ in one's bonnet
4 See 87-Down
5 Library area
6 Poetic stanza
7 Many a vaudevillian
8 Listed
9 Polished off
10 Question from one in another room
11 Bad marks
12 Because of
13 Roast go-with
14 The "it" in the lyric "turn it on, wind it up, blow it out"
15 Campus drillers
16 C
17 Frozen food brand
18 Ad-filled weekly
25 4 on a phone
28 Cool sorts
30 Computer option for a document
33 Singer Washington
35 *Ernest and Julio Gallo product
37 Regulars on VH1
38 Asia Minor
39 Model
41 The Whale constellation
45 Pro ___
47 Enzyme regulating blood fluid and pressure
49 Cabbage dishes
51 Original "Wagon Train" network
53 Classic McDonnell Douglas aircraft
56 Goes bad
57 *Usual amount to pay
59 Act like a protective mother
61 Hit one out of the park, say
62 Sap
63 Innocent
66 Actress Knightley
68 "The ___ Tailors," Dorothy L. Sayers mystery
71 N.Y.C. landmark
73 Trite
75 Ignore, in a way
78 Fishing line fiasco
80 Tick off
82 Monterrey Mrs.
85 One with endurance
87 With 4-Down, $MgSO_4.7H_2O$
89 Fingers, for short
91 Source of many English words that come to us via French
93 "Strap yourselves in, kids . . ."
95 *Part of a boxer's training
96 Time it takes to develop a set of photos, maybe
97 Scrupulously followed, as the party line
98 No-win situation?

by Kay Anderson

100 One living off the land, maybe
101 One-piece garment
105 Where kids get creative in school
107 *It's pitched for a large audience
111 Fifth of eight
113 Learn to get along
115 Bit of smoke
117 *Common secret
119 Smelly
120 Israeli conductor Daniel
121 After-dinner drink
123 Iowa college
125 Margery of rhyme

DON'T!

ACROSS

1 Group working on a plot
6 Seurat painted in one
10 "Look what ___!"
14 One of Santa's team
19 Old Olds
20 Biblical shepherd
21 Alma mater of football great Roger Staubach
22 Opt for the window instead of the aisle?
23 Don't . . . !
26 Ottoman relative
27 Lover of Bianca in "Othello"
28 See 3-Down
29 Plea to the unwelcome
31 Loo
33 Bug-eyed primates
35 "Dream on"
37 Priestly robe
38 Don't . . . !
40 Us, e.g.
42 Attack like a bear
44 First person in Germany?
45 Stir up
46 "___ is life . . ."
47 Like some wrestlers' bodies
48 "___ for Cookie" ("Sesame Street" song)
50 It's not good when it's flat
51 Word processing command
52 Don't . . . !
56 Skirt chaser
57 Good news for a worker
58 It's passed down through the ages
59 Like some old-fashioned studies
60 Homeric cry?
63 Apothecary weight
64 More, in scores
65 Bass in a barbershop quartet, e.g.
66 Old Tokyo
67 Do-it-yourselfer
69 Filing aid
70 Open
72 Established facts
73 Don't . . . !
78 Person with a code name, maybe
79 Puts words in the mouth of?
80 A trucker may have one: Abbr.
81 Hurricane of 2011
82 Advanced sandcastle feature
83 Target of some pH tests
84 Org. for some guards
86 Famous Georgian born in 1879
87 Camera operator's org.
88 Don't . . . !
92 30, for ⅕ and ⅙, e.g.: Abbr.
93 Start without permission?
95 Possible result of a defensive error in soccer
96 Rogers on a ship
97 Sharpens
98 E-mail from a Nigerian prince, usually
99 Now or never
101 Indulge
103 Don't . . . !
108 Distanced
109 Biblical twin
110 Filmmaker van Gogh
111 One of the Allman Brothers
112 Harry Potter's girlfriend
113 Trick out, as a car
114 In view
115 Palais du Luxembourg body

DOWN

1 Trade's partner
2 ___-American
3 One may be seen on a 28-Across's nose
4 Indo-European
5 Stats on weather reports
6 Sunbathing sites
7 Can't stand
8 "Automatic for the People" group
9 iPod type
10 Liquid, say
11 "Matilda" author
12 "___ had it!"
13 Poor character analysis?
14 Building material for Solomon's Temple
15 Shade of green
16 Don't . . . !
17 UV index monitor, for short
18 Total hottie
24 Shipwreck spot, maybe
25 Ones with crowns
30 End of a series: Abbr.
31 Biblical twin
32 Basic skateboarding trick
34 "If only!"
35 It has a crystal inside
36 Brand for people with milk sugar intolerance
38 Got started
39 Figure of speech
41 Not the ritziest area of town
43 Small dam
46 "Ditto"
48 France's equivalent to an Oscar
49 Two who smooch, say
50 Mawkish
51 Gilbert Stuart works
53 Hacking tool
54 Spanish newspaper whose name means "The Country"
55 Bring up
56 Done in
59 Packer of old
60 He was named viceroy of Portuguese India in 1524
61 "Heavens!"
62 Don't . . . !
65 Look down
68 A big flap may be made about this
69 Possible change in Russia
71 Banks on a runway
73 Briton's rejoinder
74 Long-armed simian, for short
75 Element in a guessing contest
76 Chilling, say
77 Concern when coming up, with "the"
79 Archetypal abandonment site
83 Corporate type
84 Inexperienced with
85 Witticisms
86 Aníbal Cavaco ___, Portuguese president beginning in 2006
88 Kind of keyboard

by Josh Knapp

89 Model used for study or testing
90 Without flaw
91 Large ___ Collider (CERN particle accelerator)
94 Bramble feature
96 Lock horns (with)
98 Dis
100 Some linemen
101 Definitely not a hottie
102 Reuters alternative
104 "Just ___ suspected!"
105 "What ___ said"
106 Uracil's place
107 Volleyball action

ACROSS

1 Bryn ___ College
5 Often-parched gully
9 Goal of phishing
13 Where the Baha'i faith originated
17 It entered circulation in 2002
18 "My heavens!"
19 1997 best seller subtitled "Her True Story"
20 Lifted
21 Result of being badly beaned?
23 Scraping kitchen gadget with nothing in it?
25 Big name in root beer
26 Drill attachment with teeth
28 Offered a shoulder to cry on, say
29 Cry after a series of numbers
32 ___ Meir Tower, Israel's first skyscraper
34 CBS's "The ___ Today"
35 "Author! Author!" star, 1982
39 Broadly speaking
41 Leonine movie star of old
45 Pale yellow-shelled sea creature?
47 Differ
49 Contraction before boy or girl
50 October haul
51 Year the Paris Métro opened
52 Front-wheel alignment
53 Vlasic pickles mascot
55 That babies come from a 53-Across, e.g.
56 Gather
57 English weight
58 Return address info
60 View the effects of a big lunch in court?
63 Promise of a sort
65 Person with a headset, maybe
66 A bit slow
67 Fluorescent candy?
75 Materialize
80 Register, to a Brit
81 It's an imposition
82 Show shock, in a way
84 Land of King George Tupou V
85 Memorable mission
86 ___ in ink
87 Jewelry setting
89 Alternative to Ole or Edvard
90 "R" card in Uno, in effect
92 "Cheers" spinoff mania?
94 Stanch
95 Eases the misgivings of
97 Star-struck entourage
98 Funny Poehler
100 Allies have one
102 Post-solstice celebration
103 Kind of tape
107 Arrives
109 Crew
113 Hapless Roman ruler?
115 Taser for children?
118 Campfire treat
119 Hit ___ note
120 Tiny-scissors holder
121 Cone former
122 Desire, with "the"
123 "Buddenbrooks" novelist
124 Trickle
125 They can be prying or crying

DOWN

1 Very, informally
2 Charismatic effect
3 St. Paul's architect
4 Downed power lines, e.g.
5 Bonded
6 Turkish V.I.P.
7 Häagen-___
8 Things to think about
9 Almost matching
10 Polyphemus, to Odysseus
11 Kind of colony
12 Giant who made "The Catch," 1954
13 "No worries"
14 Mil. educators
15 Sheltered
16 Quiz bowl lover, say
19 Corrupts
20 Mirror image
22 Over again
24 Daydreams, with "out"
27 "Why not!"
30 Black Watch soldier's garb
31 Vast, old-style
33 Scavenging Southern food fish
35 Stockpile
36 Foamy mugful
37 Climbing aid
38 Falls into line
40 Clear
42 "The only rule is that there ___ rules"
43 Pittsburgh-based food giant
44 Soprano Fleming
46 Glut
48 Take a whack at
51 My, in Bretagne
54 Garrulous Garrison
56 Entrees sometimes prepared in crockpots
59 Charles, e.g.
61 Tipping point?
62 Subj. of the 2005 Pulitzer-winning book "Ghost Wars"
64 Hags, e.g.
67 Picks up
68 Possible lagoon entrance
69 Serious
70 Unemployed persons with full-time jobs
71 California's ___ Castle
72 O.T.B. conveniences
73 Slender fish
74 1983 Woody Allen film
76 Less fortunate
77 China's Zhou ___
78 Visually transfixed
79 Reviewers' comments on book jackets, typically
83 Distrustful
87 God, with "the"
88 Cut-off pants?
91 Not consent
92 Like some chickens
93 Mea ___
96 Cheer for
99 Swamp
101 "My heavens!"

by Paul Hunsberger

103 Mosquito
    protection
104 Cartridge filler
105 "Great" red
    feature of Jupiter
106 Fat unit
108 The __ Owl, "L.A.
    Confidential"
    coffee shop

110 Fix
111 Golf great
    Ballesteros
112 Timeline segments
114 When repeated,
    name in old
    Hollywood
116 Outstanding
117 Goose egg

43 MASQUERADE

ACROSS

1 Tierra en el agua
5 Horror movie locale, in brief
10 Run ___ of
15 "Whoa! Calm down!"
19 Be featured (in)
20 Words on a Spanish valentine
21 Temerity
22 Choir part
23 Rods on a cowboy's truck
25 Environmentally sound keyboard
27 Prepare the soil for planting, perhaps
28 Multicapable
29 DLXXVI doubled
30 Lily type
32 Foreign visitors?
33 Only nonsentient zodiac symbol
36 In style
37 Voting to pass
38 Empathetic words
40 Password preceder, generally
41 Example, for instance: Abbr.
42 007 strategy
44 High card up one's sleeve
46 Baltimore daily, with "the"
47 ___ voce
48 French river or department
49 Web programs
53 Property claims
55 Some sexy nightwear
60 Clingy wrap
61 Ties up
63 Memo abbr.
65 "To Live and Die ___"
66 Narrow overhang
68 Government resister standing ready
70 It might be in a belt
71 More than attentive
72 Immature egg
73 East Coast rte.
74 Was sincere
76 Strong point
78 It often involves a Snellen chart
80 ___ about
82 All, in old-time stage directions
84 Modern address
85 Shock a fairy-tale monster
89 Nocturnal birds liable to keep people awake
91 Take most of
94 Burglar discouragers
95 Billiards shot
97 Fannie ___
98 "Pastorals" poet
99 Former Portuguese colony in China
100 Certain game-ending cry
101 Industrial hub of Germany
103 1983 domestic comedy
104 Like invalid ballots
107 Fries, e.g.
109 Soup spoon designed for shellfish
111 Last costume at a costume party
113 Requiem hymn word
114 Visibly stunned
115 Michael and Sonny's brother in "The Godfather"
116 Cleaner target
117 Five-spots
118 Transport, as across a river
119 1999 Broadway revue
120 Seasonal worker, say

DOWN

1 U.N. member since '49
2 Like some newly laundered shirts
3 Ointment base
4 Bitterly cold
5 Californie, e.g.
6 Collection of specialized words
7 Green-headed water birds
8 What wavy lines may indicate in a comic strip
9 Lean-___
10 Celestial being, in France
11 Actor José
12 Trilogy that includes "Agamemnon"
13 Eye layers
14 Carnival follower
15 When the events in flashbacks took place
16 Field with unknowns
17 RR stop
18 "___ knight doth sit too melancholy": "Pericles"
24 Part of "the many," in Greek
26 Canola, for one
28 Clears out of, as a hotel room
29 Hosts, briefly
31 Cheerful and spirited, as a voice
34 Singer Ocasek
35 Fruit drink
37 It might have serifs
39 Before long
40 Straight
42 ___ Vista (Disney video distributor)
43 Boiled cornmeal
45 Cashew, for one
46 Hit hard, as brakes
49 Northeastern Indian state
50 ___ d'Or (film award)
51 Italian "first"
52 Many a "Damn Yankees" role
54 Mutely showed respect
56 Truck fuel
57 Paper collector
58 Kagan of the Supreme Court
59 "The Crucible" locale
62 Pooh-bah
64 Business card abbr.
67 Gets the water out of
68 Many Monopoly spaces
69 They might atone
72 Moved like water into plant roots
75 Very, very funny
77 Short answers?
79 Festive time
81 Note to self
83 "___ in the kitchen with Dinah" (old song lyric)
85 Bad situation
86 Suffix with Cray-
87 Unfilled spaces
88 Mesmerized states
90 Newspaper section that competes with Craigslist
91 Hockey team's advantage
92 Smallish marsupial
93 Prize
96 Elk's weapon

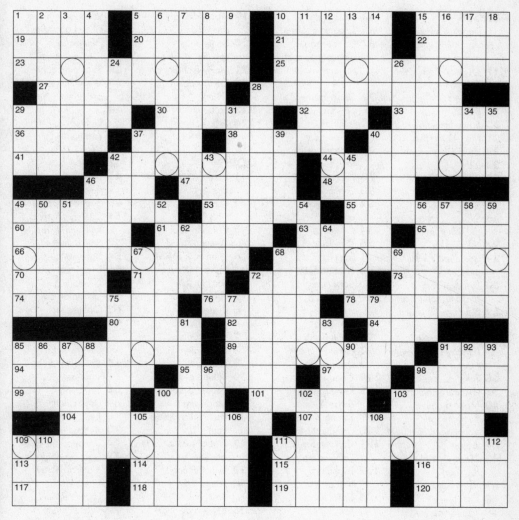

by Eric Berlin

44

GRIN AND PARROT

ACROSS

1 Dancing misstep
5 Time's 1981 Man of the Year
11 Churchill item
16 Chattering bird
19 Subject of a blurry photo, maybe
20 Some terminals
21 Mild 11-Across
22 Ice climber's tool
23 Ride
24 Détente as a means of self-preservation?
26 World Factbook publisher, in brief
27 Floored by
29 Some extra bills, maybe
30 Symbols of a budding romance
32 Big name in office supplies
33 "The ___ Bride" (Rimsky-Korsakov opera)
36 Take ___ (rest)
37 Like most churches
40 Make a homie's turf unfit for habitation?
44 Adjust
45 "Today" rival, for short
47 Veep Agnew
48 Off
49 Thai money
50 Dissertation
53 Where the 34th Infantry Division fought: Abbr.
54 Joint legislative assemblies
55 Israel's Weizman
56 Seven, for one
58 Songs for one
60 Eye part
61 Diminutive of a common Russian man's name
63 Antiulcer pill
65 Juice component
67 Lay out some newspaper copy the old-fashioned way?
71 Debating two options, say
72 Whine
73 Barrel part
75 Match closers, for short
78 Tucson sch.
80 Quickly
82 "While you ___ out . . ."
84 Go off
86 They're laid by aves
88 Shiny, hollow paperweight
89 Prefix with venous
90 Star men?
91 Churchgoers
93 Electoral map shade
94 Blender maker
95 Rhombus on an award?
99 Taking drugs
100 Dead letter?
101 Concert for ___ (2007 event)
102 Highflier's home?
104 Derailleur settings
106 Cartoon character whose last name is Höek
107 Dressing place
111 P
112 What a mysterious restaurant critic has?
116 1968 live folk record
117 Company with Patch Media
118 Sourpusses
119 Precipitation prediction
120 Something special
121 Many a shampoo
122 Court nobleman in "Hamlet"
123 Bottoms
124 "Mr. Roboto" band, 1983

DOWN

1 Banks raking in the money?
2 Criticize severely, with "out"
3 Chichén ___ (Mayan ruins)
4 Getaway where Italian pies are consumed?
5 Crumpled (up)
6 Close to, in poetry
7 Skyscraping
8 Dutch city
9 Mailed
10 Setting of the castle Rocca Maggiore
11 Early third-century year
12 France's Belle-___-en-Mer
13 Vacancies
14 Foe of the Pawnee
15 Cyrano de Bergerac wooed her
16 Strength required to lift a car?
17 Revolutionary line
18 What a raised hand may mean
25 "Can't beat that contract"
28 Duke ___, Rocky's manager/trainer
31 1986 Indy 500 winner
34 Weapon in Clue
35 Ticked-off states
37 "Quién ___?" ("Who knows?")
38 Shopping center
39 What PC gurus provide
40 Some New Guineans
41 Army units
42 "Yes ___?"
43 Couple
45 Scholastic measure: Abbr.
46 Seder serving
51 Title character in love with Elvira
52 Snitch's activity
54 Light on the stove
56 Drag-racing fuel
57 Grubs, e.g.
59 Ukrainian city
62 Obliterates
64 Last thing a fellow actor says, maybe
66 Awards won by shrimps?
68 Surround
69 Drop a letter or two
70 Actress Mimieux
74 Dropped the ball
75 Dole's running mate of 1996
76 Like some contraception
77 Where your opinion on "One lump or two?" counts?
79 Skirt
81 Nascar Hall-of-Famer Jarrett
83 Spots for hammers and anvils
85 Sharp irritation
87 Berry in some energy boosters
89 Slice of old Turkey?

by Brendan Emmett Quigley

91 Bird hangouts
92 Target competitor
96 Intl. humanities group
97 Bowler's target
98 Refrain bit
99 End of a pricing phrase
102 Japanese beer
103 Fire-___ (carnival performer)
104 Home for a certain old woman
105 Tattoo removal reminder
108 Like some sparkling wines
109 Side (with)
110 Sauce thickener
111 Car wash need
113 A single may get you one, briefly
114 PC key
115 Like some flat-screen panels, for short

45

GETTING IN SHAPE

ACROSS

1 Small amount
6 Nab, as a base runner
13 Well-known maze traveler
19 Slings
20 "I kid you not!"
22 "Things Fall Apart" author Chinua ___
23 Full-length
24 See highlighted letters intersected by this answer
26 Game hunters
28 Business card abbr.
29 Friend of Fifi
30 Fleur-de-___
31 Frozen beverage brand
32 One in debt
34 Author ___ Hubbard
35 Guess on a tarmac: Abbr.
36 Geological feature on a Utah license plate
38 Polite
40 Some batteries
41 Speak horsely?
43 ___ hall
44 Tennis's Berdych
45 Type
46 Golfer nicknamed "The King"
47 Year Michelangelo began work on "David"
48 As ___ (usually)
49 Charades participant, e.g.
52 Newsroom workers, for short
53 "Unfortunately, that's the case"
55 "Hurry!"
57 Obedient
58 Umpire's ruling
60 "I ___ the day . . ."
61 Priestly garment
64 Folkie Guthrie
65 Repeated musical phrases
67 Mazda model
69 Facility often closed in the winter
71 Home state for 86-Across: Abbr.
72 Soviet space station
73 Zig or zag
74 Home to the Venus de Milo
76 "Easy as pie"
80 Majority figure?
82 Texans' org.
85 Palindromic vehicle
86 Cheney's successor
87 82-Across stats
88 Launch
90 Jack or jenny
91 Beginning of un año
92 Eggs in a sushi restaurant
93 Freshen, as a stamp pad
94 Isn't wrong?
96 Popular pie flavor
97 Ends
98 PC key
99 1977 thriller set at sea
100 Comedy Central's "___.0"
101 Prefix with -gon
103 Pointed tool
104 ". . . . ___ saw Elba"
105 Co. that owns Moviefone
106 Commonly called
109 See highlighted letters intersected by this answer
114 Child's pet
115 Phenomenon associated with the Southern Oscillation
116 Message seen after 13-Across dies
117 Setting for van Gogh's "Cafe Terrace at Night"
118 Phillies div.
119 Drama has it
120 Shooting sport

DOWN

1 So
2 Character in "The Hobbit"
3 See highlighted letters intersected by this answer
4 Critical situation
5 Cosmetician Lauder
6 They have mtgs. in schools
7 Not std.
8 Share
9 Harvey of "Reservoir Dogs"
10 Two-for-one, e.g.
11 Flunk
12 Media watchdog org.
13 "Going Rogue" author
14 Rheumatism symptom
15 1969 film with an exclamation point in its title
16 When the table is set
17 Missing parts
18 Realizes
21 Jewel holder
25 Book after Joel
27 Cousin of an oboe
32 See highlighted letters intersected by this answer
33 Sassy
34 Site of a key battle in the War of 1812
35 Flotsam or Jetsam in "The Little Mermaid"
36 Fleet
37 He played the candidate in "The Candidate," 1972
39 "___ in the Morning"
40 '10 or '11 person, now
41 Buster
42 Shop posting: Abbr.
44 Follow
45 Aviation pioneer Sikorsky
46 Designer of the pyramid at the 74-Across
50 See highlighted letters intersected by this answer
51 It's for the birds
54 Garlicky mayonnaise
55 "___ for Cookie" ("Sesame Street" song)
56 Totaled
59 Ashanti wood carvings, e.g.
62 See highlighted letters intersected by this answer
63 Reason to doodle
66 Apple debut of 1998
67 "I'm less than impressed"
68 Mouse in a classic Daniel Keyes book
70 Contact ___
73 RCA products
75 "I didn't mean to do that!"
77 Quite a schlep
78 "Do the Right Thing" pizzeria owner
79 Thomas who lampooned Boss Tweed
81 "You have no ___"
82 "Tell Me More" network
83 Age-old philosophical topic
84 Fictional reporter
86 Buzzers
89 ___ Park, home for the Pittsburgh Pirates
94 Cézanne's "Boy in ___ Vest"
95 Bonus to something that's already good

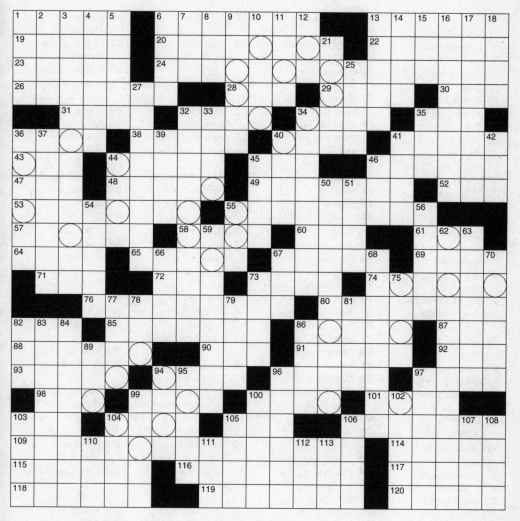

by Joel Fagliano

96 Spanish chickens
97 Active
99 Doubting words
100 Representative
102 Musical symbols that
    resemble cross hairs
103 Gulf of ___
104 A very long time
105 Top

106 "Show Boat"
    composer
107 Writer James
108 The "S" of TBS: Abbr.
110 Unaccounted for,
    briefly
111 Take sides?
112 Prefix with culture
113 Boss of bosses

46

TAKE IT FROM THE TOP

ACROSS

1 Onetime propaganda source
5 Portmanteau
8 Obstruct
13 Brings in
18 Funny Johnson
19 See 6-Down
20 Queen City of the Rockies
21 Prefix with light or sound
22 Holiday purchase, informally
24 Tone setters for conductors
26 Item in a certain e-mail folder
28 A couple of Spaniards?
29 E-mail alternatives
30 Source of the Amazon
31 South Carolina's state bird
32 Neurotic Martin Short character
35 Not discounted
36 Give up
38 Start of a 1957 hit song
40 Press and fold, say
41 Pecking order?
42 Oxidized
43 Agree (with)
44 Cousin who's "altogether ooky"
45 Vague early afternoon time
47 Like certain investments
49 Soaked
53 To the point, to lawyers
55 Times ___
57 Succeed
59 Bridge expert Culbertson
60 Go back and forth
62 Some are cohesive
64 Territory
65 1985 film based on "King Lear"
66 How some games finish
67 How some cars screech
69 Plant known as "seer's sage" because of its hallucinatory effect
71 Loser
72 Skinny
74 Screenwriter Ephron
75 Somme place
76 Prefix with magnetic
77 Old fishing tool
79 An instant
81 Blowup, of a sort
82 ". . . but possibly untrue"
84 Peeper protector
86 Wield
88 Uncorking noise
90 His debut album was "Rhyme Pays"
91 Grating
92 W. Hemisphere grp.
95 Queen's land
97 Like average folks, in Britain
98 Enthralled
99 ___ Park, classic Coney Island amusement locale
100 V formation?
102 Shop chopper
104 Bounce (off)
105 Mil. officers
106 Avg. level
107 Change quickly
110 Incredibly nice
115 Matter in statistical mechanics
116 Bulldog
117 Dispatch boats
118 Neighbor of Oman: Abbr.
119 "Pride and Prejudice" actress Jennifer
120 9-Down holder
121 Pickup line?
122 One of the Chaplins
123 Underworld route

DOWN

1 Transference of property to pay assessments
2 Asian republic
3 Gets up for the debate?
4 Certain poetic output
5 Reveal
6 With 19-Across, far back
7 Beats it and won't explain why?
8 Proof that a "Jersey Shore" character has an incontinence problem?
9 Heady stuff
10 Entire "Reservoir Dogs" cast, e.g.
11 Athlete's attire, informally
12 Pampers maker, informally
13 Arrests an entire crime syndicate?
14 Inits. in '70s and '80s rock
15 Slayer of his brother Bleda
16 Like some majors
17 Impudent
20 Longtime ESPN football analyst Merril ___
23 Protected images, for short
25 Russian novelist Maxim
27 Fancified, say
32 Singer Gorme
33 Eschews Mensa material when going to parties?
34 "Drag ___ Hell" (2009 movie)
36 "Star Wars" character ___-Gon Jinn
37 SALT party
39 Dashboard choice
42 Contents of Lenin's Tomb, e.g.?
46 Settle in
47 Aquatic nymph
48 The Wildcats of the N.C.A.A.
50 Merits at least a 20% tip?
51 "Airplane!" woman
52 King or queen
53 Hard Italian cheese
54 Slower to pick up
56 Phone button trio
58 ___ Minor
61 Break down
63 A bar may offer it
68 One-dimensional: Abbr.
70 Flat flooring
73 Minute
78 Scout's mission
80 Assertive comeback
83 118-Across is in it
85 Super Bowl IV M.V.P. Dawson
87 Scoring stat for N.B.A.'ers
89 Wallop
91 Motorola phone line
93 Departure from the norm

by Joe DiPietro

94 Untraditional, as some marriages
95 Charges
96 Give a hard time
99 Soup kitchen implements
100 They're shown by X's, O's and arrows
101 Luggage attachment
103 Some annual bills
104 Major org. representing entertainers and athletes
108 Anita of jazz
109 Desideratum
111 ___ Fit
112 Brooklyn's Flatbush, e.g.: Abbr.
113 Go unused
114 Symbol for electric flux

ACROSS

1 "Right back at cha!"
9 Unclear
15 Sandcastle engineering equipment
20 Took one step too many, maybe
21 She was beheaded by Perseus
22 "Dallas" Miss
23 One of St. Peter's heavenly duties?
25 "The Untouchables" villain
26 "How's it ___?"
27 Ship part
28 Roast slightly
29 Mujeres con esposos
31 Place for un béret
33 Conquer
36 Kitty, in Segovia
37 Singer Cassidy
40 One side of a quad, maybe
42 "Snakes on a Plane," e.g.?
46 Brand of tea
48 Term on a tide table
50 Subject of a Magritte painting
51 Doc workers' org.?
52 What a lazy mover prefers to carry?
56 Projections on some globes: Abbr.
57 Your, in Tours
58 Blues instrument
59 Harsh cry
60 Cheap and flimsy, as metal
62 Big bump
63 Poet Mark

64 "___ Fan Tutte"
65 Bob, for one
67 Workout class on a pleasure cruise?
74 William Morris workers
75 Cousin of an ampule
76 Things rings lack
77 Egg foo ___
78 Makeshift Frisbee
81 Film special effects, briefly
82 Rangers' venue, for short
85 Ax
86 Number of X's in this puzzle's answer
88 Unbelievable court infraction?
91 Game with 108 cards
92 Mouselike animal
94 Fictional Jane
95 Biblical dancer
96 Cabby's nonstop patter?
100 Key with four sharps: Abbr.
102 Curt
103 "Family Guy" wife
104 Melodic passages
106 Provide a gun for, maybe
108 "Shakespeare in Love" star
111 Anthem contraction
112 Crystal on the dinner table?
114 Bloke
118 Dickens's Drood
119 Guests at a Hatfield/McCoy marriage ceremony?
123 Appropriate
124 Playground retort
125 Classic Freudian diagnosis

126 Stinger
127 Stonewallers?
128 Looks down on

DOWN

1 Single partygoer
2 Classical Italian typeface
3 Christmas party
4 Occurring someday
5 Daughter of Loki
6 Horror film locale: Abbr.
7 Garnered
8 "The Simpsons" teacher Krabappel
9 Letters of surprise, in text messages
10 Classmates, e.g.
11 Lets in
12 City that was the site of three battles in the Seven Years' War
13 Org. with a sub division
14 Has a beef?
15 Mark Twain and George Sand, e.g.
16 1960s-'70s San Francisco mayor
17 Opera whose second act is called "The Gypsy"
18 Singer Ford
19 Cinco follower
24 Limb perch
30 "Raiders of the Lost Ark" locale
32 College in Beverly, Mass.
34 Fine fiddle
35 Rat-a-tat
37 Orly birds, once
38 "You're so funny," sarcastically
39 "Family Ties" son
41 It's west of 12-Down: Abbr.

43 "You put the ___ in the coconut . . ."
44 Marcos of the Philippines
45 "Morning Train" singer, 1981
47 Ancient May birthstones
49 Thing that may break people up
53 Rtes.
54 Polar hazard
55 Money-related: Abbr.
61 Automaker since 1974
62 Triangular sails
63 "Shoot!"
65 1997 winner of Wimbledon and the U.S. Open
66 Step down, in a way
67 Union concession
68 Creature whose tail makes up half its body's length
69 World heavyweight champion who was once an Olympic boxing gold medalist
70 Egg: Prefix
71 Feudal estate
72 "Et violà!"
73 Geom. figure
78 ___ sci
79 Peeper problems
80 Doing injury to
82 Othello, for one
83 Basic arithmetic
84 Lottery winner's feeling
86 Easy eats
87 Poorer
89 Word with level or devil
90 Arrow maker
93 Mendes of "Hitch"
97 Charge, in a way
98 Chips away at

by Andrea Carla Michaels & Patrick Blindauer

99 Given false facts
101 Co-star of Kate and Farrah, in 1970s TV
105 Belted one
107 Ho-hum
108 Celebration
109 Theory
110 Did laps

113 Cries in Cologne
115 One of a pair of towel markings
116 17-Down piece
117 Challenge for jrs.
120 Ballpark fig.
121 Turndowns
122 Jeanne d'Arc, for one: Abbr.

ACROSS

1 Number of coins in la Fontana di Trevi?
4 Singer Bryan
9 Formal occasion
13 Power option
17 Roasted: Fr.
19 Invader of 1066
21 Logan of "60 Minutes"
22 ___ fide
23 Muscat's land
24 Focus of Gandhi's philosophy
26 Sweet's partner
27 Radioactivity figure
29 Plans to lose
30 S'pose
32 Uppity sort
33 Degs. from Yale and Harvard
35 TMC competitor
36 Fried chicken choice
37 "Odyssey" temptress
39 Infinite
42 Chem. unit
43 Turkish title
45 Mediterranean isl.
46 Makes a scene
49 "Humbug!"
50 Feminine suffix
51 And others
53 Credit card bill nos.
55 Wearing a wig and shades, say
57 Marriage site
60 Baseball's Bando
61 "The Boy Who Cried Wolf" storyteller
62 Classic jetliner
64 Old hi-fi records
66 Accurse
68 Big grocery store chain
69 Tagalong

70 On the double
72 "Pinwheel and Flow" artist
74 "Fee, fi, fo, ___"
75 Ratchet bar
77 "Cheers!"
78 How you might get change for a twenty
79 Perfumery rootstock
81 PJ-clad mansion owner
83 Henry ___ Lodge
85 "Paper Moon" girl
86 It means nothing to the French
87 Musician who won a 2011 Presidential Medal of Freedom
89 Shake, rattle or roll
91 Poetic preposition
92 Brightly colored lizards
94 Museum hanging
95 It has banks in St. Petersburg
96 Bugs, e.g.
97 Peak leaf-peeping time in Pennsylvania
100 Certain antibody
102 Raise, as a topic
105 Part of a Q&A: Abbr.
106 Hurt
108 "Be silent," in music
111 Cheesemaker's supply
112 Empty spaces
114 Subdued
116 Have ___ for (desire)
117 Police protection
120 Dust Bowl witness
121 English general in the American Revolution
122 About

123 Personal contacts?
124 Dangerous speed
125 Bygone spray
126 Gets in the pool, say
127 Like bell-bottoms or go-go pants
128 Barbecue sound

DOWN

1 Not having quite enough money
2 Circus Maximus patron
3 Schokolade
4 Years, to Tiberius
5 Manna, according to the Bible
6 Synthetic fiber brand
7 Year of Super Bowl XXXIX
8 Declared
9 Huge amounts
10 Pirate's demand
11 "The Lord of the Rings" menace
12 The "mode" of "à la mode"?
13 Math coordinates
14 Bakers, e.g.
15 Canine shelter
16 Certain huckster
18 How Hershey's Kisses are wrapped
20 "There is ___ in team"
25 Anne Rice vampire
28 P.O. box item
31 In the past, once
34 Corp. alias abbr.
38 No-___-do
40 Wooded area near the Rhine Valley
41 One of the Alis
42 Area known to the Chinese as Dongbei

44 ___ Building, New York landmark north of Grand Central
47 Pastry chef creations . . . and a hint to 12 other answers in this puzzle
48 Children and more children
49 Tries to get at auction
50 Squishy dish cleaner
52 Woman of one's heart
54 Less abundant
56 Suffix with human
58 Drag
59 Córdoba cordial
61 Word before republic or seat
63 ___ Beach, Hawaii
65 Spartan walkway
67 Former call letters?
71 Photo developer
73 Inc., abroad
76 "___ loves believes the impossible": Elizabeth Barrett Browning
80 So to speak
82 Followers of some asterisks
84 Girl's holiday party dress fabric
87 Cause for bringing out candles
88 Constriction of pupils
90 High beam?
93 Cheese fanciers
95 Atomic energy oversight agcy.
96 MTV's owner
98 Gambol
99 Not so tough
101 Orchestra section: Abbr.

by Elizabeth C. Gorski

102 "Moon Over Parador" actress
103 Coat of paint
104 Russia's ___ Bay, arm of the White Sea
107 "The Planets" composer
109 Sends forth
110 Bed cover
113 FedEx rival
115 Former U.S. gas brand
118 Follower of Ernest or Benedict?
119 Austin-to-N.Y.C. path

ACROSS

1 Followers of William the Conqueror
8 ___ Pepper
11 African menace
14 Part of a sentence: Abbr.
17 Tracing paper, e.g.
18 Twosomes
19 Partner of raised
21 Who said "Learn from the masses, and then teach them"
22 Students err?
24 Bonus reel fodder
26 Punk offshoot
27 Pistil complement
28 "10" in a bikini
29 Oklahoma city
31 Medusa killer takes his agent to court?
33 Feel that one's had enough, say
37 Temptation
38 Singsong syllable
39 Part of N.C.A.A.: Abbr.
40 Rig
41 Foreign tender?
44 Open hearings in courts
46 Reinforced ice cream container?
51 What Eng. majors pursue
52 Kay of "Rich Man, Poor Man"
53 "That's it!"
54 Info on modern business cards
56 Just sort, supposedly
58 Inferior tour vehicle for Snoop Dogg?

63 One side in a bullfight
66 Em and Bee, e.g.
67 Up
68 Recollection from a winter tourist in Poland?
71 Cut, in a way
73 It serves a duel purpose
74 Flip of a flop
75 Bit of progress
76 One encountered in a close encounter
79 Disparaging Argentine leader badly injured?
87 Ads
88 Perks
89 "Shucks!"
90 Actress Thurman
93 With 65-Down, stuck
94 The old man
95 "We totally should!"
97 One-on-one job for a ladies' man?
102 Spin meas.
103 Place to buy stage props
104 Stanza alternative
106 Former J.F.K. line
109 Rug type
110 "Son of Darius, please confirm my dog is male"?
113 Hip-hop's ___ Def
114 Rein in
115 Denizens: Suffix
116 Risk
117 Approx.
118 Guitar great Paul
119 Emergency broadcast
120 "Do it"

DOWN

1 "Don't think so!"
2 Ooplasm locale
3 Take back
4 Picture of health, for short?
5 Best effort
6 Long Island county west of Suffolk
7 Part of GPS: Abbr.
8 1970 #1 R&B hit for James Brown
9 Not be spoken aloud
10 Rx qty.
11 French clergymen
12 Way passé
13 One who gets things
14 1998 Masters champion Mark
15 It may be settled over beers
16 Nativity figure
18 Stopping point?
20 A lack of compassion
23 Come full circle?
25 "Reading Rainbow" network
28 "That . . . can't be . . ."
29 Busy
30 Send out press releases, e.g.
32 The Auld Sod
33 Former N.B.A. star Spud
34 A pastel
35 "Shoot!"
36 It's stunning
42 Pres. Carter's alma mater
43 Candy company whose first flavor was Pfefferminz
44 Federal org. with inspectors
45 Cry with a forehead slap, maybe

47 Pipe fitting
48 Drains
49 Cities, informally
50 Down in the dumps
55 Dashed fig.
56 They may be sore after a game
57 Nest egg option, briefly
58 Big ___
59 Italian article
60 Start of an aside, to tweeters
61 Jah worshiper
62 Total
63 Hampshire mother
64 SoCal squad
65 See 93-Across
66 Italian vineyard region
69 "Too bad!"
70 River islands
71 Whom Han Solo calls "Your Worship"
72 Constantly shifting
75 TiVo, for one
76 Press
77 They may be metric . . . or not
78 Dedicated offerings
80 Deluxe
81 Completely flip
82 Scaloppine, usually
83 Show, as something new
84 Curio displayers
85 Sound dumbfounded
86 Their necks can turn 270 degrees
90 Repulsive

by Jeremy Newton and Tony Orbach

91 Skirts smaller than minis
92 Having a policy of reverse seniority?
94 Top 40 fare
96 Lead's counterpart
98 Wedded
99 Producers of scuff marks
100 "New Sensation" band, 1988
101 Former telco giant
105 Get back to
106 "That's a fact"
107 "#1" follows it
108 Given the heave-ho
110 Sorority letters
111 Roxy Music co-founder
112 A street drug, for short

50 FIGURE IT OUT

Note: In some squares of this crossword (as indicated by slashes), the Across and Down answers do not actually cross. Write both parts in the squares. Then use the central Across answer to interpret them properly to spell an appropriate final word.

ACROSS

1 ___ World Tour (sports circuit)
4 Stew
8 Comedian Nora
12 School hall feature
18 Rank in kendo
19 Article's start, to a journalist
20 Former New York governor Cuomo
21 Like some moving estimates
22 Justice Fortas
23 Computer animation option
25 Some harvesters
26 Calculator symbol
28 The "B" of B&N
29 Lincoln ___ (L.A. neighborhood)
31 "___ You Glad You're You?"
32 Fill-in
33 Teeing off
34 Mountain in Deuteronomy
36 X-ray units
37 Settee settings
39 Gourmet's treat
41 Paid, with "up"
42 Within the grace period?
45 Thuggish sorts
49 Armored truck company
50 Is persistent at an auction
51 Alternately
52 Ill-gotten gains
53 Signs
54 Dieter's unit: Abbr.
55 The Great Commoner
56 Front of a coin: Abbr.
59 Aunt ___ ("Star Wars" character)
60 Lead-in to 1812 or attrition

62 Stat that may be "adjusted"
63 How to get this puzzle's final word
69 Suffix with malt
70 You can believe it
71 Way off
72 Furthermore
73 Burned out
75 You go by one in Québec
76 Strike down
77 Season Pass offerer
81 Some ninths
83 Rattlesnake, at times
84 Singer Morissette
86 2011 International Tennis Hall of Fame inductee
87 Bob Marley's group, with "the"
88 Vodka source
89 Not ethereal
91 County northwest of San Francisco
92 Traumatize
95 Men in the middle of the peerage
96 Takes a bit off
99 La Città Eterna
101 Trojan War figure
103 "I'd never have suspected!"
104 Veep before Spiro
105 Gurus' titles
106 Oscar winner for "Cocoon," 1985
108 "My sources say no" source
111 Years, to Yves
112 Word with note or case
113 Like some accents
114 Item to thrust
115 "Details forthcoming": Abbr.
116 Pants

117 Prudential Center team
118 -
119 "___ questions?"

DOWN

1 Make fit
2 Dinner date request
3 Zithromax treats it
4 Sitcom waitress
5 Cardinals
6 Awards with a "Best Fact Crime" category
7 Will's ex-wife on "Glee"
8 Morse bits
9 Swiss canton
10 Seasonal saint
11 Hole in the head
12 Cap
13 Fit to be called up
14 Fruit-flavored soft drink
15 Emperor Taejo united it
16 Correct
17 Is quiet
20 Video file format
24 "Dear ___ Landers"
27 Watching without being watched
30 Jiffy
34 Minds
35 Sci-fi series set in the 23rd century
38 "Yikes!"
39 It was first broken in 1954
40 Monitor inits.
41 "Independent Lens" network
42 Puzzler
43 Come back from adjournment
44 "Awake in the Dark" author
46 Wasn't lackadaisical
47 ___ nous

48 Chi Cygni, for one
51 Italian province or seaport
54 Desk chair features
57 Short while
58 One step up from a four-cylinder
60 King, for example
61 Rock's ___ Fighters
63 Politicians' supporters, sometimes
64 Incorporating
65 Singer Marie
66 Grandson of Adam
67 Send away
68 Certain muscles
74 Oscar-nominated sci-fi film of 2009
76 Besmirches
78 Ladylove
79 Thiamine
80 Spanish bear
82 Intel interpreter, for short
83 TV award discontinued in 1997
84 Ardent adherents
85 Actor Chaney
87 Electrical worker
90 Conversation stopper
91 Over-the-shoulder garment
92 Sends millions of unwanted messages, say
93 Animal crackers animal
94 Georgia Dome, e.g.
96 Color whose name is French for "flea"
97 Blood type system

by Trip Payne

98 Rise up
100 Appraise
102 Most-quoted
author in the
O.E.D.: Abbr.
104 #1's, e.g.
107 Chicago trains
109 Kind of course
110 CBS's Moonves

ACROSS

1 Test-drive
5 Scintillate
10 Who wrote "By their own follies they perished, the fools"
15 Name of nine Thai kings
19 Name of five Norwegian kings
20 Dogpatch yokel
21 Name on a B-29
22 "What ___?"
23 Pirates of the Caribbean, e.g.
24 Full of strong feelings
26 Instinctive desire
27 Villainous role for Montalbán
28 Bedelia of children's literature
29 Fearsome creature with plates on its back
31 Something to enjoy on a beach
34 More foamy
35 "Let's make ___ true Daily Double, Alex"
36 Two on a line
39 Razz
40 Sleaze
43 Mata ___ (spy)
47 Contented sighs
49 Start of many Portuguese place names
50 Family ___
51 Gloomy
53 Irving Berlin's "___ Be Surprised"
55 Area 51 holdings, supposedly
58 Flavor enhancer
59 Representatives in a foreign country
60 Italian woman
62 Amount past due?

63 N.C.A.A. part: Abbr.
64 Absorbed, in a way
65 Breach
66 Qatari bank note
67 It has a crown
68 Turner who led a rebellion
69 Musician's asset
71 Where the vice president presides
72 Grp. with the 1973 gold album "Brain Salad Surgery"
73 Windy City rail inits.
74 Dud
75 Green hue
76 Perfection, for some
77 Opus
78 Rams, but not dams
79 Rice-___
80 All together
82 Dismiss
83 Abbr. on a B-52
85 Dance partner?
86 Early online forum
87 Gillette brand name
88 Gift in "The Gift of the Magi"
90 Classic soft drink brand
92 Land o' blarney
93 Words on an information desk
94 Crow with a powerful voice
97 Guidelines: Abbr.
99 Moo ___ pork
100 Seaside
102 He might put chills up your spine
110 Perfectly
113 Edith's cranky husband

114 Not straight
115 Dept. of Labor arm
116 Started sneezing and sniffling, say
118 Sorvino of "Mighty Aphrodite"
119 Opponents of us
120 Architect Jones
121 Singer Susan with the 2009 #1 album "I Dreamed a Dream"
122 Wood alternative
123 "No problem!"
124 Fancy car starter?
125 Family of Slammin' Sammy
126 Some shooters, for short

DOWN

1 Uncool set
2 Root of politics
3 Lady's address
4 Digit protector
5 Bygone Las Vegas hotel/casino with a roller coaster
6 Certain W.M.D.
7 Lay to rest
8 Writer Zora ___ Hurston
9 Singer Tennessee ___ Ford
10 Sly laugh sound
11 Low dice roll
12 Castle guard
13 Some cobblers of lore
14 Sci-fi zapper
15 "The Social Contract" philosopher
16 Suffering from nyctophobia
17 Author Cervantes
18 On the ground, in ballet
25 Flabbergast

30 Some of Keats's feats
32 Neighbor of Sudan: Abbr.
33 "Bambi" character
37 Walter Mitty, e.g.
38 Lock
40 Master criminal of books and film
41 Establishes
42 Weighing hardly anything
43 Time in Hawaii, maybe
44 MGM motto starter
45 Question asked to one with a hangover
46 Malcolm X adopted it
48 Kuomintang co-founder
51 Is protective of
52 Particularly: Abbr.
54 "CSI" procedure
56 Grilling procedure
57 Bit of stage scenery
59 "Cheers" waitress
61 Coeur d'___, Idaho
70 British weights
71 One of a standard group of five
75 Little bit of French?
81 Singer DiFranco
84 "Bad!"
87 Ring of Fire perils
89 Eight bits
91 It may precede a kiss
93 Yellowfin tuna
94 Skedaddles
95 Island south of Tsugaru Strait
96 Italian automaker since 1906
98 Adirondack chair element

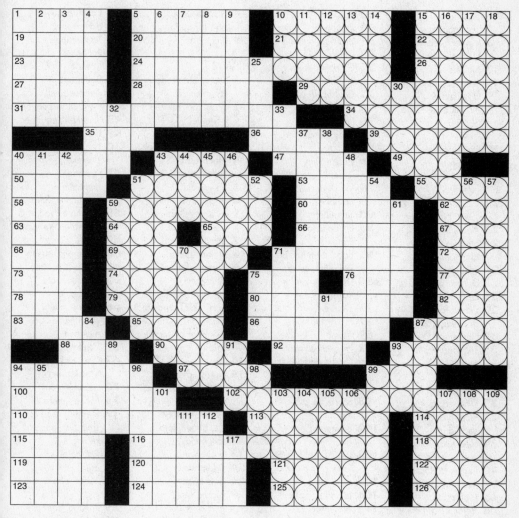

by Jeff Chen

SWAPPING PARTNERS

ACROSS

1 Secretaries, e.g.
6 Modern record holder?
10 Bucks
15 Take ___ (doze)
19 Dow Jones industrial with the N.Y.S.E. symbol "AA"
20 Cataract site
21 "The Ten Commandments" role
22 ___ contendere (court plea)
23 Anaïs Nin, e.g.?
25 Seizure at Sing Sing?
27 Title girl in a 1979 Fleetwood Mac hit
28 Reverse
29 Cause for a kid's grounding
30 Heavenly: Prefix
31 Tech marvel of the 1940s
33 "Adam-12" call, briefly
34 Pioneering
37 Rice may be served in it
39 Heavenly voice of conscience?
43 Figure in Raphael's "School of Athens"
45 Going to hell
46 Verbally attack, with "at"
51 Old switch attachment?
52 Wrong
54 Due
56 House of ___ (European dynasty)
57 Sailors' spars
59 Specialty of a couples therapist?
62 "___ see it my way" (Beatles lyric)
63 Razzed
64 Adams and Falco
65 Israel's Dayan
68 Dear
71 Capital and largest city of Ghana
72 Gathering of spies
73 Fjord, e.g.
74 Very good, in slang
76 Courtroom jacket?
79 Work in a chamber, say
83 Scrutinizer
84 Prone to acne, say
85 Food item prized in French cuisine
86 De Matteo of "Desperate Housewives"
87 Put right
89 "Yeah, r-i-i-ight!"
92 Hypnotist Franz
94 Circus performer in makeup?
97 Fashion inits.
98 Starts, as a big meal
102 Business partner, often
103 Reciprocal function in trig
105 Very sore
106 Island hopper?
108 No voter
110 Herr's her
113 Storyteller for Satan?
116 Improvement of a Standardbred's gait?
118 "The ___ lama, he's a priest": Nash
119 Biology lab stain
120 Dense
121 Rend
122 Moolah
123 Prefix with history
124 Gorilla skilled in sign language
125 Kicks back

DOWN

1 Many Little League coaches
2 "Popular Fallacies" writer
3 One starting a stampede, maybe?
4 Much-read collection of verses
5 Suppose
6 Rub with ointment, as in a religious ceremony
7 Skewbald
8 Bread spread
9 Burrow, for some
10 Qualified
11 "___ and the Real Girl" (2007 movie)
12 Up
13 Criminal patterns, briefly
14 Hostess ___ Balls
15 Up in arms
16 "WarGames" grp.
17 "The George & ___ Show" (old talk series)
18 Submarine
24 Dilemma
26 Sets to zero
29 Name sung over and over in a Monty Python skit
32 The last Pope Julius
33 Década divisions
35 Decorative tip on a lace
36 ___-thon (literary event)
37 English channel, familiarly, with "the"
38 Mark's replacement
40 Counterpart of advertising
41 Antarctica's ___ Ice Shelf
42 Votary
44 Became discouraged
47 NyQuil targets
48 "Hamlet" courtier
49 Downright
50 Nickname for Theresa
53 "Leather," in baseball
55 Generous leeway
58 Onetime Procter & Gamble shampoo
59 Churl
60 Be contiguous to
61 Pages (through)
63 Kind of force
65 Corner joint
66 How some sandwiches are made
67 Wallowing sites
69 Cause of a breakdown
70 ___ of Venice
75 Movie genre
77 Element used for shielding nuclear reactors
78 Rank below capt.
79 Möbius strip, e.g.
80 Troops' harvest?
81 Athletic supporters?
82 Title below marquis
85 Big name in faucets
88 Balcony window
90 "What's it gonna be?"
91 Whip
93 Some "Men in Black" characters, for short

by Kelsey Blakley

95 Card game akin to Authors
96 Time for the balcony scene in "Romeo and Juliet"
98 Managed
99 "The Faerie Queene" character
100 It may punctuate a court order
101 Fence straddler
104 Annual advertising award
107 It may come in buckets
108 First name at Woodstock
109 Barnes & Noble electronic reader
111 Stuck in ___
112 Tag callers?
114 "Get it?"
115 Bunch
116 Reproachful cluck
117 Mess up

ACROSS

1 Routine responses?
6 1961 Charlton Heston/Sophia Loren film
11 "Who ___?"
15 Goes back
19 Words of certainty
20 Unit of energy
21 Sculpture garden setting in N.Y.C.
22 Response to freshness?
23 Technical trouble
25 Uncle of Levi
26 Author John Dickson ___
27 Puts together
28 Items at one's disposal?
29 Prefix with thesis
30 Actor/comic Brad
32 Helper in herding
37 Bird with meat high in protein
38 Not e'en once
40 Not straight up
41 Sideshow features
42 Collectible book
45 Block legally
47 Carrier in the Star Alliance
48 Cassette knob abbr.
49 Yokel's laugh
50 Big name in trading cards
54 Indonesian vacation spot
56 Bao ___ (former Vietnamese emperor)
57 Line in London
60 Symbol of a boring routine
62 Special ___
63 Cassette button abbr.
64 Key: Fr.
65 Split

66 Like many an online password
69 World Cup cry
70 Service
71 Rose who rose to fame in the 1980s
72 50-50, e.g.
73 Small carriage
76 It might have a theater and planetarium
79 Campers, for short
80 "Love surfeits not, ___ like a glutton dies": Shak.
81 Show expanded to four hours in 2007
82 Chess opening?
83 Itinerary word
84 Marxist, e.g.
85 Bars
87 Singer who played Cyrano in "Cyrano de Bergerac"
93 Caesar, e.g.
96 When daylight saving begins: Abbr.
98 Commercial time of day
99 "___ House," 1970 Crosby, Stills, Nash & Young hit
100 Introvert or extrovert
103 Grenache, for one
105 ___ fruit
106 They may be flipped
107 Off
109 Start
110 "Come here often?", e.g.
111 Protector
115 Kin of -ess or -trix
116 Future platypi
117 Offer one's thoughts
118 "Somewhere in Time" actor

119 Suffix with prank
120 Part of 58-Down: Abbr.
121 In a stack
122 Approvals

DOWN

1 Boozehound's sound
2 "Just ___!" ("Hold on!")
3 Prosaic
4 On the say-so of
5 Gift from the well-endowed
6 Bounced
7 Old tales
8 What a mummy might have
9 Agcy. of the U.N.
10 "___ Kommissar" (1983 hit)
11 "Bam!" man in the kitchen
12 Petered out
13 Very successful
14 Seine filler
15 Way out in space
16 Football Hall-of-Famer George
17 Composer of "The Miraculous Mandarin"
18 Parsley parts
24 Some pupils
28 Swedish-born "Chocolat" actress
30 Cowlick tamer
31 Confidant, peut-être
33 Get exactly right
34 'Vette alternative
35 Little newt
36 Hot
39 Play featuring Mrs. Malaprop, with "The"
43 Española, e.g.

44 Demoiselle's dressing
46 Sudden turns
49 Not just noteworthy
51 Embroidery loops
52 What a forklift may lift
53 Disapproving look
54 Depp title role
55 Famous 12-book story
56 Brooklynese, e.g.
57 Wannabe
58 Alma mater of some engrs.
59 "Cheers" actor Roger
60 Word in many bank names
61 Year that Emperor Frederick I died
67 Not even once, in Nürnberg
68 For nothing
71 "Moving on then . . ."
74 Simple
75 German import
77 Resident of New York's Murray Hill, e.g.
78 Batch that's hatched
83 Seductress
84 Relative of fusilli
86 Vessel in an alcove
87 Kitchenware
88 Not in the profession
89 Made fractions . . . or factions
90 Pests
91 T. S. Eliot's "Theatre Cat"
92 What's mined to keep?
93 Sonatas and such
94 University V.I.P.

by Patrick Blindauer and Tony Orbach

95 Dahl of "A Southern Yankee," 1948
97 Most outspread
101 True
102 Brick-and-mortar alternative
104 Dancer Jeanmaire
108 "Rule, Britannia" composer
110 Bit of neckwear
111 Herd of elephants?
112 Initials in news
113 1950 Anne Baxter title role
114 Évian-___-Bains, France

As Elmer Fudd Would Say . . .

ACROSS

1 House extension
8 Deadly African biter
13 Container holding slips of paper with tasks written on them
19 Like a bogey or double bogey
20 Commonplace
21 "Shouldn't have done that!"
22 "Amahl and the Night Visitors" composer
23 Part of a biblical warning against growing onions?
25 Garden with an apple tree
26 Livens (up)
28 Ages upon ages
29 French wine classification
30 Some locker room tomfoolery?
33 See
34 What a mare bears
35 Turn-___
36 Jerusalem's Mosque of ___
37 Letters
38 Arduous travels
39 Down
40 Bio for a Looney Tunes coyote?
45 Bakery trayfuls, say
48 Philosophy
49 Cartesian conclusion
50 "___ Ben Jonson!"
51 Radio features
52 OPEC unit: Abbr.
53 Closet item, in brief
56 Politico Ralph's fishing gear?
60 Light of one's life
62 Lots
63 Georgetown hoopster
64 The ___ One (sobriquet for Satan)
65 Buck
66 Razed
68 Pretty fat, actually?
72 Victorian ___
73 Sounds at a vaccination center, maybe
74 Garb for Gandhi
75 First Baseball Hall-of-Famer, alphabetically
76 Intent
77 Tabriz native
79 Marco Polo's destination
80 React to a bitter mouthwash?
84 Big hirer of techies
85 Mae West's "___ Day's a Holiday"
86 2003 disease scare
87 Battle of Normandy town
89 Egg container, of sorts
92 PBS staple since 1974
93 Barney of Mayberry
94 Sloven in the coven?
98 Author Umberto
99 Timbales player Puente
100 Loose smock
101 '33 Chicago World's Fair style
102 Advice to someone going to the Egg-Beaters' Convention?
105 Blanket
108 Thinks
109 Reduce to mush
110 Traditional
111 Spotlight sharer
112 Assists
113 Some dollhouse miniatures

DOWN

1 Recover from a blackout
2 Photographer Richard
3 Gets more InStyle, say
4 Lying
5 Make a choice
6 Singer
7 Singer Yearwood
8 Singer's accompaniment
9 "Put ___ in it!"
10 Nine daughters of Zeus
11 Curmudgeonly cries
12 ___ king
13 Actress Meadows
14 ___ of Solomon
15 Maker of the Z4 roadster
16 Snoopy's hip alter ego
17 So-so
18 Turn off
21 Totally wasted
24 Things letters have
27 Added-on Medicare provisions
31 Courtesy car
32 Saddam reportedly hid them, briefly
33 Tips, in a way
34 ___-flam
37 Beer brand originating in Brooklyn
38 Marshy tract
39 Collected
41 Gossipy Hopper
42 Nobel laureate Wiesel
43 Stereotypical debate outburst
44 Calf bone
45 Be philanthropic
46 Clay, e.g.
47 Golden Globe winner Pia
52 Rite for a newborn Jewish boy
53 1958 #1 hit by Domenico Modugno
54 King Arthur's burial place
55 Solidify
57 "Prove it!"
58 Knocks dead
59 "The Fountainhead" writer Rand
60 New Deal inits.
61 "To life!"
64 So-called "Giant Brain" of 1946
67 Bit of crochet work
68 Détentes
69 "___ soit qui mal y pense" (old motto)
70 "Put ___ writing!"
71 English archer's weapon
74 Rapper with the 6x platinum album "2001"
76 Taj Mahal city
77 Spaced out
78 Fits one inside another
79 Unctuous
80 Kind of code
81 Shade of green
82 Cancels

by Ed Sessa

83 The way things stand
88 Everything
89 Nicks on a record?
90 Sign of stress
91 Farmer's to-do list
93 Moral ___
94 Renaissance ___ (historical reenactment)
95 "No more for me, thanks"
96 Takes a shine to
97 Many people in People
99 "Cheerio!"
100 Carp family fish
103 "Mangia!"
104 New Deal inits.
106 Any of the Marquises, par exemple
107 Child-care writer LeShan

ACROSS

1 Ready for publication
7 Flag
13 Certain Internet connection: Abbr.
16 Things refs raise their arms for
19 Full chromosome set
20 Pairs' debarking point
21 Joy
23 234, as of July 4, 2010?
25 Cash in the music business
26 1950 noir film
27 Perfect specimens
28 Divided
30 ___ Bros.
31 Unit of force
32 Workers in a global peace organization?
35 Hard look?
38 Pass off as genuine
39 Hip
40 Unconventional
41 Remove from a talent show, maybe
42 Come under criticism
47 What gumshoes charge in the City of Bridges?
52 Kid
53 Native Coloradan
54 Some court evidence
55 Signs of spoilage
56 Group following a star?
57 Left at sea
59 Drinker's problem, for short
60 Word that comes from the Greek for "indivisible"
61 Not stay long for shots?
62 Symmetrical power conductor for appliances?
67 Hole
70 Makes holes
71 Sounds of understanding
72 Wrapped garment
76 Nimble
77 Any singer of "Hotel California"
79 "Stop!"
81 Grp. of connected PCs
82 What's borne at a funeral
83 Too much guitar work by a professor's helper?
86 Like some English muffins
88 Scullers' needs
89 Best
90 Aquatic shockers
91 "The Addams Family" co-star
93 Most easily sunburned, maybe
94 "Pay in cash and your second surgery is half-price"?
99 Small islands
100 Nuevo Laredo store
101 Get along
102 Singer Fitzgerald
103 Galoot
106 Second
108 Typical termite in a California city?
112 Inactive state
113 Using fraudulently altered checks
114 Sharpie alternatives
115 Preceder of 116-Across
116 Follower of 115-Across
117 Pack rat
118 "Opening" word

DOWN

1 "Good grief!"
2 Art ___
3 Quechua speaker
4 Low digit
5 What many older parents face
6 Locking lever
7 Rogues
8 Tulsa sch.
9 ___ Cruces
10 Elocutes
11 Seasoned stew
12 Harsh
13 "___ Fuehrer's Face" (1942 Disney short)
14 Dawdler
15 Explorer who claimed Louisiana for France
16 Thin-toned
17 Recipient
18 Bergen's foil
22 Poi ingredient
24 General dir. of Sal Paradise's return trip in "On the Road"
29 Peach ___
31 Gossip
32 Grillers' grabbers
33 On dope
34 Things that drawbridges bridge
35 Absorb
36 Headquarters of the Union of South American Nations
37 Speak
38 "Hansel and Gretel" setting
41 CNN's Sanjay
43 Northern inlets
44 Any tail in a cat-o'-nine-tails
45 Lhasa ___
46 Not spoil
48 Not well
49 Thick soups
50 Miley Cyrus and Lady Gaga, e.g.
51 Tomato type
56 Hole number
58 Some short-term investments, briefly
60 Seed coverings
61 ___ nova
63 Adherent: Suffix
64 Advantage
65 Site of some paintings
66 Informal exchanges
67 Li'l Abner creator
68 Food thickener
69 Loathsome
73 1967 Dionne Warwick hit
74 Some constructions on "Survivor"
75 Certain detail
77 Bobby Fischer, once
78 Words before "kindness" and "the Apostles"
79 Be of use
80 Like diabetes
83 Refinement
84 Tiny bit
85 Woes
87 Cross or star, often
91 Dexterous
92 Apparently do
93 Rice dishes
94 Steps that a farmer might take
95 Brown and Turner

by Robert W. Harris

96 "The defense ___"
97 Stake
98 Prepares to play pool, say
99 Tie indicator
102 Many an M.I.T. grad
103 "Che gelida manina," e.g.

104 Salon option
105 Celtic tongue
107 Nautical rope
109 Novy ___, Russian literary magazine
110 Low digit
111 International grp. since 1948

ACROSS

1 "Silas Marner" foundling
6 They're schlepped on tours
10 Bruce who played Watson in Sherlock Holmes films
15 Equal
19 PBS figure from 1968 to 2001
21 Eyes
22 As well
23 Cause for Adam to refuse the apple?
24 Congested-sounding
25 Weapon in Clue
26 Feature of some Greek buildings
27 Feudal holding
28 Precamping preparation?
30 Tests for srs.
32 One-time connection
34 BMI rival
35 Christmas, for Christians?
41 Alibi, e.g.
45 Antique restorer's need, for short
46 Locale in a 1968 Beatles song
47 Beaks
48 "Really?"
49 British P.M. during the creation of Israel
51 Bountiful harvest?
55 Good source of protein
56 Saudi Arabian province
57 __ gin fizz
58 Article in Die Zeit
59 Robert Downey Jr. title role
62 Prom rental
65 Place to pray
67 Independence Day barbecue serving?
74 Auel heroine
75 Prefix with plasm
76 Girl in a Willa Cather title
77 Shelter grp.
81 Cut
83 Serving with gâteau, maybe
85 P.T.A. member?: Abbr.
86 Unnecessary part of a jacket?
90 When streetlights go on
92 Refuse
93 The Road Runner, for one
94 Freezer brand
96 Caviar
97 Makeshift stepladder
98 Ultimatum from a spouse who wants nicer digs?
102 Single-celled organism
104 PC key
105 Some chorus members
106 Refusing to watch football on New Year's Day?
111 Tijuana fare
113 Genesis victim
117 1970s–'80s horror film franchise, with "The"
118 Lofty retreat
119 Nathan's annual hot-dog contest, e.g.?
121 It may be framed
122 __ Chaiken, creator and writer of "The L Word"
123 Concerning
124 Eye __
125 Grayer, perhaps
126 Scorch
127 Magnetic induction unit

DOWN

1 Pair of ruffians?
2 Rear end
3 Coin with a profile of José María Morelos
4 Conference clip-ons
5 Suffix with ranch
6 Ones prejudiced against 125-Across people
7 One subjugated by Cyrus the Great
8 Kind of housing, for short
9 1040 datum: Abbr.
10 Bar __
11 Self-motivational mantra
12 Composer Mahler
13 Slip by
14 Eye shadow shade
15 Property that costs $350
16 Patron saint of goldsmiths
17 Where to find "Baseball Tonight"
18 Nicolas who directed "The Man Who Fell to Earth"
20 Umbrage
28 Shire in Hollywood
29 Treasure hunter's find
31 See 110-Down
33 It's WNW of Grand Canary Island
35 Interference
36 Figure at una corrida
37 Represent
38 Municipal laws: Abbr.
39 Maker of the trivia-playing computer program Watson
40 Those, in Toledo
42 Longfellow's bell town
43 "The heat __"
44 Look down
48 Trinity component
50 Sally __ (teacake)
52 Agitate
53 Needing tuning, maybe
54 Mr. Peanut prop
56 Hunting lodge decoration bit
60 Bird that is no more
61 "As I was saying . . ."
63 Casual slip-on, casually
64 Plans
66 Young newt
68 "Cactus Flower" Oscar winner
69 Alternative to chestnut
70 1940 Fonda role
71 Hesitant
72 Willowy: Var.
73 Ruth, once
77 Does, say
78 Blog comment
79 First name in fashion
80 Personal
82 Alternative to grounding
84 Media exec Robert
87 Person with a serious conviction
88 Sandal's lack
89 Great Lakes mnemonic
90 Eternal
91 Perfectly

by Alan Arbesfeld

95 There's a national park named for one
98 Old phone company nickname
99 Scented
100 Station identification?
101 Alternative to Cialis
103 Marsh of mysteries
106 "Uh-uh"
107 Big picture?
108 Lawless role
109 Shiraz, for one
110 Look from a 31-Down
112 Gillette product
114 "On&On" singer Erykah
115 CPR experts
116 Some summer births
119 Winter hazard in Munich
120 Stand-up staple

ACROSS

1 Grinder toppings
7 Supreme Court justice nominated by Reagan
13 Real-life actor Joe who is a character in Broadway's "Jersey Boys"
18 Bunny's covering?
19 Bent nails
20 Furniture retailer ___ Allen
21 Put a few monarchs on the scale?
23 "Orlando" novelist
24 Sister of Charlotte and Emily
25 All wrong
26 Huggies rival
28 Gaza Strip org.
29 Wrinkly dog holder?
33 Espresso topping
35 Engage in debate
36 "I said - ___!"
37 Firecracker's trajectory
38 Obama whose Secret Service code name is "Rosebud"
40 Snobbery
42 Location for a fall
45 Bank claims
47 Location for the Fall
48 Helped with the laundry
50 Political appointee
51 Cords behind a computer, often
54 Word with a German request
57 Blew by a drummer, maybe
59 Played the tourist
61 Hurting
62 Smoking character
65 Relative in the barrio
66 The golden ratio
67 Line score letters
68 Gel
69 Golfers' wear
71 N.B.A. All-Star Artest
72 Tractor-trailer
73 One with a pupil
74 Amsterdam air hub
76 Puppeteer Tony
77 Company that merged with Sony in 2001
80 Brunonian rival
81 Compromise of 1877 president
82 1996 Grammy winner for the album "The Road to Ensenada"
83 Camper's rental
85 Alternate road
88 Robert of "The Sopranos"
89 Poll answer choice
91 Famed Fokker flier
95 Toward the middle
98 "Why is this happening to me?!"
100 Its cap. is Beirut
101 Prefix with tour
102 Mensa and others: Abbr.
103 With honor
105 Floral garland for whoever?
108 Kangaroo ___
109 Character with a prominent back
110 Gillette model
111 Many P.T.A. members
112 Duel overseer in "Hamlet"
114 Indecisive wolf's question?
120 John Mason ___, English priest who wrote "Good King Wenceslas"
121 Accustoms
122 Hair-texturizing tool
123 Heretofore
124 Overage
125 Observation

DOWN

1 Battle site of 1945
2 River on the Benin border
3 -like equivalent
4 Available for purchase
5 Biomedical research agcy.
6 Secure, with "in"
7 Breastbone-related
8 Clumped
9 "Prince ___" ("Aladdin" song)
10 Basketball coach Kruger
11 Hearth
12 Take as a given
13 Sunday seats
14 W.W. II zone: Abbr.
15 Mist from a mall?
16 Leonard Bernstein called her "The Bible of opera"
17 Enlighten
18 Brazilian mister
21 "I ___ ready!"
22 Things shepherds shepherd
27 Miss who parks cars?
30 Military chaplain
31 Suffix with stink
32 Only thing between you and an open window?
33 In hell?
34 ___ close second (almost won)
35 Arterial implant
39 "Attack!"
41 Baking spuds
43 "The scavenger of misery," per Shaw
44 Served seconds, say
46 Yearbook signers: Abbr.
49 Cuts up, in a way
52 Punjabi capital
53 Oil family of TV
54 Oil unit
55 First player to hit an inside-the-park home run during an All-Star Game, 2007
56 Generous carhop's prop?
58 Brawl at a ball?
60 "Am ___ fat?"
62 Leno's necklace?
63 Mousse pie ingredient, maybe
64 Oily substance
68 Prynne of "The Scarlet Letter"
70 Absolute
75 Hardly a fan
76 ___ Lee bakery
78 Bird and others, once
79 Publisher of Shooting Illustrated, for short
81 When doubled, "I like!"
84 "___ in Calico" (jazz standard)

by Brendan Emmett Quigley

86 Prefix with copier
87 River to the Baltic
90 Game in which it's easy to make a mess
92 Change tags on
93 Mop brand that "makes your life easier"

94 Whooping
95 Dos Equis competitor
96 Clears
97 Louse
99 Austrian title
104 Where hip-hop was born, with "the"

106 F.D.R. veep John ___ Garner
107 Parkinson's battler
109 Entertainer born Tracy Marrow
110 Cries made in passing?
113 Saint-Martin, e.g.

115 Winning Super Bowl XXXVII gridder
116 Exist
117 Surgery sites, for short
118 20%, maybe
119 "I didn't need to know that," in modern lingo

ACROSS

1 One-named teen idol of the late '50s/early '60s
7 Fashionably nostalgic
12 Came out even, in a way
19 God who killed the dragon Python four days after his birth
20 Bygone shampoo brand
21 Heads
22 See circled letters in 96-Down
24 Dow Jones publication
25 Can
26 Join the crew
27 Kind of acid found in spinach
29 Hook's right-hand man
30 Frankfurt term of address
32 Demanding overseer
34 Tennis's Nastase
36 New York subway inits.
37 In order (to)
39 . . . in 79-Down
42 Teen's room, stereotypically
44 Like some proverbial milk
46 Dweller on the Baltic
47 Two-baggers: Abbr.
48 People holding signs at airports
51 Dwellers on the Baltic
53 Why
55 Noted wine region
56 Underworld bosses
57 Take off
58 Stephen of "The Musketeer"
60 Does some freestyling
61 . . . in 13-Down
63 Big letters in fashion
64 CBS show with Laurence Fishburne
65 Very reverent
67 "Charles in Charge" co-star
68 Mathematical ordinal
69 "What was ___ think?"
70 . . . in 62-Down
74 Star turns
75 River to the Rhône
76 ___ place
77 New Balance competitor
78 Flatware finisher
80 Furniture mover
82 On-base percentage and others
83 At the earliest opportunity
84 Will of "The Waltons"
85 Florida city, for short
86 Word with love or honey
87 Row of stables, in Britain
88 . . . in 89-Down
91 Telecom hookups
94 Highway hazard
95 Spree
97 Inside flight
99 Mane, for a female lion, e.g.
101 Concerning
103 Lieu
106 Gluck works
108 Spider-Man's aunt
109 Igneous rock
111 . . . in 1-Across
114 Home to Mount Chimborazo
115 Brachyodont perissodactyls
116 One of the Kennedys
117 Some carry-on items
118 Apple purchases
119 Tot tender

DOWN

1 Palestinian party
2 Climbers' goals
3 1928 musical composition originally called "Fandango"
4 Québec's Grosse-___
5 River in "Kubla Khan"
6 Tiring problem for bicyclists?
7 Soak back in
8 Drink from a bowl
9 Cycle attachment?
10 Jazz phrase
11 Aware of
12 Art installation
13 They can always be counted on
14 TiVo, for one, in brief
15 Relative of -ists
16 . . . in 65-Across
17 Actor Ed and family
18 Microwave button
20 Lincoln Center institution
23 Bottom-fishes
28 Melodic speech
31 Some Jamaicans, for short
33 TV marshal who frequents the Long Branch Saloon
35 Sets off
38 Job detail
40 Silly ones
41 Some sporty cars
43 P.G.A.'s Ernie
45 Heat source?
47 "The Wreck of the Mary ___"
48 Cross of "Desperate Housewives"
49 Band composition
50 . . . in 48-Down
51 Not in
52 Make a choice
53 Like a successful dieter's clothes
54 Candy giant, informally
56 Brilliant successes
57 Goes for, as a fly
59 Jazz great nicknamed Jumbo
61 #2 or #3
62 Rash remedies
65 Boycott, e.g.
66 ___ peace
71 "Coming at you!"
72 Jason who plays Lucius Malfoy in Harry Potter films
73 River island
74 It has a bottom but no top
78 Don Ho fan fare?
79 Laze
81 Singers do it
82 "Mamma Mia!" song
83 Shepherd of "The View"
85 Unadorned
86 Arrowhead Stadium team
87 One of the friends on "Friends"

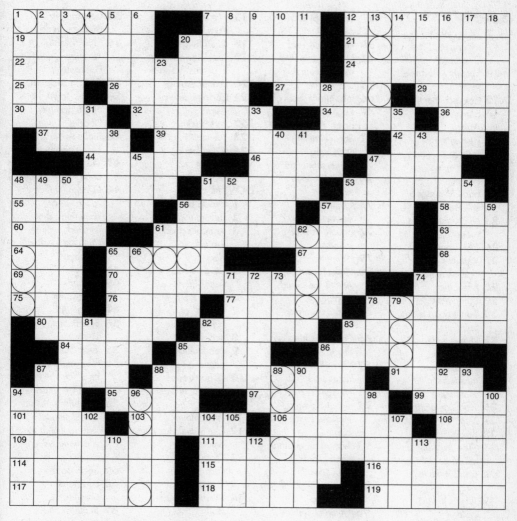

by Pamela Amick Klawitter

88 Works a wedding, maybe
89 Wee
90 Heists
92 "Anything you say!"
93 "Make yourself ___"

94 Leader succeeded by his brother Raúl
96 Prevent
98 Wise ones
100 Orchestra leader Kay
102 Part of Q.E.D.

104 Theater opening
105 60 grains
107 Feng ___
110 Swear words in a swearing-in
112 Pronunciation guide std.
113 Cause of a big bang

ACROSS

1 Writer of the short story "The Overcoat"
6 Sitcom with three stars
10 Compos mentis
14 Some Latinas: Abbr.
19 Hersey novel setting
20 Cream, e.g.
21 Angel
22 Parts of many a still life
23 Underachiever's motto?
26 SALT topic
27 Vladimir Nabokov novel
28 It's noble
29 Sol mates?
30 Some court pleas, for short
31 U.N.-created land: Abbr.
33 Places where masseurs massage
35 Trouble's partner
37 Milk containers
38 Being debated
41 "The Mystery of ___ Vep," 1990s Off Broadway play
42 E is its lowest note
43 Majorcan affirmation?
47 She-bear: Sp.
50 7-0 record, e.g.
51 Something for a kid to keep on hand?
52 Portuguese wines
54 Worthy of mention
56 "The lowest form of humor," per Samuel Johnson
57 Grps. that know the drill?
58 Roam and raid
61 Not yet acquired, as knowledge
65 ___-all
66 Inhabitant: Suffix
67 Registering a poodle?
71 Steve Martin's "boy king"
72 What atoms do
74 Liza Minnelli's father
75 Contents of sleeves
77 N.S.A. concern, for short
79 Ultimate
80 Hulk Hogan or Andre the Giant, slangily
83 "Vitruvian Man" artist
85 Part·of batting instruction
87 "Twin Peaks" actor Jack
91 Misspeak, e.g.
92 Guy holding a Hostess snack cake?
95 Canadian curling championship, with "the"
97 Procrastinator's response
98 Decimal system
99 The beginning
101 Dom ___, "Inception" hero
102 ___ Ed
104 Letter run
105 Skyscraper support
106 300 to 3,000 MHz range
107 ___ fixe
109 Popular fragrance
112 Slithering menace
113 Words of caution from Rodolfo?
118 "___ I might . . ."
119 "___ Diana's altar to protest": Shak.
120 Dinner crumbs
121 Certain Central Asian
122 Puts back in
123 Politico Gingrich
124 [Over here!]
125 Bounce

DOWN

1 Group of whales
2 Harem room
3 Annual parade subject
4 "Go ___!"
5 Fin de siècle writer Pierre ___
6 V.J.'s employer
7 The "A" of sports' A.F.L.
8 Begets
9 Red Skelton persona
10 Organizer of many a sit-in: Abbr.
11 Windblown
12 Like Bob Dylan's voice
13 Opposite of Thanatos, to Freud
14 More thin and frail
15 Modify, as software
16 Reservation at a Johannesburg restaurant?
17 Mail
18 112-Across sound
24 Follow
25 Hors d'oeuvre follower
31 Pet food company since 1946
32 Worry
34 Constant, in product names
36 "Toe" of the Arabian Peninsula
37 Coll. in La Jolla
39 Tuscan town, home of the painter Duccio
40 Biblical correspondent
41 Very emotional
42 Designer Versace
44 Gently roast . . . or something that's roasted
45 Out of the office, perhaps
46 Blue pixie
48 Hipbone attachment
49 Ledger list
53 Sports org. since 1894
55 Year Columbus returned from his final voyage to the New World
56 Something that's "Miss" titled?
58 Where the driver is driving Miss Daisy
59 Sorry soul?
60 Landlord's ultimatum?
62 Sculptor Maya
63 Board, in a way
64 Purveyor of nonstick cookware
68 Bit of air pollution
69 Div. of biology
70 Actresses Kristen and Graff
73 Locale for a trophy display
76 Astronomer Tycho ___

by Daniel C. Bryant

78 Traditional church celebration
81 Univ., e.g.
82 Held in reserve
84 First president of South Korea
85 Supercilious sort
86 Nearly worthless
88 Almost

89 What's expensive in Paris?
90 Time on end
93 Currently
94 Must
96 Try to scare off, in a way
99 Library shelfful: Abbr.

100 End early
101 Work that's no fun
102 Jury members
103 Track meet events
106 Japanese noodle
108 Sell-off, say
110 Play money?

111 Key with five sharps: Abbr.
114 It has a blast
115 Mar. weekend shortener
116 ___ and cheese
117 Operator of the original N.Y.C. subway

ACROSS

1 "Come to ___!"
5 Of wrath, in a Latin hymn
9 Throws in
13 "La Resurrezione" composer
19 Film about a corrida participant put to pasture?
21 Mount ___ (volcano in Mordor)
22 Too
23 . . . a candy-sharing confederate?
25 Lake Erie city west of Cleveland
26 As bad luck would have it
27 Vivacity
28 . . . a small-minded lady?
30 "Casino" actor Joe
32 TV producer MacFarlane
34 1942 Harry James hit "___ My Guy"
35 Bowler's assignment
36 ___ Day & the Knights (band in "Animal House")
38 The mythical tree Yggdrasil, for one
40 Finback whale
41 Museum piece
43 Cut off
44 . . . an embarrassingly one-sided tennis match?
48 David Sarnoff's company
51 Political theorist Hannah
53 "Evita" narrator
54 The Beatles' "___ Got a Feeling"
55 Some solos

57 One who keeps things from going up?
59 Geometric shape whose perimeter has infinite length
62 The Colosseum was completed during his reign
63 Paramecium's propellers
65 Part of N.F.L.: Abbr.
66 Base
67 . . . decorative furniture elements being blown off with dynamite?
75 Army division
76 "Lying thief," e.g.
77 ___ Dame
78 Actress Perez
80 Speaks nonsense
83 Record keeper
87 Practices, as a trade
88 Helpfulness
89 Lunch, e.g.
91 "Rainbow Six" author
92 California city name starter
93 . . . a demonic horse?
98 Continuity problem
99 Western star Lee Van ___
101 Center of a daisy, e.g.
102 Shuffleboard stick
103 Pixar title character
104 Recitation by Scheherazade
106 "Time ___ . . ."
108 Yukon, e.g.: Abbr.
110 Makes an effort
112 . . . drink garnishes?
115 Work like a dog
117 Rhenium or rhodium
120 Inability to appreciate music
121 . . . a seedy Hollywood bar?

124 Antipathetic
125 ___ Cakesters (Nabisco offering)
126 . . . skinned knuckles?
127 Tenant
128 Home in the sticks?
129 Weather-stripped item
130 Sicilian province

DOWN

1 Gentle touches
2 Turkish title
3 One whose music is easy to follow?
4 What intersecting lines create
5 Maker of the Roadrunner supercomputer
6 "What nonsense!"
7 Wing-shaped
8 Novelist Bret Easton ___
9 1969 literary heroine who says "I like the words damozel, eglantine, elegant. I love when you kiss my elongated white hand"
10 Intelligent swimmer
11 Founder of an Oahu plantation
12 Tommy of ESPN
13 Papal office
14 Acknowledge
15 ___ oil (perfumery ingredient)
16 Bomb detector?
17 Name in 2000 newspapers
18 Country singer Shelby
20 Fellas
24 "Baby, It's Cold Outside" composer
29 Bygone Toyota
31 Hybrid farm animal

33 Afternoon meal, across the pond
36 Count ___ (2004 Jim Carrey role)
37 Singer/songwriter Amos
39 Ad ___
42 Exam for would-be attys.
44 Univ. overseers
45 Part of a TV dial
46 "What he said"
47 Where Excalibur was forged
49 Make watertight
50 Beasts of burden
52 Upscale restaurant requirement, maybe
56 "To Catch a Thief" setting
58 Sharpie tip
60 Author Malraux
61 Flagged vehicle
64 St. Clare's home
67 Consumer reports?
68 ___ Gay
69 Renders reluctant
70 "The Sandbox" playwright
71 Central point
72 Hip 1960s teen
73 "New and Improved!" might appear on one
74 Song syllables
79 Carlisle Cullen's wife in "Twilight"
80 Boisterous laugh
81 Mention
82 ___ volatile
84 Swallowing of food, e.g.
85 Hustle
86 Paper slip?
90 Personal quirk
94 English churchyard sight
95 Plants with stinging hairs

by Patrick Berry

96 Indian mulberry product
97 Sailor's sword
100 Hand brakes, e.g.
103 Conifer leaf
104 Unqualified
105 Registering a pulse
107 Electronic game fad of the 1980s
109 Gives deep massage therapy
111 Web site for cinephiles
113 What lotus-eaters enjoy
114 "I'd be glad to!"
116 Russian figure skater Kulik
118 Major publisher of romance novels
119 Helen of Troy's mother
122 Wanting to be near one's fans?
123 Last in a series

ACROSS

1 Like villains
6 Middleton who sang with Louis Armstrong
11 They might carry babies in nappies
16 Muckety-mucks
19 Cell phone feature
20 Auditorium features
22 *Kid constantly switching schools, maybe
23 *Age-revealing method
25 Headless Horseman's wear
26 The Wildcats, for short
27 Kind of expression
28 Real cutup
29 *Stale air removers
33 *Supposed results of stress
35 Danielle Steel novel about a European princess
36 Lisa with the #1 hit "Stay (I Missed You)"
38 Barks
39 "Gee," in Glasgow
42 Newer, as a car
46 "Ladies and gentlemen . . . ," e.g.
50 Biblical kingdom
52 Big name in dinnerware
53 "Conversations With God" author ___ Donald Walsch
56 British American Tobacco brand
58 *Embezzlement, e.g.
60 *Pet shop purchase
62 Gamble
63 Not an imit.
65 Makes one
66 Reuters competitor
67 Words a house burglar doesn't want to hear
68 *Party bowlful
71 Highest point on the Ohio & Erie Canal
73 "___ moment"
74 Thunderbirds' org.
76 Like peacocks
77 "___ a Woman?" (Sojourner Truth speech delivered in 1851 in 71-Across)
78 *Pluto, e.g., before it was plutoed
81 *Harlequin romance, e.g.
85 Isthmus
86 Wine order
87 Protuberant
88 ___ precedent
89 Title dog in an Inge play
91 Delicate skill
94 Cover some ground
95 Cards once traded for Gehrigs, say
98 Part of Q.E.D.
99 ___-Boy (brand of furniture)
101 *Leadfoot's downfall
106 *It's got some miles on it
112 Some World Cup cheers
113 Was two under
115 Flair of pro wrestling
116 Matey's libation
117 *Annual sports event since 1997
120 *Beginning of time?
122 Bagel request
123 Online mag
124 Arrive continuously
125 Religious council
126 Around the Clock is a version of this
127 Solomons

DOWN

1 Antiseptic agent
2 Zip
3 "You bet!"
4 "Cabaret" lyricist
5 Navy, e.g.
6 Cleaner, for short
7 Went by
8 Newswoman Logan
9 "Sex and the City" character also known as John
10 Egyptian god of the universe
11 Rice source
12 Small inlet
13 "Per ardua ad ___" (Royal Air Force motto)
14 900 years before Queen Elizabeth was crowned
15 Mister abroad
16 Tempo
17 Own, in the past
18 Double ___ (Oreo variety)
21 Some police personnel: Abbr.
24 About
30 Web address
31 Donation location
32 Cozy spot
34 Cable inits. for sales pitches
37 Oscar winner for "Life Is Beautiful"
39 Skipping
40 Carries on
41 Is not as easy as it seems
43 Atlantic City hot spot, with "the"
44 Musician Brian
45 Court cry
47 Purchase at a booth: Abbr.
48 Soldiers home from service, e.g.
49 Start of a popular children's rhyme
51 Hog
54 Elementary figure: Abbr.
55 Corrosive cleaning agents
57 Where the limbo dance originated
59 Object
60 Be a ___ heart
61 Chris with the top 10 hit "Wicked Game"
64 Woolgathering
68 Where the Senegal River begins
69 "___ all possible"
70 Citation's end
72 White wine cocktails
75 Like aprons, at times
79 Squeeze (out)
80 Nancy Drew's beau
82 Locale of an 1805 Napoleon victory
83 Supermarket with a red oval logo
84 Low-cost, lightweight autos of the 1910s–'20s
87 Lesage book "Gil ___"
90 Gymgoer's pride
92 Sensible
93 Derisive call

by Derek Bowman

96 "Time ___" (1990s sci-fi series)
97 Gave under pressure
100 Many a path up a mountain
101 Foments
102 Wields
103 Teeny-tiny
104 "Dónde ___ los Ladrones?" (1998 platinum album by Shakira)
105 Square
107 Temperance proponents
108 ___ Cong
109 ___ de cacao
110 Petty and Singer
111 Von Furstenberg of fashion
114 Kuwaiti dignitary
118 Alternative rock genre
119 Parisian possessive
121 Actor Stephen

TURNING BACK

ACROSS

1 Math class, for short
5 Future doc's exam
9 Its slogan begins "15 minutes could save you . . ."
14 How stocks may be sold
19 Snack with a floral design
20 Ship written about by Apollonius of Rhodes
21 International relief org.
22 Went for
23 Taking the dimensions of busybodies?
26 Encircle
27 Medicare add-on
28 Fair
29 Short-billed rail
31 Starting material in coal formation
32 Some wedding guests
34 Image format
36 Her feast day is Jul. 11
38 Eminem song that samples Dido's "Thank You"
41 __ germ
42 Done swimming?
45 Giving an award to the wrong person?
48 Capital of Albania
49 Freshen, in a way
50 Lipstick hue
52 Tofu base
53 Add (up)
56 Indian guy in National Lampoon's "Van Wilder" movies
57 Get on
59 Sense

61 Italian sculptor Nicola
63 Follower of White or Red
65 "That feels good!"
67 Wielder of the sword Tizona
69 More likely to get gifts from Santa
70 Slandering a Thanksgiving dish?
74 Othello, before Act V, Scene II?
76 "Enoch __," Tennyson poem
77 Plum relatives
79 Palindromic preposition
80 Map abbr. before 1991
81 Many Maurice Sendak characters
83 Kazakh land feature
86 Large cask
88 Professional org. with a House of Delegates
90 It has a big mouth but can't speak
91 Friendship ender
93 Loy of "The Thin Man"
95 Custom-make
97 Awaited judgment
99 Comment in a women's mag?
101 Summary of "Raiders of the Lost Ark"?
105 Like Beethoven's "Kreutzer" Sonata
106 January 13, e.g.
107 So far
108 Site of the oldest university in South America
109 Joins

111 Letter opener
112 Fervent
115 Character in "I, Claudius"
117 Carne __ (roasted meat dish)
121 Marion's "La Vie en Rose" character
123 Pious spouse's ultimatum?
126 Bank manager?
127 Hyundai sedan
128 Had a hunch
129 Drink in "My Big Fat Greek Wedding"
130 Wand waver, old-style
131 Like Ymir
132 Ymir, for one
133 One-eighties

DOWN

1 Give for free
2 Word with gray or rest
3 The Duke of Albany's father-in-law
4 Surname of TV's George, Frank and Estelle
5 Disfigure
6 Champagne often mentioned in hip-hop songs
7 Undecided, in a way
8 Getup
9 Suffix for shapes
10 Antiship missile used in the Falklands War
11 "It slipped my mind"
12 Cloak, in Córdoba
13 Siberian city
14 "Mein Gott!"

15 Wearer of a famous ring
16 Fruit with a thick rind
17 Crumbly cheese
18 Netflix movie
24 "__ Roi" (Alfred Jarry play)
25 Brief stay
30 F equivalent
33 Bouquet of flowers
35 Metamorphose, as a larva
37 Keeping an eye on
38 It may cause a scene
39 One who keeps one's balance?
40 Sneaker with a Jumpman logo
43 Made-up
44 Hit 1989 biographical play
46 Z follower
47 Samoan dish
51 Put to sleep
53 Dish with greens and ground beef
54 A nonzero amount
55 Unit of pressure
58 Grub
60 "__ on parle français"
62 Family of games
64 Classic Jags
66 Piece keeper?
68 Reputation ruiner
70 Brand advertised as "the forbidden fragrance"
71 Beseech
72 Go to waste
73 Overflow
75 Gray, e.g.
78 Cuckold's purchase, perhaps

by Will Nediger

82 Confessional user
84 Charcoal alternative
85 One-point Scrabble tiles
87 "Me, ___ cheerful twinkle lights me": Robert Burns
89 Torah holders
92 Agcy. that may order recalls
94 "Is it not so?"
96 Sweetheart's telephone comment
97 Egyptian coin
98 Rescue
100 Bogey
101 ". . . is fear ___"
102 "Search me"
103 Certain PC storage area
104 Apple products
110 Roosevelt or Hoover
113 Mathematician Turing
114 Doofus
116 City in Nevada
118 Flu symptom
119 Ready for a nap
120 Big deals
122 "Get your hands off me!"
124 Popular middle name for a girl
125 Shorn female

ACROSS

1 Obstinate type
4 Electronic music pioneer Robert
8 Boost
13 Straw hat
19 Cry after poor service?
20 River with the Reichenbach Falls
21 Some commercial signs
22 Remove ropes from
23 Bad news on Wall Street
25 What Fels-Naptha banished, in old ads
27 Where N.B.A. coach Rick Pitino played college ball
28 Relating to songbirds
30 Boost
31 French ice cream flavorer
33 "So nice!"
34 Excited call to a crew
36 Three squares
39 Classic camera maker
44 How to address a brother
47 Large group in a 23-Across
48 Heavenly body that humans will never set foot on
52 Alderaan royal
54 Jet boat brand
55 Alternatively, in Internet lingo
56 When said three times, a W.W. II cry
57 Followers
59 Like some doughnuts and windows

61 Unit of star measurement
62 Beckett's "Krapp's Last Tape," e.g.
65 Deli nosh
66 High-fiber, low-fat cereal ingredient
67 Mandela's presidential successor
72 Hazards for marine life
75 Blow it
77 Arc de Triomphe and Nelson's Column
81 Bet in craps
82 Strong
83 Part of MHz
84 Company that introduced NutraSweet
87 Botanical bristle
88 Tough rubber?
90 Relax
92 Angelo or Antonio
93 Connect with
94 Neutral space
97 Diminish
101 Mezzanotte is one
102 Crime scene evidence
106 Merely routine
110 Levels
113 Works in the music business
114 April, May and June
116 Blah-blah-blah
118 Subject of the 2008 biography "Somebody"
119 Bête ___
120 "Super!"
121 Object of many a court order
122 Some flowering shrubs
123 Overthrow, e.g.

124 Hair goops
125 Like a three-card monte player

DOWN

1 Contents of a sleeve
2 Request for face time
3 David Bowie single with the lyric "if we can sparkle he may land tonight"
4 Reed sites
5 Flavor associated with Chardonnay
6 Treat in a blue wrapper
7 Contends for valedictorian, say
8 See 9-Down
9 James known for playing an 8-Down
10 "Let's hear it!"
11 It does a bang-up job
12 Singer K. T. ___
13 Relative of Rover
14 Doing really well
15 Assert without proof
16 Butler's place
17 Those, to Tomás
18 "Seven Seas of ___" (early Queen hit)
24 Galaxy sci.
26 Squelch
29 "___, I'm sure"
32 Disgorges
35 About equal to
37 "___ Gold"
38 Kyushu volcano
40 "Do I dare to ___ peach?"
41 "Rinkitink ___" (L. Frank Baum book)
42 Smear with wax, old-style
43 Slightly

44 Hooch holder at a ballgame
45 Intel mission
46 Provençal sauce
49 Take ___ for the worse
50 Japanese noodle
51 Throat stuff
53 Frightens
58 Swiftian brute
59 Unhip sort
60 Farm newborns
62 "L'Après-midi d'un faune" poet Stéphane ___
63 Lift innovator
64 "ER" network
66 ___ orange
68 Crude qty.
69 Mournful songs
70 ___ Kinte of "Roots"
71 "Um . . . well . . . it's like . . ."
73 "___ la Douce"
74 Fabrications
75 He taught Mowgli the law of the jungle
76 Depletes
77 Slightest amount
78 Emporio ___
79 Actress Sommer
80 Sports competition
81 Dividing fairly, say
84 South of France
85 Check person
86 Brand for hay fever sufferers
89 Watts who hosted a 1990s talk show
91 Implants
95 Behind bars
96 Quick swims
98 Mathematician Paul
99 Smugness
100 It joins the Rhône at Lyon

by Paula Gamache

103 Places for some newborns
104 "Perry Mason" scene
105 Tear-jerking
106 Chem. pollutants
107 In short supply
108 Pearl Buck heroine
109 George Manville ___, English adventure writer
111 "Comin' ___ the Rye"
112 Chick's tail?
115 Neither's partner
117 Permitted

64

MUSICAL PLAY

ACROSS

1 Diner fixture, informally
5 Not stopping the draft, say
9 Cathedral feature
13 Once-popular Olds
18 Producer of a colorful ring tone
19 It mentions the Prodigal Son
20 ___ Men ("Move It Like This" group)
21 Kind of season
22 "Carmen" composer-turned-dam builder?
25 Passé
26 It hangs around the Amazon
27 Not straight
28 Not neat
29 Embrace more than just a family of Baroque composers?
33 Org. in the "Bourne" series
34 Union representative?
35 Hawaiian fish, on some menus
36 Mine entrance
38 These, overseas
39 Romantic overindulgence in nocturnes and mazurkas?
46 Distills
49 Some gridiron yardage
50 Zoo heavyweight
51 Buzz in a rocket
52 Oblast bordering Kazakhstan
53 ___ harp
55 Singing a "Messiah" piece too quickly?
60 Sightseer?
61 Song lead-in to "di" or "da"
62 Opposing
63 It's eight hours off from 49-Down: Abbr.
66 Countrywide music celebration in Hungary?
73 If all else fails
76 Fortune
77 "This isn't looking good . . ."
78 Missionary Junipero ___
79 It might start a rumor
81 Ohio city named for a queen
83 Part of a children's game with the Father of the Symphony?
86 Place of corruption
87 Ja's opposite
88 Poet depicted in art alongside the Scythians
89 ___ economics
92 Otolaryngology: Abbr.
93 Grand nuptials whose only music was "Peer Gynt"?
101 Climactic
102 Cousin of a goldeneye
103 Some old runabouts
104 Physicist Schrödinger and others
105 Try to capture the Waltz King?
110 Upscale upholstery
111 Hint
112 Geezer
113 Laguna composition
114 Twisty turns
115 Command
116 Dame ___
117 Honey Nut ___

DOWN

1 It might be found in a plant
2 Longtime news inits.
3 Second baseman Matsui, to fans
4 Aromatic resin
5 Purchase of 1867
6 "Even if it'll never happen again . . ."
7 Alias
8 Taxpayers' hopes
9 Noisy counters
10 Smoothed over
11 Succubus
12 Pink Mr. Potato Head piece
13 Gossip topic
14 Hindu god of thunder
15 Work ___
16 It's measured at arm's length
17 Gets in the game, say
21 Peaceful protest
23 Peewee
24 Highland tongue
28 "Funny meeting you here!"
29 How current events may happen?
30 It helps you change the locks
31 Strummed instruments, for short
32 Lager sources
33 Wine order
37 Garr of "Tootsie"
39 Till fill
40 Bring up
41 Last thing
42 It can be popped
43 Upstate N.Y. school
44 Spill-fighting grp.
45 Years on end
47 Bass part
48 They're worth their weight in gold
49 See 63-Across
52 Wink ___ eye
53 1998 film featuring Princess Bala
54 Mad person?
56 Something of yours you'll never see
57 Mel's Diner waitress
58 Greet loudly
59 Opposite of a ques.
63 Many a Little Leaguer
64 Setting forth
65 Monocrat
66 France's ___-Pas-de-Calais
67 ___ Islands, group at the mouth of Galway Bay
68 Bide-___
69 Publicist's headache
70 Choreographer Lubovitch
71 ___ Beta Kappa
72 Port SSE of Sana
73 Contents of some cones
74 Crumpet's go-with
75 Not straight
79 "This ___" (Michael Jackson album)
80 It may extend about a yard
81 Persian's call
82 News anchor Cooper
84 Sell quickly
85 Like the Ford logo
86 Track event for gamblers
89 #2

by Kevin G. Der

90 "Glory, Glory" singer
91 It's often carried around a gym
93 Irish novelist Binchy
94 W.W. I battle site
95 Gets the ball rolling?
96 "Uncle!"
97 Offspring's inheritance
98 One thrown from a horse
99 "In my opinion . . ."
100 Singer of sewing machine fame
105 Grunts
106 Mann's "Der ___ in Venedig"
107 Cry of distaste
108 Go after
109 Big band member, for short

65

LOCATION, LOCATION, LOCATION

Note: Each set of circled letters is described by an answer elsewhere in the grid.

ACROSS

1 When repeated, a resort near the Black Forest
6 How things may be remembered
11 Beginning
15 Caboose, for one
18 In ___ (unborn)
19 Homeric hero
20 Part of Q.E.D.
21 ___ Miss
22 Specification in a salad order
25 A lens fits in it
26 Swell
27 Certifies, in a way
28 U.S.M.C. barracks boss
29 XXX
31 Homeric genre
32 Address part
34 Unit in measuring population density
40 As a friend, to the French
42 Relative of Manx
43 Michael who once headed Disney
44 Grab bag: Abbr.
46 Some stakes
48 Dreadful feeling
49 Worker who may create a stir?
53 Following
56 Opening
57 Opening for an aspiring leader
59 Fine and dandy, in old slang
60 "I don't give ___!"
62 Zing
63 Writer/critic Trilling
65 Hit computer game with the original working title Micropolis

68 First name alphabetically in the Baseball Hall of Fame
70 President who said "I'm an idealist without illusions"
71 Giggle
72 Suffix with lumin-
73 Hard, boring efforts
74 Directional suffix
75 Diagonals
79 "Mazel___!"
82 Fix, as a shoelace
84 Complete
85 Country singer Griffith
87 Name on 1952 campaign buttons
89 Romance of 1847
90 Errand runners
91 Mid 12th-century year
93 Cool, very red celestial body
97 Carp or flounder, typically
99 Highly rated security
101 Hungarian city
103 Actress Ward
104 Fashion inits.
105 You might wait for it to drop
109 Three-wheeled vehicle
114 Spanish bruin
115 Go-between
117 Rapper ___-A-Che
118 Same: Fr.
119 Convict
120 Relative of a canary
121 Cinch ___ (Hefty garbage bag brand)
122 "Idylls of the King" lady
123 Falls (over)
124 Breast: Prefix

DOWN

1 Melville's "Billy ___"
2 Italian bell town
3 Dead ends?
4 Formerly, once
5 Public knowledge
6 Ph.D., e.g.
7 Barge ___
8 "Don't give ___ lip!"
9 Beverage that may be foamy
10 A wishbone has one
11 Director Vittorio
12 48th state: Abbr.
13 Begins energetically
14 Explosive trial, for short
15 Place for a date, frequently
16 "___ Restaurant"
17 Not likely
19 ". . . ___ the queen of England!"
23 "And to those thorns that ___ bosom lodge": Shak.
24 St. Patrick's land
30 One of the 12 tribes of Israel
33 Shipwreck locale
34 Ship locale
35 Last dynasty of China
36 Links org.
37 Susan who co-starred in "Five Easy Pieces"
38 Actor Neeson
39 "Cómo ___?"
41 Shopping locale
45 Indulged
47 Pre-broadcast activity
49 David Cameron, e.g.

50 Normandy battle town
51 More ___ enough
52 Dark time, in verse
54 Just got (by)
55 Trust, with "on"
57 Honey badger
58 Dinner spreads
61 Engine type
64 Employed
65 "Fer ___!"
66 French noun suffix
67 Cause of thoughtlessness?
68 Dog of old films
69 Didn't just pass
70 Noted Bauhaus artist
72 Dallas-to-Memphis dir.
73 High-hats
76 Large food tunas
77 Bausch & ___ (lens maker)
78 Langston Hughes poem
80 "The ___ Gave My Heart To" (1997 Aaliyah hit)
81 Tapers, briefly
83 Peculiar: Prefix
85 Bedouins' trait
86 It's like "-like"
88 "Next . . ."
90 Dimwit
91 City chiefs
92 Cinnamon tree
94 Swarmed
95 Indian tourist city
96 Challenger astronaut Judith
98 Chief dwelling?
100 "I'm innocent!"
102 Liechtenstein's western border
106 Certain engine
107 "This round's ___"
108 List-ending abbr.

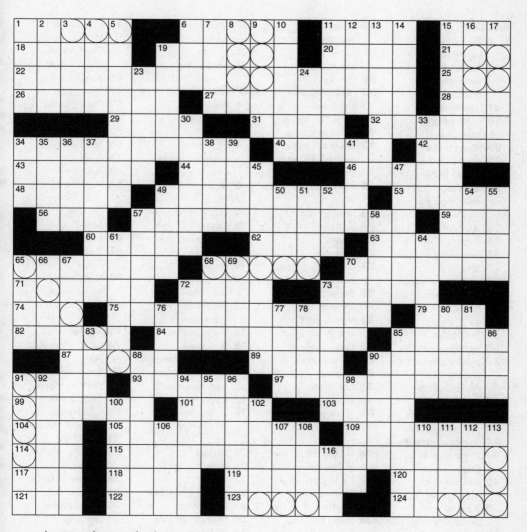

by Pamela Amick Klawitter

110 Notion
111 Mil. leaders
112 Came to
earth
113 "There Shall ___
Night" (Pulitzer
winning Robert E.
Sherwood play)
116 Elevs.

66

CAN I CHANGE PLACES?

ACROSS

1 "This can't be happening!"
6 Apple's instant-messaging program
11 Headquartered
16 Anatomical pouch
19 Spanish fowl
20 Headquarters
22 Inquire about private matters
23 Lewis and Clark expedition, for the 1800s?
25 "Monsters, ___"
26 Student
27 Elite group, with "the"
28 Like some exams
29 Turn red, say
30 "___ you!" ("Just try it!")
32 Search the heavens
35 Spoiler of a parade for Ahmadinejad?
40 Racing boat
41 Charlie Brown's curly-haired pal
44 January birthstone
46 Attaches with string
49 Like most city blocks: Abbr.
50 Parisian possessive
53 Andrea ___ (lost ship)
54 Like some kicks
55 "___ From Hawaii," 1973 Elvis album
57 Top butcher's title?
60 Pull
61 WXY buttons
62 Sultan's group
63 Santa Barbara-to-Las Vegas dir.
64 Blemish
65 Hosiery shade
66 "Climb ___ Mountain"
67 ___ en scène (stage setting)
69 Her: Ger.
70 "Independence Day" fleet
71 Singer DiFranco
72 Brewery sights
73 South American shrubs with potent leaves
75 T-shirt sizes, in short
76 Destroyers of les forêts?
79 Glide
80 Aplenty
82 Surgeon's procedure
83 Super ___ (game console)
85 Minute fraction of a min.
86 Cave dwellers
87 Menu option
89 Upbeat
91 Chocolate substitute
93 What a family court judge enforces?
96 Where sharks are in their food chain
99 Plant ___ of doubt
100 Glimpsed à la Tweety Bird
103 Luke's princess sister
104 Yellowish-brown
109 Convert, as metal into a melt?
111 Prefix with skeleton
112 Admonishment at a Surrealist museum?
115 Delivery means
116 "West Side Story" fight scene prop
117 More awesome, to a rapper
118 Slalom figure
119 Lab holder?
120 Darling
121 Like many mosaics

DOWN

1 Went (for)
2 ___ toad
3 Cold look
4 Grab bag
5 Moved on wheels, as a movie camera
6 Afraid
7 Et ___
8 Regal letters
9 Opposite of sans
10 Practical school, for short
11 Uncle ___
12 Pennies are small ones
13 Staples of action scenes
14 Poetic contraction
15 Humorless
16 Decorative piece of George Harrison tour equipment?
17 Ball's partner
18 Spring, summer, fall and winter, e.g.
21 Big suit
24 Stale
28 Eyes
31 Grade school subj.
33 Play opener
34 Wishing undone
35 Restrains
36 Boo ___, recluse in "To Kill a Mockingbird"
37 Forster's "___ With a View"
38 Crucifix letters
39 Unlikely response to "Sprechen Sie Deutsch?"
41 Actress Drescher
42 Chart showing highs and lows
43 Paintings of Marilyn Monroe, Che Guevara and the like?
45 Rests
47 Shoe insert
48 Grown-up eft
51 Anesthetic gas
52 Sharpener residue
56 Sun Devils' sch.
58 Screw up
59 Actually
64 Words said with a shrug
67 Tiki bar order
68 Medit. state
69 Suffix with robot
70 Grp. concerned with courses
71 Playground retort
72 Volunteer
74 Cabinet member: Abbr.
76 Parisian business partner, maybe
77 Squeeze (in)
78 "___ Nagila" (Hebrew folk song)
81 Site of the College World Series
84 Cornea neighbor
88 RR stop
90 Didn't shrink from the challenge
92 1990s war site
94 Member of the prosecutor's office: Abbr.
95 Fyodor Karamazov, for one
96 Advil rival
97 U.S.S. ___, first battleship to become a state shrine

by Daniel A. Finan

98 ZaSu of film
100 Peewee slugger's sport
101 Tree-lined walk
102 Kooky
105 Permanently mark
106 Japanese drama
107 Gists
108 Rights org.
110 Year Boris Godunov was born
112 Broadband letters
113 Be behind
114 Witch

ACROSS

1 "Applesauce!"
6 The pulp in pulp fiction
11 "That ticked me off!"
16 Bob and pageboy
19 1987 #1 Heart song that starts "I hear the ticking of the clock"
20 Sauce made with garlic and olive oil
21 Adrenaline producer
22 Dog show org.
23 YOUR TAX DOLLARS AT WORK . . .
26 Call of support
27 Some run to get in it
28 "Batman" fight scene sound
29 Blender brand
31 Hold 'em bullet
33 MERGING TRAFFIC . . .
38 Files that don't go far from home
40 Removed fold marks
41 Places to pray
42 Know-it-___ (cocky types)
43 Cuzco native
44 Range rover
45 STOP . . .
51 Some '50s Fords
55 Suffix with hatch
56 Special ___
57 Reply from a polite young'un
59 It's often pointed in gymnastics
60 Ermine, e.g.
61 CONGESTION NEXT 10 MILES . . .
65 Wearers of jeweled turbans

71 Neurotransmitter associated with sleep
72 NO THRU TRAFFIC . . .
76 However, briefly
77 Genetic material
78 Open mike night format, perhaps
80 From ___ Z
81 Wizened woman
84 Winged celestial being
88 STAY IN LANE . . .
91 Kind of translation
93 Setting for the biggest movie of 1939
94 Sailing
95 Number system with only 0's and 1's
98 Cheesesteak capital
101 Earthlings
103 NO STOPPING OR STANDING . . .
106 Ultimate degree
107 Like some legal proceedings
108 Has an angle
109 Syrian president
111 Comprehend
112 SPEED LIMIT 65 M.P.H. . . .
119 Guffaw syllable
120 "None for me, thanks"
121 Field Marshal Rommel
122 Feeling when called to the principal's office
123 Literary monogram
124 Cockeyed
125 Requiring an umbrella
126 Brings in

DOWN

1 Unchallenging reading material
2 ___-mo
3 Roughhousing
4 Egyptian symbol of life
5 Online program
6 City in a "Can-Can" song
7 Common inhalant
8 Creator of the detective C. Auguste Dupin
9 Architectural addition
10 Oriole who played in a record 2,632 straight games
11 Small crustacean
12 Low-level position
13 Queen of double entendres
14 Cannonball's path
15 Took an alternate route
16 The Wright brothers' Ohio home
17 Michael of "Caddyshack"
18 Gobbles (down)
24 Mortgage figs.
25 Part of 24-Down
30 Awakens
31 Swiftly
32 Kind of commentator
34 Pub order
35 Don Marquis's six-legged poet
36 Lion or tiger or bear
37 Tony Hillerman detective Jim
39 ___ Intrepid
43 Connections
44 Investment unit

46 Roadies work on them
47 First name in TV talk
48 Spanish bear
49 Actress Thurman
50 Gallivants
52 School for Prince Harry
53 Anderson of "WKRP in Cincinnati"
54 Spotted
58 Harm
60 Troll dolls or Silly Bandz
62 Gambino boss after Castellano
63 Group values
64 Place with feeding times
65 Supermarket V.I.P.'s: Abbr.
66 Best-of-the-best
67 Frozen dew
68 Betty, Bobbie and Billie followers on "Petticoat Junction"
69 Bandleader Shaw
70 Woodlands male
73 "The Situation Room" airer
74 Japanese vegetable
75 Slowpoke
79 "The Power of Positive Thinking" author
80 "I get it now"
81 Like some matching pairs
82 Representative
83 Grind together
85 Anacin alternative
86 Famed Russian battleship
87 "That's just ___ feel"
89 "___ Little Tenderness"

by Patrick Merrell

90 Houston after whom the Texas city is named
92 Toilet tissue superlative
95 Worry for a farmer
96 Leader whom Virgil called "the virtuous"
97 Jean-Paul who wrote "Words are loaded pistols"
98 Particular form of government
99 Jabba the ___, "Star Wars" villain
100 Bond offerer, e.g.
101 It may wind up at the side of the house
102 All the pluses
104 "Criminy!"
105 Sideshow worker
110 Taj Mahal site
113 Bird in New South Wales
114 New Deal inits.
115 Breathalyzer determination, for short
116 One, for Fritz
117 It's often picked up at the beach
118 QB's stat.

ACROSS

1 Alaska senator Murkowski
5 Sean who played the title role in "Rudy," 1993
10 Start to frost?
15 Pan handler
19 El océano, por ejemplo
20 Shakespeare's Lennox, Angus or Ross
21 Bitter
22 Aries or Taurus
23 Hoop grp.
24 They may be split
25 Singer with the #1 country hit "Hello Darlin'"
27 When repeated, a calming phrase
28 A whole lot
29 Debate side
30 Cartographic extra
31 Egg protector
32 Easy as falling off ___
33 Salon, for example
35 Listens, old-style
37 Suspenseful 1966 Broadway hit
43 Grp. that conducts many tests
46 Biblical liar
48 See 39-Down
49 Actress ___ Chong
51 Least welcoming
52 Wait upon
53 Gathered
54 ___ Coty, French president before de Gaulle
55 Stick in the mud
57 Subtracting
59 Cassandra, for one
60 Repeatedly raised the bar?
63 Long piece of glassware
67 N.F.C. South player
70 Noggin
71 Still product: Abbr.
72 On the safe side
73 Wave function symbol in quantum mechanics
74 Items of short-lived use
76 Racy best-selling novel of 1956
79 Take ___ (rest)
80 Hindu titles
82 Speed-skating champ Johann ___ Koss
83 Out of
87 Like an egocentric's attitude
91 Flammable fuel
93 Part of a postal address for Gannon University
95 Carry out
96 Moon of Saturn
97 Barbecue cook
98 Football linemen: Abbr.
99 Fast-talking salesman's tactic
102 Itsy-bitsy
103 Explorer ___ da Gama
104 Shout from one who's on a roll?
106 ___ loss
107 One to a customer, e.g.
110 Prime
113 Camping treats
115 B.M.O.C.'s, often
116 X Games competitor
118 Rikki-___-tavi
119 Tanned
120 Zoom
121 Florida univ. affiliated with the Catholic Church
122 ___ the hole
123 ". . . and ___ it again!"
124 "Twilight," e.g.
125 ___ manual
126 Gull relatives
127 Spat

DOWN

1 Common patio sight
2 Bliss, it is said
3 1, 2, 3, 4, 5, 6 or 7, in New York City
4 Prominent tower, for short
5 Massachusetts industrial city on the Millers River
6 Trails
7 Follow too closely
8 Dictator's phrase
9 Dread loch?
10 Spotted cavy
11 H.S. class
12 Didn't buy, perhaps
13 Don Herbert's moniker on 1950s-'60s TV
14 Lessen
15 "Educating Rita" star
16 Sheds
17 Novel conclusion?
18 Track star A. J.
26 Gave a sly signal
28 Good spot for a date?
34 "Dies ___" (hymn)
36 Prepare for a dubbing
38 Yucatán "you"
39 With 48-Across, mediocre
40 Insomniac's TV viewing
41 "The Chairs" playwright
42 Former Fords
43 Showing, as a deck member
44 Square sorts
45 Peace Nobelist Sakharov
47 Cost for getting money, maybe
50 Common settler
52 Bowls
56 ___-Tass news agency
58 Bread, milk or eggs
61 Tech stock
62 Elk
64 Folk singer Jenkins
65 Miracle Mets pitcher, 1969
66 Shamus
67 Person who's visibly happy
68 On deck
69 Rubs
75 Sweeping story
77 Schubert's "Eine kleine Trauermusik," e.g.
78 Use Turbo Tax, say
81 Comedian Foxx
84 Movie producer's time of stress
85 Tariffs hinder it
86 Oscar-winning actress for "The Great Lie," 1941
88 With freedom of tempo
89 Conditions
90 Some service stations
92 Black bird
94 Devotional ceremonies
97 Pickle type
100 Noggin
101 Ring around the collar
103 Lead-in to harp or phone

by Patrick Blindauer

105 Dancer's controls?
107 W.W. II craft
108 Furniture giant
109 Largest employer in Newton, Iowa, until 2006
111 Not e'en once
112 Winged Greek god
113 Ballpark figure
114 Cheese lovers
117 The Sun Devils of the N.C.A.A.
119 Magnanimous

ACROSS

1 Charitable contributions
5 Bungalow roof
11 Part of an ice skater's shoe
18 One of the Three B's
19 Friend of Hamlet
21 Film festival name since 1990
22 London-based place to play the ponies?
24 Firm part
25 Street bordering New York's Stuyvesant Town
26 "___ Athlete Dying Young" (A. E. Housman poem)
28 8-point X, e.g.
29 Laughing
30 J.D. Salinger character's favorite game?
37 Golfer John
38 Doughnut shape
39 Asian royalty
40 Letters on an Olympics jersey
42 Busy
44 Like Nasser's movement
48 Game played with dice set on fire?
52 "Mad Men" actor Hamm
53 "99 Luftballons" hit-maker of 1984
54 Spoilage
55 Short and detached, in mus.
56 Diva Renata
59 One-third of a game win
60 "I'm ___ you!"
62 Libido
64 One-armed bandits?

66 Arabian Peninsula native
68 Sideways on a ship
70 Participants in an annual run
71 Relative of a bingo caller?
75 Insurer's offering
79 Author McCaffrey
80 Antiquity, quaintly
81 Mitch Albom title person
82 Losing tribe in the Beaver Wars
84 Psychologist LeShan
85 Crumhorn, e.g.
87 Dearie
88 Card game played Reynolds's way?
93 Leaves high and dry
95 Poe's "rare and radiant maiden"
96 On a roll
97 "I'm not the only one?"
99 Actress Langdon
101 ___ ghanouj
105 "Please consider playing the wheel again"?
109 "Life of Brian" outfits
110 Stereotypical lab assistant's name
111 Alphabetically first inductee in the Rock and Roll Hall of Fame
112 Arriviste
114 Split personality?
118 Pot with a pile of chips?
122 Offered in payment
123 Vine-covered colonnade
124 Emphatically
125 Nods

126 Radio ___
127 Gym gear

DOWN

1 "All ___!"
2 8-Down's home
3 TV character with dancing baby hallucinations
4 Climb, as a rope
5 What you used to be?
6 Big gun
7 The Iguazu Riv. forms part of its border
8 1960s chess champion Mikhail
9 L overseer
10 Alluded to
11 When repeated, an admonishment
12 Mich. neighbor
13 Capital until 1868
14 Like politics, by nature
15 Hole just above a belt
16 Flashlight battery
17 Worked (up)
20 N.B.A. star nicknamed the Candy Man
21 World capital almost 1 ½ miles above sea level
23 Bit in trail mix
27 Part of a plot
31 "The Epic of American Civilization" muralist
32 Stuff of legends
33 Effort
34 Begins to transplant
35 "Lost" shelter
36 Squishy place
38 Art collector's asset
41 Snake's warning

43 Rock band with an inventor's name
45 Football special teams player
46 Tropical menace
47 Roadster's lack
48 Frogs
49 Seven-line poem
50 One who's all there?
51 Bygone geographical inits.
52 Scribble
57 Give for free
58 Frequently, in brief
61 Well-known Tokyo-born singer
63 "The Open Window" story writer
64 Talk to the flock: Abbr.
65 Mau ___ (forever, in Hawaii)
67 School: Suffix
69 Former Buffalo Bills great Don
72 Hall & Oates, e.g.
73 1974 top 10 hit whose title means "You Are"
74 Canvases, say
76 Coach Dick in the N.F.L. Hall of Fame
77 The Altar
78 Recess
83 Prefix with warrior
86 Do some quick market work
89 Tacit
90 Smooth operator
91 Early smartphone
92 Basically
94 Neighbor of Swe.
95 Trial of the Century defendant
98 "Shanghai Express" actor

by Brendan Emmett Quigley

100 Mathematical sequence of unknown length
102 Annual award for mystery writers
103 Most meager
104 Texas nine
105 Mandates
106 Meanies

107 Common times for duels
108 0.5 fl. oz.
109 "Your safety is our priority" org.
113 Bit of theatrics
115 "Taps" hour

116 N.Y.C. subway line
117 1950s political inits.
119 Actress Graynor
120 Metric weights: Abbr.
121 Big stretch?

70

FANGS FOR THE MEMORY

Note: When this puzzle is completed, connect the circled letters in alphabetical order from A to R to show the outline of an 84-Across.

ACROSS

1 Home of "Hardball"
6 "Love is blind," e.g.
11 Moolah
16 Even
17 Doltish
21 Odd Fellows' meeting place
22 Kind of acid
23 1922 Max Schreck film
24 Words of empathy
25 Heavyweight
26 High-water mark
27 "Enough, Jorge!"
28 Super ___ (old game console)
30 It might come after you
31 ___ Balls (Hostess snack food)
32 As written
33 Tijuana table
36 Parking spot
38 Actor McGregor
40 "Beetle Bailey" dog
44 Lover of Isolde
46 Oodles
50 Cozy place?
52 Wagnerian opera setting
54 Crime scene matter
55 Saturnalia participants
56 1995 Eddie Murphy film
59 Tech whiz
61 Athenian porch
62 Some gravesite decorations
63 Arctic herder
66 Composer Ned
68 1931 Bela Lugosi film
72 Fix, as laces
73 Coolers, for short

74 System of beliefs
77 "The Rights of Man" writer
78 Mauna ___
80 Argentine article
81 Furry adoptee
82 Water brand
84 [See instructions]
85 Cobb of "12 Angry Men"
86 A bit of cheer?
87 Like some fondue pots
89 Halloween cry
90 Compel
92 When Italian ghouls come out?
93 Poodle's greeting
95 Bygone flightless bird
96 ___ Bator
97 1979 George Hamilton film
105 "Fine"
108 Stage direction that means "alone"
109 Ring figures
113 1987 Adrian Pasdar film
116 ___ Tin Tin
117 2008 Robert Pattinson film
119 Bones also called cubiti
120 "Piece of cake!"
123 Pianist/composer Schumann
124 Tandem twosome
125 1986 Brad Davis film
126 George who wrote "The Spanish Gypsy"
127 Walk the earth
128 "___ Ben Adhem"
129 Belonging to you and me
130 Many visitors to Legoland

DOWN

1 Coconut filler
2 Acreage fig.
3 When French ghouls come out?
4 Fruit-based fountain treat
5 Make a copy of
6 Sucks up
7 Crusoe's creator
8 Breezed through
9 Grade school door sign
10 Noted New York eatery
11 Russian pancakes
12 What Chippendale furniture was made in
13 Cheese ball?
14 "Slumdog Millionaire" locale
15 Subpar grades
17 Gershwin's "Concerto ___"
18 Canine cousin
19 "Do ___!" ("Stop procrastinating!")
20 Maestro's sign
29 Skull caps?
32 Sly sorts
33 "Jersey Shore" airer
34 All alternative
35 Medal of valor
37 Like the inside of a coffin
39 Used, as a dinner tray
41 Bernard Malamud's first novel
42 Rocky pinnacle
43 Saturn's wife
45 Souvenir from Scotland
47 Early fifth-century year
48 "Slander" author Coulter
49 Bit of Vaseline

51 Communication syst.
53 Longtime Yankee nickname
55 Roman squares
57 O.K. Corral figure
58 Exclude, with "out"
59 Bunch at a grocery store
60 Epoch in which mammals arose
64 One getting hit on at a party?
65 Female fowl
67 Selfish person's cry before and after "all"
69 Common rhyme scheme
70 "Later!"
71 Biblical preposition
72 N.F.L. defensive lineman B. J. ___
75 ___ soda
76 ". . . And I'm the queen of England!"
78 Serving on a stick
79 Sushi bar order
83 Sarah McLachlan hit
85 It may be hidden at a hideout
88 Shopping center regulars
91 Kind of warfare
94 Units of cream: Abbr.
95 Slush pile contents: Abbr.
98 Least typical
99 Cold war broadcasting inits.
100 Gift giver's words
101 Epic translated by Alexander Pope

by Elizabeth C. Gorski

102 Reaches altogether
103 "Vous êtes ___"
104 Sprinkled with baby powder
105 Like a locked lavatory
106 Old-style fax
107 Hawaiian veranda

110 Question shouted in exasperation
111 Spasm
112 Some of the fine print on sports pages
114 1988 #1 country album

115 Newsman Marvin
117 Layer
118 Jazz saxophonist/ flutist Frank
121 Ontario's ___ Canals
122 "A ___ tardi" ("See you later," in Italy)

71

LEADING ARTICLES

ACROSS

1 Oscar-nominated actor with the given name Aristotelis
8 Preserves holder
14 Annapolis frosh
19 "Fine, tell me"
20 Slide sight
21 Steve who played the title role of Hercules in a 1959 film
22 Trying to stay awake?
24 Fervid
25 Stockholder?
26 Deck for divining
27 No Mr. Nice Guy
28 It has 21 spots
31 Features of some jeans
33 Reads the riot act
35 Connections
36 Pinned down?
40 "Beauty and the Beast," e.g.
41 Bunch
43 Spot overseer
44 Air bag?
46 Working hard on
50 Vigorous
52 Not worth debating
54 Popular word in German product packaging
55 Requested
56 Shaggy locks
58 Get rid of
60 Lay on
62 Debussy subject
65 Northern hemisphere?
67 Took a card
69 Like grizzlies
70 Classic theater name
72 Really enjoy going to carnivals?
75 Home to fly into
76 Noncommittal reply
78 "Darn!"
79 Work, in a way
81 Un-P.C. suffix
82 Star-___
84 Early Beatles songs are in it
86 Foe of 130-Across, at birth
88 Call to a dog
89 Vinegar
91 Twice-a-month tide
93 It was developed by Apple, IBM and Motorola
97 Seemingly without end
100 Sudden fancy
102 Lake ___ City, Ariz.
103 Site of the brachial artery
104 Prepresidential title for Bill Clinton or Woodrow Wilson: Abbr.
106 Straddling one's opponent?
108 Moreover
110 They have duel purposes
113 First near-Earth asteroid to be discovered
114 Addams Family cousin
115 Skin layer
117 Scaling tool
119 Peripheral
122 Mark who won the 1998 Masters
123 Frisking Dracula?
128 First name on "60 Minutes"
129 Rake
130 Lex Luthor alter ego, once
131 Takes nothing in

132 One of the Crusader states
133 A sixth of the way through the hour

DOWN

1 Letter start
2 Gray
3 With 4-Down, in relation to
4 See 3-Down
5 For fear that
6 Activity with flags
7 Spunk
8 Bender
9 Part of a Latin conjugation
10 Conger cousin
11 Razzed
12 Smirnoff competitor
13 Refuse to shut up
14 Jewelry designer Elsa
15 Mother of Helen and Pollux
16 Mechanic's task?
17 Neighbor of Nigeria and Togo
18 Opera singer Simon
21 Arthur C. Clarke's "Rendezvous With ___"
23 Kingdom overthrown in 2008
28 Couple
29 May event, informally
30 British P.M. between Churchill and Macmillan
32 Film you don't want to see
34 Stockholders?
37 Entrance requirement, sometimes
38 Didn't go

39 The "K" of James K. Polk
42 Partway home
45 Handyman's exclamation
47 Island do
48 Good-looker
49 Plain homes?
51 Sentence structure?
53 Gang's area
57 Any minute now
59 Furniture material
61 It may involve punitive tariffs
62 Sitcom role for Brandy Norwood
63 Ready for publication
64 What the dissatisfied female giftee might do after Christmas?
66 Certain gamete
68 Sleep unit?
71 "Goodness me!"
73 George Orwell's alma mater
74 Take in
77 Gym number
80 85-Down is part of it
83 Ocean areas
85 Home of the highways H1 and H2
87 Big name in denim
90 It may be elementary
92 Snowman's prop
94 Sitarist Shankar
95 H.S. junior's exam
96 Kind of film
98 Call makers
99 Freeloaded
101 Fool
105 Take to the cleaners
107 Nutty treat

by Will Nediger

108 Unpopular baby name
109 Site of Hercules' first labor
111 "Well, old chap!"
112 Goldman ___
116 Fountain order
118 Classic sports cars

120 Nobel Prize subj.
121 Frolic
124 Writer Levin
125 Portrayer of June in "Henry & June"
126 "Illmatic" rapper
127 Blaster

72

DOUBLEHEADERS

ACROSS

1 Buggy versions, maybe
6 Big yard area
10 Expresses disbelief
16 "The Big Bang Theory" network
19 Went beyond
21 Truck driving competition
22 Muesli tidbit
23 Factors to consider while trying to sleep on a campout?
25 Upper mgmt. aspirant
26 Superior
27 You might come up for this
28 Epitome of ease
29 Arabian Peninsula sultanate
30 What the marshal declared the moonshiner's shed to be?
35 L on a T?
37 A.E. Housman's "A Shropshire ___"
38 Smelted substances
39 Preventive measure
40 Submerge
43 Upper support
44 Attend to a plot
47 "Pardonnez- ___!"
48 Ohio State athlete who forgot his uniform?
53 Fighting fighting
56 Coxswain's lack
57 Relative standing
58 Publishing hirees, for short
59 Part of P.T.A.: Abbr.
60 From ___ Z
61 Name for a persona non grata

62 One who puts U in disfavor?
63 C.E.O.'s tricycle?
69 Start over on
70 Chain of life?
71 Local news hour
72 Keel's place
73 Dudgeon
74 Prologue follower
76 Request upon finishing
77 As a group
81 Wild Bill Hickok holding his aces and eights?
85 Spell
86 Respectful bow
87 Criminal charge
88 Picture that shows you what's up?
91 Platoon members, briefly
92 Competed
94 Unit of current
96 Places to plug in peripherals
97 Garbage receptacle that you and I insult?
103 Promising good things
104 Music genre prefix
105 Ancient Rome's Appian ___
106 "What a shame!"
107 Rose of rock
108 "That high lonesome sound," as played by Atlantic crustaceans?
115 Uma's "Pulp Fiction" role
116 Many a Monopoly property
117 Singer of the 2008 #1 hit "Bleeding Love"
118 Seat facing the altar

119 Worked on in the lab
120 Cornerstone abbr.
121 Put up

DOWN

1 Rise and fall repeatedly
2 Big day precede
3 Red Sox legend Williams
4 Call into court
5 Followed the game
6 Crooked
7 Rebel org.
8 Soprano Tebaldi
9 Went around in circles, say
10 Opposite of post-
11 Landscaper's roll
12 Zimbabwe's capital
13 Pueblo structures
14 Army-McCarthy hearings figure
15 Roman sun god
16 "Borrows peremptorily
17 Founder of Celesteville, in children's lit
18 Roadside shop
20 Indication of teen stress, maybe
24 "Turn up the heat!"
29 Missouri's ___ Trail
30 Common dessert ingredient
31 Tess's literary seducer
32 Offers a few directions?
33 "Dies ___" (Latin hymn)
34 By surprise
35 City where TV's "Glee" is set
36 In a moment
41 Discountenance
42 Called upon
43 Fragrant cake

44 Round container
45 Singer Gorme
46 Cheeper lodging?
49 Eucalyptus eater
50 Defense grp. headquartered in Belgium
51 Pharmacopoeia selection
52 It bounces
54 Shakespearean character who says "I am not what I am"
55 Nashville-to-Memphis dir.
61 Diverse
62 Composer Bartók
63 Kentucky college
64 pV = nRT, to physicists
65 Geraint's wife in "Idylls of the King"
66 Aircraft, informally
67 Like a Chippendales dancer
68 Massachusetts' state tree
69 Frees (of)
74 Covered
75 Business address ender
76 Army of the Potomac commander, 1863-65
78 Pool hall pro
79 Quatre + trios
80 Former union members?
82 1989 Oscar-winning title role for Jessica Tandy
83 Took a card
84 Census form deliverer: Abbr.
89 Sequin
90 Crayon wielder
92 Moral standards

by Patrick Berry

93 Focused
94 Fit for cultivation
95 Invitees who didn't R.S.V.P., say
97 Cargo vessel with no fixed route
98 ___ Hart, showgirl in "Chicago"
99 Deliver at a farm
100 Bygone rival of Delta
101 Harass nonstop
102 "Take ___ Train"
108 Be up
109 Ham helper
110 Spectrum segment
111 Auction purchase
112 What the sublime inspires
113 Verbatim quote addendum, possibly
114 J.F.K. arrival of old

73

HAVING ASPIRATIONS

ACROSS

1 Judge's no-no
5 Like some responsibilities
10 German-born tennis star Tommy
14 Start of "A Visit From St. Nicholas"
18 Spree
19 "The Bad News Bears" actress
20 Film character who actually does not say "Play it again, Sam"
21 "Take it easy!"
22 Robbers' gain
23 "Winnie-the-Pooh" character
24 Signal for a programmer's jump
25 One side in the 1973 Paris Peace Accords
26 Macho guys like their pie cold?
30 Second
31 Some dates
32 "___ Day Will Come" (1963 #1 hit)
33 You might play something by this
34 Ignore
37 Potential cause of a food recall
39 Name often followed by a number
41 Bad actor's philosophy?
47 "___ doubt but they were fain o' ither": Burns
48 Org. with the motto "For the benefit of all"
49 Fair-hiring inits.
50 Kim Jong-il, for one

53 James or Jackie of Hollywood
56 Carrier with a frequent flier program called EuroBonus
59 It may be snowy or spotted
61 Emmy-winning actress ___ de Matteo
62 Johnny ___
63 Concerns of middle-aged guys in lower Louisiana?
67 Cute
71 Org. for electing candidates
72 Whales, at times
73 Lengthy military sign-up?
76 Cpl.'s inferior
77 Presidential straw poll city
78 Bauxite, e.g.
79 Place for mounted antlers, maybe
80 Club Meds, e.g.
84 Way in
87 Conductors of many exams, for short
89 R.E.M.'s "The ___ Love"
91 Chit
92 Put the dentures aside while gardening?
98 ___ Park, Queens
99 News show assemblage
100 Eye parts
101 Disco fan on "The Simpsons"
104 Reed in music
105 Shiites or Sunnis
106 View from Catania
108 Starboard food fish?
116 Contest

117 Away from the storm
118 What a beatnik beats
119 Kind of theater
120 Not so tied up
121 Sail problem
122 Maine college
123 [sigh]
124 "___ of the Storm Country"
125 Lawn starters
126 Wear away
127 Vetoes

DOWN

1 Atom modeler
2 "Dies ___"
3 Content of la mar
4 Course outlines
5 Out of one's mind, in a way, with "up"
6 Vacuous
7 Hawk
8 "Were I the Moor, I would not be ___"
9 Loud ringing
10 It's symbolized by caviar and Champagne
11 Athol Fugard's "A Lesson From ___"
12 1930s film pooch
13 Portuguese-speaking island off the African coast
14 Like some spicy food
15 Pain result
16 Honolulu's ___ Stadium
17 More cunning
21 Very religious
27 Bearing
28 Chaucer piece
29 Actor Dennis
34 Diminutive suffix
35 List ender

36 "Get ___ hence": I Kings 17:3
37 Replies from the hard of hearing
38 Stop
40 Give due credit
42 Not smooth
43 Result of some time in a bed?
44 Cry of delight
45 Scrub over
46 Seine tributary
51 Nostradamus, for one
52 Soviet news group
54 One who takes people in
55 A Lennon
57 Xanadu river
58 Sobersided
60 Back talk
63 "Alas"
64 Part of a Molière play
65 Snag
66 Huggies competitor
67 Quick-like
68 Item in a music producer's in-box
69 Cricket units
70 MGM symbol
74 Bordeaux, e.g.
75 Benjamin
80 Old touring car
81 Fair attraction
82 Feature of much ancient Roman statuary
83 Goes after
85 Artist's workplace
86 Gain access, in a way
88 Roman square
90 Org. with a 2004-05 lockout
93 Chewy treats
94 Apiece

by Clive Probert

95 1976 rescue site
96 Go after
97 Dodge
101 Give a raw deal
102 Third planet from le soleil
103 Impulses

105 Hogan contemporary
106 Pushed, with "on"
107 "___ were the days"
109 Streets of Québec
110 Fleischmann's product

111 Surf sound
112 Word after bang, break or bump
113 Letters of faux modesty
114 Title for Helen Mirren
115 Couples no more

ACROSS

1 Passes with flying colors
8 Home of Hells Gate State Park
13 A lot of an orchestra
20 Really, really want
21 Break off
22 "Are we not joking about that yet?"
23 Sounded sheepish?
24 Roulette bet
26 How pets may fly
27 Came to realize
28 Avant-garde composer Brian
29 Quick flight
30 Something groundbreaking?
31 N.B.A.'er Smits, a k a the Dunkin' Dutchman
32 Amaze
33 Shed thing
36 Source of some rings
38 Felt in the gut
41 Richard Gere title role of 2000
42 Peach, e.g.
45 Onetime "S.N.L." regular Tina
46 Snack food with a Harvest Cheddar flavor
50 "Butter knife" of golf
51 Deem
56 Austin-to-Waco dir.
57 Frozen, perhaps
59 Escapee from a witch in a Grimm tale
61 Swingers' grp.
62 It may be put down on a roll
64 Up for bidding
68 Strong aversion, colloquially
70 Kind of moment
71 10 Downing St. figures
73 R.V. refuge org.

74 Reflux
76 Places for needles
77 Go by
79 Exactly right
82 Mythological triad
83 Porker's place
84 Creatures known to lick their own eyeballs
86 Itty-bitty
88 "Cómo es ___?" (Spanish "Why?")
89 Nuts about
90 It guards the heart
94 Kind of romance between actors
96 One of the Gandhis
99 ___ Grand
101 Vegas opening?
102 ___ Na Na
104 What might go for a dip?
108 Worked up
110 Big name in late-night
112 "Don't try any more tricks!"
114 Brooks or Blanc
115 When repeated, an old sitcom farewell
116 Cry of self-pride
117 Beginning
118 Preceders of xis
119 Stretched figures
121 R&B funk trio with the 1990 hit "Feels Good"
124 One using twisted humor
126 Is worth doing
127 Trattoria topper
129 Letter-shaped support
131 Provides service that can't be beat?
132 Stave (off)
134 Part of a sunbow
136 Shih ___ (dog)
137 Blue stuff
139 Bitter quarrels
142 Input

144 Beatles' last studio album
148 Annual Manhattan event (represented symbolically in this puzzle)
151 Transmission repair franchise
152 Footnote abbr.
153 Zero
154 Christmas ___
155 Leader of the Silver Bullet Band
156 Lillian of silents
157 Seek damages
158 Org. that infiltrated Nazi Germany
159 Rx amount: Abbr.
160 In thing

DOWN

1 Doesn't shut up
2 Razzle-dazzle
3 With 5-Down, when 148-Across traditionally takes place
4 Pirate's realm
5 See 3-Down
6 Ceaselessly
7 Intense heat
8 La Palma, e.g.
9 Canned foods giant
10 Cosmetics giant
11 Title for Judge Judy
12 Cookie with creme
13 Wakens
14 Picker-upper
15 Where 148-Across takes place
16 "Yes, Virginia, there ___ Santa Claus"
17 Traditional centerpiece of 148-Across
18 "Diary of a Madman" author
19 December fall
24 Dinner in a can
25 "Whip it" band
34 Discus path

35 Mount in myth
37 Here, in Dijon
39 "Deus ___ "(1976 sci-fi novel)
40 Low-___
43 Hardly a plain Jane
44 Capital of Iceland?
46 Winds
47 Detach, in a way
48 Movie co. behind "Wordplay" and "My Big Fat Greek Wedding"
49 Ready
52 Blind guess
53 French seasoning
54 Texas A&M athletes
55 Asserts something
58 Magnetic disruption in space
60 1960s girl group, with "the"
63 Literary inits.
65 It's picked in Maui
66 Part of an ear
67 Torque's symbol
69 Gate projection, for short
72 Man in the hood?
75 One-named rock star
78 Stream of consciousness, for short?
80 Chu ___ (legendary Confucian sage)
81 What it must do
82 PX patrons
85 Fraudster
87 Frenchman's term of address
89 Shtick
91 Swell
92 Echo producer
93 "Right there with you"
95 Chinese "way"
96 Clean again, as a floor
97 Tiny creature
98 Like St. Nick

by Jeremy Newton

ON A ROLL

ACROSS

1 Hearty drinks
7 Midwest city named for an Indian tribe
12 More sentimental
19 Major diamond exporter
20 Closing to some letters
21 Trapped
22 It makes the hair stand on end
23 First step of instructions for what to do with this finished puzzle
25 N.Y.C.'s ___ of the Americas
26 Goal of a screen test
28 Many an extra on "Star Trek": Abbr.
29 Vacation conveniences, for short
30 Vitamin C source
31 Raise a big stink?
33 Kids
35 "___ Us," 1995 Joan Osborne hit
37 Path of enlightenment
38 European leader?
39 Black
40 Flavor
42 Part of PIN: Abbr.
44 Make up
46 "Where does it ___?"
47 Is
48 '60s–'70s 114-Across locale
51 Web browser provider
52 ___ fide
53 Part of every month
54 Reveals
56 Instructions, part 2
63 Prohibition's start
64 ___ Little, "The Wire" gangster
65 Old Philadelphia stadium, informally, with "the"
66 Earthen pot
67 Bygone Starfire, e.g., informally
68 ___ Rebellion of 1857-59
70 Evicts
72 Org. in 2005's Oscar-winning "Crash"
73 Hightail it
74 Alternative to plata
75 Cellar item
76 Bedouin
77 Instructions, part 3
82 Demagnetize, say
83 St. in a children's rhyme
84 Coupling
85 Previously
87 Half of many a business partnership
88 Ticks off
91 Plug's place
92 It's between green and black
95 Viceroy, e.g.
96 Snap
97 Aware of
98 Nile biters
102 "We shun it ___ it comes": Emily Dickinson
103 "Beat it!"
105 Little bit
106 Moolah
107 Except for
109 Certain thankful
110 ___ alai
112 Some funerary ware
114 See 48-Across
115 Last step of the instructions
119 Tie up
121 Cell phone plan units
122 "Pick me! Pick me!"
123 Long fights
124 Least puzzling
125 Pedestal toppers
126 Barrels along

DOWN

1 Doha native
2 Lopsided
3 Said "yea"
4 The Beatles' " ___ No One"
5 Edsel
6 1984 Olympics site
7 The Cowboys of the Big 12 Conf.
8 Portions
9 Connecticut town named for an English river
10 Coop group
11 Wall St. worker
12 Second place
13 "___ it goes"
14 Bud
15 Dr. ___
16 Charges, in a way
17 Honda model
18 Begrudges
20 Follows through with
24 Ripley's last words?
27 Insurgent group
32 Pond fish
34 Acme product in Road Runner cartoons
35 Long-running hit TV show based in Chicago
36 ___ -upper
40 Farrier
41 Polly of literature, e.g.
43 Fade, maybe
45 Condé ___
47 Revises
48 Doze
49 Artemis' twin
50 Pea observer
52 Time for a party, in brief
53 Rapper with the 1988 platinum album "Power"
55 Plummet
57 Board
58 Latin lover's word
59 Elicit
60 Alpaca relatives
61 Home of minor-league baseball's Diablos
62 Depress
68 Undersides
69 Greek god whose name is one letter off from 118-Down
70 Soak up rays
71 Second-largest city in Kyrgyzstan
75 "No problemo"
76 "On tap" sign, sometimes
78 Affirms
79 Depressing darkness
80 Scuttlebutt
81 Device for winter sidewalks
86 Virtue
88 Take for granted
89 Superstate in Orwell's "1984"
90 Good rolls in craps
91 One-named singer/actress
92 "___ -la-la!"
93 Stampede
94 [That's awful!]
96 The rite person?
99 Waste
100 Finished second

by Ben Pall

101 Gray hair producer, they say
104 Superman's closetful?
105 Vista
108 Pin holder
110 King in II Kings
111 Brouhahas
113 Trim
116 Packed away
117 Head, in slang
118 Greek goddess whose name is one letter off from 69-Down
120 Virginia's ___ Highway

ANSWERS

1

(1)W	A	R	E	■	J	A	N	E	T	S	■	(9)H	A	B	I	T	A	T
T	I	M	O	N	■	E	R	A	S	E	S	■	C	O	R	O	N	A	D	O
O	D	I	N	G	■	W	I	N	K	A	T	■	A	R	T	L	O	V	E	R
P	E	N	C	I	L	(5)E	N	E	R	S	■	U	N	I	O	N	I	S	T
■	O	N	A	■	T	I	R	E	■	O	S	S	E	■
O	(4)E	■	E	N	A	T	E	■	R	I	S	E	■	R	A	Z	O	R	(14)
L	T	R	■	E	C	L	A	S	S	■	H	A	S	H	■	V	O	L	E	S
D	E	N	■	R	E	L	S	■	T	H	O	M	■	A	S	I	N	I	N	E
P	R	E	T	E	R	(6)	■	K	E	E	P	A	(10)L	O	O	K	O	U	T
R	E	S	O	D	■	A	U	E	L	■	E	L	O	N	■
O	R	T	S	■	H	Y	P	E	R	I	N	(8)I	O	N	■	S	C	O	T
■	C	E	O	S	■	C	O	L	S	■	(12)L	A	K	E
(2)E	A	R	T	H	S	O	C	I	E	T	Y	■	A	L	S	O	R	A	N
C	A	P	E	E	S	H	■	E	L	S	A	■	(11)F	E	E	■	D	P	S
A	V	I	L	A	■	I	S	L	E	■	R	E	T	O	O	L	(13)I	E
R	E	A	L	M	S	■	C	T	R	L	■	V	E	R	V	E	■	S	S	S
■	I	S	I	S	■	A	C	E	D	■	I	C	C	■
(3)O	B	J	E	C	T	S	■	(7)B	O	R	N	C	I	T	I	Z	E	N
T	R	U	E	L	I	E	S	■	G	I	D	E	O	N	■	I	R	A	N	I
O	C	O	T	I	L	L	O	■	A	L	E	T	T	E	■	O	R	N	O	T
N	A	Y	S	A	Y	E	R	■	S	E	X	T	E	T	■	N	I	E	L	S

(1) FLAT (2) FLAT (3) SHARP (4) FLAT (5) SHARP (6) NATURAL (7) NATURAL (8) FLAT (9) NATURAL (10) SHARP (11) FLAT (12) NATURAL (13) SHARP (14) SHARP

2

M	A	O	R	I	■	S	P	U	D	■	T	A	C	I	T	■	W	E	B
A	S	H	E	N	■	O	P	I	N	E	■	H	A	L	V	E	■	E	A	R
K	I	N	G	J	A	M	E	S	A	V	E	R	S	I	O	N	■	I	S	O
E	S	O	T	E	R	I	C	A	■	O	R	E	■	M	R	A	P	R	I	L
■	C	A	T	T	■	R	U	N	A	W	A	Y	M	O	D	E	L
A	L	C	O	T	T	■	R	O	A	R	E	D	A	T	■	T	O	R	Y
L	E	A	P	■	Z	U	N	I	S	■	W	E	M	E	T	■
G	E	N	T	L	E	A	M	E	N	■	A	M	A	S	S	M	E	D	I	A
A	R	T	I	S	A	N	■	S	Y	R	I	A	■	N	E	R	U	D	A
■	C	U	R	I	E	■	A	D	R	E	P	■	R	Y	D	E	R
O	U	R	■	P	E	P	P	E	R	A	C	O	R	N	■	E	S	P
U	N	I	T	Y	■	S	A	U	T	E	■	N	E	O	N	S	■
S	T	J	O	E	S	■	M	A	R	I	N	■	T	R	U	C	K	E	D
T	O	N	Y	A	R	O	M	A	S	■	D	A	R	T	A	B	O	A	R	D
■	S	H	I	V	A	■	D	O	P	E	Y	■	U	L	N	A
H	E	R	R	■	E	N	A	M	E	L	E	D	■	B	A	T	B	O	Y
A	R	O	U	N	D	R	O	B	I	N	S	■	R	O	A	D	■
M	A	S	S	E	U	R	■	B	L	T	■	N	O	P	R	O	B	L	E	M
P	S	I	■	A	N	A	B	O	L	I	C	A	S	T	E	R	O	I	D	S
E	E	N	■	L	E	T	I	T	■	S	I	Z	E	S	■	N	O	M	A	R
R	R	S	■	E	D	E	N	S	■	T	A	I	S	■	S	T	A	M	P

3

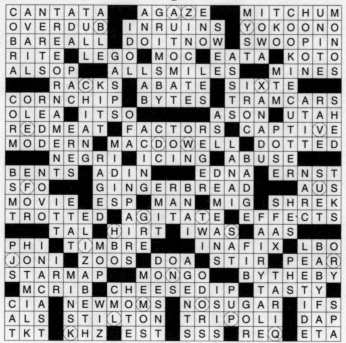

```
CANTATA   AGAZE    MITCHUM
OVERDUB  INRUINS  YOKOONO
BAREALL  DOITNOW  SWOOPIN
RITE  LEGO  MOC  EATA  KOTO
ALSOP    ALLSMILES   MINES
    RACKS  ABATE   SIXTE
CORNCHIP  BYTES  TRAMCARS
OLEA  ITSO    ASON   UTAH
REDMEAT  FACTORS  CAPTIVE
MODERN  MACDOWELL  DOTTED
    NEGRI   ICING   ABUSE
BENTS  ADIN   EDNA   ERNST
SFO   GINGERBREAD    AUS
MOVIE  ESP  MAN  MIG  SHREK
TROTTED  AGITATE  EFFECTS
    TAL  HIRT  IWAS   AAS
PHI  TIMBRE   INAFIX   LBO
JONI  ZOOS  DOA  STIR  PEAR
STARMAP  MONGO   BYTHEBY
  MCRIB  CHEESEDIP  TASTY
CIA  NEWMOMS  NOSUGAR  IFS
ALS  STILTON  TRIPOLI  DAP
TKT  KHZ  EST  SSS  REQ  ETA
```

4

```
PHDS   SARAN   PBJ   ABEAM
SEEIFICAROM  OUI   GOLDA
HYPNOTICTRANSOM   AGAIN
AJA  RODE   VEIN   STAYED
WORSEN    STEMTOSTERNUM
  ETAL  STERNO   HOSTESS
    GETAWAY     VOW
CAP  GALES   OFFICEMAXIM
BLOB  LOL   BREAK   OLIVE
SILICONVALIUM    STONED
  EARN  ERA  IMO  KONG
RINSES    BRUTEFOURSOME
ACTED  SEOUL    YSL  OURS
HEADOFHAREM   MOCKS   TIP
    LOU    EURASIA
ACHEFOR   BUMMER   DXCV
THELIONSDENIM    PEERED
BEANED  NOAH   TARA   UTE
EATIN  PARTICLEBOREDOM
SPEND  IRA  PIEALAMODEM
TODOS  GEL   GOLEM   NYSE
```

5

Grid 5:

S	T	I	L	T		C	L	A	R	I	C	E		C	E	R	A	M	I	C
T	O	G	A	E		A	E	R	O	S	O	L		A	V	O	C	A	D	O
O	S	A	K	A		D	O	N	T	P	L	A	Y	M	A	T	C	H	E	S
R	E	V	E	R	S	E			I	T	E		C	R	E	A	M			
K	E	E	P	U	P	T	H	E	J	O	N	E	S	E	S		A	R	L	O
		O	P	A		E	A	C	H			L	A	W						
	F	E	W		C	O	A	S	T	E	R		D	U	L	C	I	N	E	A
G	R	E	E	N	E	N	V	Y		D	A	T	E	D	E	S	T	I	N	Y
E	A	R	L	E		S	E	A	S		T	A	R	E			E	C	C	E
S	T	Y	L	I	Z	E		E	A	T	M	E		Z	E	R	O	E	S	
			G	E	T	T	H	E	P	R	O	G	R	A	M					
G	O	E	T	H	E		A	O	R	T	A		E	P	I	C	U	R	E	
A	N	T	I		M	L	L	E		P	H	E	N		L	A	T	E	N	
S	E	A	L	E	D	A	K	I	S	S		I	M	T	H	E	B	A	N	D
P	A	T	T	E	R	N	S		S	T	A	N	D	E	E		A	H	A	
		K	I	N			O	L	D	E		N	I	L						
A	Q	U	A		P	A	S	S	F	L	Y	I	N	G	C	O	L	O	R	S
M	U	L	L	S		O	I	L			R	E	N	E	W	A	L			
I	O	N	L	Y	W	A	N	N	A	B	E	Y	O	U		I	R	E	N	E
S	T	A	I	N	E	D		U	K	U	L	E	L	E		Z	O	N	E	D
H	A	R	N	E	S	S		S	E	M	I	N	A	L		E	S	S	E	S

6

Grid 6:

C	O	L	D	C	A	S	E		Z	A	P	S		P	H	A	S	E	R
O	P	E	R	A	T	O	R		I	D	E	E		P	H	A	L	A	N	X
C	A	S	T	L	E	I	N	S	P	A	I	N		S	O	R	B	E	T	S
A	L	T		I	M	S		T	I	M		S	A	I	N	T	E			
			E	M	O	T	I	C	O	N		O	L	D	B	A	G			
A	T	C		H	B	E	A	M		T	O	R	T		G	E	O	R	G	E
L	O	A	F	E	R		S	A	F	E	S		I	T	R	Y		O	R	S
U	R	B	A	N	E		O	T	I	S		M	P	A	A		W	N	E	T
M	E	L	D		A	N	N	A	N		T	E	E	U	P		A	X	E	S
N	A	E		T	K	O	D		A	I	R	E	R		H	E	R	B	
I	T	S	R	A	I	N	I	N	G	C	A	T	S	A	N	D	D	O	G	S
	I	T	E	N		X	Y	L	E	M		P	R	E	Y		M	O	E
M	A	T	E		G	R	O	P	E		C	L	I	M	E		E	B	O	N
A	B	C	S		T	E	N	D		F	A	I	R		D	W	E	E	B	S
D	O	O		P	H	I	L		K	A	R	M	A		L	E	G	R	E	E
A	D	M	I	R	E		I	N	I	T		E	N	D	E	D		S	R	I
M	E	S	M	E	R		N	O	M	I	N	A	T	E						
		L	A	U	P	E	R		G	A	D		L	G	A		L	I	V
M	I	R	A	C	L	E		D	E	U	S	E	X	M	A	C	H	I	N	A
E	P	I	T	H	E	T		I	G	E	T		E	A	R	M	A	R	K	S
H	O	N	E	Y	S		C	O	S	Y		D	R	Y	E	R	A	S	E	

7

```
S P R   C P A   M O M E N T   W I N E D
T H E B A R D   O R A T I O N   A M A T I
R O M A N O V   N I G H T W A T C H M A N
U N I T E D   S I G M A   B U L K I E S T
G O T H M U S I C I A N   A S C O T
      C O N A N     G R E     W R Y
E M I R   T A G   C H I   A P A C H E S
R I T E S   P O A C H E R S   E L A I N E
A N A L O G   F L O R A L A R R A N G E R
S I L I C O N   A R O D   W I C K
  M O T I V A T I O N A L S P E A K E R
    A I D A   N I C E   E N Z Y M E S
A L G E B R A T E A C H E R   T A L O N S
P A E L L A   U N C L E S A M   M E T E R
O U T S E L L   T H E   S O O   S E W S
D D S       A S S     E L T O N
      C H E S T   V I L L A G E I D I O T
S E A H O R S E   O L I O S   P L A Q U E
T V P E R S O N A L I T Y   W A L N U T S
E I S E N   S T R A F E D   B I G G I E S
P L O P S     S T R E S S   C R O   T R A
```

8

```
S L U E   B I G D   I N A N E   O R B
E I N E   S I N A I   C O R A L S   R I A
S P I K E H E E L S   E M A R K E T I N G
A T V   M A R V   C A M E B Y   N O O S E
M O A T E D   E R O D E     L I O N E L
E N C O R E P R E S E N T A T I O N
    O G R E   E T S   R O W E R   S U P
I R A T E   Y A L U   M A N I A   P A R E
O A T H   C T R S   I O N E X C H A N G E
C H O P C H O P   E M U S   R A I D E R
    M A Y A N S   D O N   A B O U N D
K R I S T I   S I F T   B A S S T U B A
H I S T O R Y B U F F   J A R S   B N A I
A C T E   L O O N Y   L U S T   B R E A M
N E S   M I K A N   B A D   A L O U
    L I F E T I M E M E M B E R S H I P
A G H A S T   A T P A R   A D H E R E
W R E S T   O H S N A P   H O N E   C O E
F O X H U N T E R S   O X Y G E N T A N K
U K E   P I R A T E   S E D E R   O T O E
L S D   P A P A S   T R E E   P E N D
```

9

```
E X T R A   S A T     D O G     A M O E B A
W I L E S   I V E     I K E     M A U L E D
E X C I T E M E N T     G A R D E N T O O L
    N O L O   D A I S Y     I S E L I N
O P S   C O N     S R I     C O S T A
R O M   O P E R A S I N G E R     Y E A H
G R O U S E   E T E S     A D A M   S A G O
    C O N T R A S T     A S A M A N   S R O
B I T S     C O N C E N T R A T E     T O P
U N H E A L E D   A V E R S     R I M E
D E F A M E D   P R I M O     S O L A R I A
    A L I A   P O E T I     G U N S T A N D
L O B   S P L I T S E C O N D     A N A S
E R R   S T E N T S       R A S P U T I N
N C I S   O D I E     H O U R     E N A M E L
T A C T     P O D D E D P L A N T     A L E
    A I D A N     E R E     R C A     L Y E
    V E R S U S     S C O U T     M I S C
B I R T H S T O N E     M O R A L T E N E T
O C E L O T     B U N     W A D     E D U C E
B E S E T S     S G T       S P A   D E M O N
```

10

```
B E L     A S H       A Z E R A     H A R I
A M A   O P T I C     C L O N E S     A P O P
D E L I V E R T H E G O O D (5) S     L P G A
C R A V E     T I D I E S T     A I S L E S
O I L E R   P E R I       O L D S T E R S
P L A Y (2) F O R A F O O L     E S T O P
    S E I S     C Y M B A L S     S N I T S
C A M   D E T       B O N A M I     E Y E
O G E E   F A C E (4) R E A L I T Y   O P E
Q U E L L   L A V I E     A Z O V   R E N
    I T S O N   T E N     L E K   R E A D S
J L O   G A M E     M E L E E     S T E I N
E E N   (3) M A R K M Y W O R D S   O R Z O
A R E   U N T I E S       E T O   (7) E R
N A S A L   D O N N I S H   S A N T
    (1) W O R M   D O N K E Y S Y E A R (8) S
S A M E N E S S     E L E A     A B U S E
A B A S E D   O U T S E L L     D A C H A
K O K O   F U L L M E T A L (6) J A C K E T
I D E M   I N A N E R     S T U D Y   U L A
S E R E   R E R A N     O P S     S F C
```

(1) BOOK (2) BOOK (3) BOOK (4) BOOK (5) BOOK (6) BOOK (7) BOOK (8) BOOK

11

```
S P L A T     B O T H     O B E R L I N
F O R A G E   M E L E E   M A R I A N A S
A H U G A N D A K I S S   G R A C E F U L
B A N E S   I D I O T I C   T S E   O S E
R V E R   T E R N S   T A H O E   D R E W
I E R   A C I D   P A T E N   M A M A S
C I S C O K I D   P I N C H   A L A
    O R E   S I X T H   M A T I L D A
  A F R O S   M U N I   I R I S H   T E S
W R A P U P   A N T E   N E A P   V A N S
A R I S T A   C K S   D A N   E T A L I A
L I R E   I R A E   P E L T   R I C K E Y
T B A   K N O W N   O B I S   U M A S S
Z A N I E S T   Y E N T E   S O N
    D R E   M A S T S   S T U N T M A N
B A S I L   G U C C I   W A W A   E C O
E S Q S   P A S H A   B A B E L   L E A P
A S U   M A B   T R E A D L E   H O R D E
D E A R A B B Y   G A R D E N M A R K E T
S T R O L L E R   O R A L S   G L E A M S
  S E C T O R S   T P K E   M O N T Y
```

12

```
L A M P S   L A C A S A   G A B F E S T S
I S A A C   E X A C T S   E V E R M O R E
P E R S O N A L S H O P   T O N I B R A X
O C T O P O D   H I M O M   N E A R E S T
    E D U C   E A T I N   T R Y
A N T I D E P R E S S   L A V   Y O W Z A
M O R N   S T I N T   V I D A L   S O I L
O N O F F   O P S   W H E E L I E   U R B
K E G L E R   P L E A S U R E P R I N C I
  L A Z E   L E N S   T R E A D O N
S C O T   B I E R S   L A P S E   M E N O
Y O D E L E R   H A I R   A M A D
P H Y S I C A L G E O G R A   D A R K E R
H I T   M C Q U E E N   O I D   J O N A H
O B E Y   A I R E S   P U R E R   C E C E
N A S A L   S E Z   A R T I C H O K E H E
    N E A   D E L T A   E L O N
B A C K E N D   R O O T S   A D S P A C E
U N D E R G R O   O N T H E W A T E R F R
R E L E A S E D   M A L O N E   A R T O O
T W I S T T I E   S L E W E D   R U S S O
```

13

```
B E S A M E ■ I L L ■ C A P R I ■ M G M ■
A P O L L O ■ C U E ■ O L O R D ■ A R O D
S I P P I N G O N A G L A S S O F W I N E
E T H S ■ ■ I N K ■ L O S T ■ ■ A S S I N
H O I ■ M A L I ■ Y A N K ■ B B S ■ S Q S
I M S T I L L C R A Z Y A B O U T Y O U
T E T R A D S ■ E K E ■ ■ L A N C O M E
■ ■ A T E ■ O S O ■ S F O ■ I O S ■
■ I C A N T L I V E W I T H O U T Y O U
T O C K ■ S A I D ■ M I X ■ A N N ■ E A R
W H I S T ■ H O U S E M A I D ■ T S A R S
O I L ■ H M O ■ A I R ■ T R O P ■ E S S A
D O Y O U R E A L L Y M E A N T H A T
■ ■ A M B ■ U S O ■ A D S ■ B O O ■
■ H A S B E E N ■ ■ S R O ■ S O L A R I A
■ I S T H A T T H E W I N E T A L K I N G
R L S ■ O N E ■ A L O E ■ D U T Y ■ P A R
E L I E L ■ ■ S C A R ■ O W N ■ ■ I P S E
I T S M E T A L K I N G T O T H E W I N E
N O T I ■ A L I E N ■ I T O ■ I M O N I T
■ P S T ■ P A D R E ■ N O D ■ S U N G T O
```

14

```
H A G ■ S N L ■ U S B ■ R E D ■ V A P O R
I N H A L E D ■ N U R T U R E ■ O R A T E
S N O W O W L ■ S C I A T I C ■ Y E N T A
S A S H A Y ■ J O H N J A C O B A S T O R
■ T I N O ■ A W A G ■ ■ E G O ■
■ O S L E R ■ U N S I N K A B L E ■ A B O
B P O E ■ K I N ■ T I E R R A ■ S N A P
O A F ■ S C O T T S ■ C E C E ■ R A I S E
C R T ■ W I N S A T ■ O P T S ■ E L G I N
A T H L E T E ■ X E R ■ S I T ■ P O H L
■ E E N Y ■ T I T A N I C ■ S E N T ■
■ S A S S ■ S O D ■ H A T ■ C O A S T A L
P A B L O ■ T H E M ■ P U T O U T ■ O V A
F L Y I N ■ A E R O ■ S P U R T S ■ R E N
C A S E ■ T H E M A P ■ N A H ■ B E R G
S D S ■ M O L L Y B R O W N ■ A L U M S
■ F A N ■ ■ I F H E ■ M A R E
E N G L I S H C H A N N E L ■ P R I M P S
S A L U D ■ E L E C T O R ■ I T S A B O Y
S T A T E ■ R U N L A T E ■ C O O L E R S
O L D E N ■ A B S ■ D E S ■ C N N ■ R E T
```

```
A P P . A L L S . R A C I S M . D I S K S
L E A N M E A T . A T O N C E . E N T E R
T O S E E A N E W D O C T O R . P L O Y S
E N S O R . S P I N . O R R . C L A W .
R A I N . D I P L O M A O N T H E W A L L
E G O . V E N E E R S . . R A T . W I E
D E N Y I N G . . T H E S A M E N A M E
. . . E S O . A G A . A M O C O . A Y E S
J U S T A V E R A G E L O O K I N G . . .
E R N . O S A G E S . . S E A T E D
L A U R A . C L A S S M A T E . E T U D E
L L B E A N . A U G U R S . N I L
. W H E N D I D Y O U G R A D U A T E
T O T E . W O R R Y . N A S . I A N .
W H Y D O Y O U A S K . I N D I C E S
A I M . N O S . A S S E N T S . O N O
Y O U W E R E I N M Y C L A S S . A L T O
. R A C K . S E A . R E S T . S P L I T
B E R R A . W H A T D I D Y O U T E A C H
Y E A T S . E A T S U P . A R R E S T E E
E L Y S E . A M O U N T . S E N T . E S S
```

```
P O S T I T S . S T I G M A . A S P S
A S T O L A T . P E G L E G . S O N N E T
W H A T S M Y B A R L I N E . I N T O N E
. T E A S E R . N O B A R F L Y Z O N E
W O E . A L S O . O O X . K A L
A S P I C . V I A . M A S T . E M I
T H E D A V I N C I B A R C O D E . R E E
T A N T R I C . O M E R T A . A L I T .
. A L I E N S P A C E B A R C R A F T
S H A G . I T E M . P L I A B L E
T E L . H O S T E L . A B R O A D . L E X
A X L R O S E . A L L Y . M E A T
C A S H B A R F O R C L U N K E R S .
. T O O K . I D A H O S . O R A N G E S
O V A . S A V E D B Y T H E B A R B E L L
P A R . E S S E . E N E . A C T I I I
O M G . I L E . A S S T . L A D
S O A P B A R O P E R A . E R E S T U
S O M A L I . M A R S B A R A T T A C K S
U S E N E T . A L G O R E . N O N U K E S
M E S S . N O O N E R . I N S T Y L E
```

```
Y O U P A Y ■ A D R E P S ■ B R I N E S ■
D Y N A M O ■ P E O R I A ■ O C T O M O M
S L O P E D ■ P A L M E D ■ S A S H I M I
■ E N A K E D L A D I E S ■ G O R A N
O M A R R ■ E A S E S ■ S L Y E R ■ A L T
D O G H A N D L E R ■ Q T Y ■ B E T T I E
S T O A ■ E A S T ■ S U I ■ G O A H E A D
■ T L E T T ■ C H O C O L A T E ■
P A S S E D ■ O N R E D ■ M I T ■ E R S T
I T A ■ B L U ■ G O D S E N D ■ A N I T A
P A B L O E S C O ■ B I E A N D K E N
E L I A N ■ A R R A N G E ■ R S T ■ K E G
R E N U ■ C R I ■ L E O N I ■ T I D I L Y
■ R O O M B R A W L ■ S P A C E ■
M A K E H A Y ■ E M T ■ C O I L ■ L O M E
A R E N D T ■ T S O ■ B A L A L A I K A S
M I I ■ E I E I O ■ L O M A N ■ T V S E T
B E L L A ■ B E L L Y U P T O T H E ■
A T L A R G E ■ D E L R I O ■ B O R D E N
S T O R M E R ■ E V E N E R ■ S M U R F S
■ A R D E N T ■ R I S E R S ■ P E S E T A
```

```
H U M V E E S ■ M I X E S ■ C H I V I E D
E N T I T L E ■ A R E N A ■ O U T I N L A
T E A C H E R ■ T O N A L ■ S P A N N E D
H A R E ■ V I E T N A M V E T S ■ C O M E
■ R A V E ■ F L E W ■ E O N S ■ R A C E ■
A T R E S T ■ D R O O L E D ■ S E V E N S
C H A R L E S ■ S O L E S ■ F L Y I N T O
E S T S ■ L A W ■ D A D ■ F R I ■ N T S B
■ A G A T E S ■ V ■ F E E D M E ■
M T V ■ A V A T A R ■ G A R N E R ■ V I S
C H I P S I N ■ R E P O T ■ C O S S A C K
C E L L ■ V I N C E V A U G H N ■ T R E E
A F L A T ■ C O A N C H O R S ■ R A I M I
B E A T I T ■ M S T ■ E U R ■ D U N C A N
E D G E D I N ■ M E S A S ■ T E N D O N S
■ E L E V O N ■ R O D ■ S U N N I S ■
L O V E D O N E S ■ V ■ W H I T E N E S S
I G O T O ■ U E L E ■ F I A T ■ R S V P S
M R I ■ V E S T A L V I R G I N S ■ E E G
A E C ■ E D E ■ S L A V E ■ O S U ■ I N T
S S E ■ R U R ■ H A T E D ■ N A P ■ N T S
```

19

```
COAGULATE   PNCPARK    MUY
OBSESSION   ROSALIE    INE
WANTEDDEADORALIVE      CBS
AMESS        DUM      PSHAW
NARC  BURNEDATTHESTAKE
     LIENEE    ARIA    REED
  HOOKEDONPHONICS      ALDO
TERSE    ATAN      EAT
SIDESTEP   ALEKEG   TIDAL
EGER  BLESSEDEVENT   ELI
THA  MALTA    NOTON   BAN
STL  CRACKEDJOKES   ARME
ESSAI  SOISEE  EMERSION
    TIO   PETA    OPEDS
FAIT  GROUNDEDFORLIFE
ALGA  REBS    AIMFOR
TOUCHEDINTHEHEAD   ASST
CHAKA      HAM      ETAPE
EAN  DRESSEDTOTHENINES
LOA  ITSONME  FOOTNOTES
LES  NESTLES  AIRCANADA
```

20

```
MCS  DENIM   TAPS    SAABS
RHO  ALONE   ISLAM   ADMIT
MARRYINGTHEKALE      FLITE
OREOS    HORSY   SPEEDUP
MOSTPASTORS   STAIRRAMP
   AWARDS   BOAST    LEE
SGT  ATE    IOUS    ARYANS
CRACKYOURPATE   PIE
CHOPPER  NIA    BACARDI
HOMERS  CANDLEWITHHAIR
ELY  MARS   INEZ    IVE
RAKINGMYMOUNDS   BOWMEN
IRONORE   HEE   NOWHERE
   RDA  GROUNDHOWLING
AFRESH  MOTH   AIL   GTE
RIO  ABACO   NAUSEA
TRAILMUCK  BETTERLOCKS
DENSEST  PIANO    PARCH
EBOLA  CHILLEDWITHFEAR
COKES  HALLE   DRAMA  ERE
OXEYE   MESS   SYNCS  LSD
```

(1) BALL (2) BALL (3) BALL (4) BALL (5) BALL

23

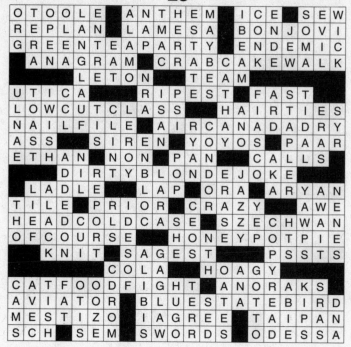

O	T	O	O	L	E		A	N	T	H	E	M		I	C	E		S	E	W
R	E	P	L	A	N			L	A	M	E	S	A		B	O	N	J	O	V	I
G	R	E	E	N	T	E	A	P	A	R	T	Y			E	N	D	E	M	I	C
	A	N	A	G	R	A	M		C	R	A	B	C	A	K	E	W	A	L	K
				L	E	T	O	N			T	E	A	M	

OTOOLE ANTHEM ICE SEW
REPLAN LAMESA BONJOVI
GREENTEAPARTY ENDEMIC
ANAGRAM CRABCAKEWALK
LETON TEAM
UTICA RIPEST FAST
LOWCUTCLASS HAIRTIES
NAILFILE AIRCANADADRY
ASS SIREN YOYOS PAAR
ETHAN NON PAN CALLS
DIRTYBLONDEJOKE
LADLE LAP ORA ARYAN
TILE PRIOR CRAZY AWE
HEADCOLDCASE SZECHWAN
OFCOURSE HONEYPOTPIE
KNIT SAGEST PSSTS
COLA HOAGY
CATFOODFIGHT ANORAKS
AVIATOR BLUESTATEBIRD
MESTIZO IAGREE TAIPAN
SCH SEM SWORDS ODESSA

24

MASHES BACKSTAB APERS
CREOLE ARISTIDE REBEL
FORGOCOLDTURKEY CROCI
LORGNETTE ATE SAILON
YMA DOONESFORBIDDING
ELEE REEK ELIO
ABIDE CAST ALLATSEA
FORGIVEUSTHISDAY ENC
OBOE IMPS NARY BUTTE
GONDOLA ELUDE PATDRY
FORAGEAPPROPRIATE
ALEUTS CHOSE ELLESSE
MINTS BLOC IONA RIPS
PVC PLAYHARDTOFORGET
SEEDCOAT TOOT MONDO
ERIN CFOS PSST
GRINANDFORBEARIT ELF
LEVITT LAE NEARFATAL
AMAZE CARRIESAFORTUNE
DINER ASSERTED PEEDEE
STANS THESSALY STEEDS

25

```
T S A . G U L A G . W A D E S . P S A L M
A O L . E R A T O . E R O D E . A L L E E
I S T I L L D O B U T I U S E D T O T O O
C O I N . S N U B S . R E S E R V O I R
H O M E R S . . S E U L . L U C I A
I N A P E D E S T R I A N S P O C K E T
. T E A M O . T I O . R E S T U P
F A D . S K I P I T . N A A N . U R I
E S A U . T H R O U G H N O T D Y I N G
N I M B L E . I N S . N O V A E
. A P O O R J U D G E O F A N A T O M Y
. A L I E N . I R E . D E W I E R
N O I T A K E T H A T B A C K . S L A P
O W N . R O U X . S T R E A M . O H M
D E T A C H . S I T . O N T O P
. S O T H A T S H O W I T C O M E S O U T
. T A R O T . M I D I . S T E R N A
S U P E R D O M E . N E E D S . U T I L
I S I N A G L A S S J A R O N M Y D E S K
D A N D D . E L S I E . E Z I N E . G O T
E R A S E . D O E S T . D E P O T . A N O
```

26

```
D E B U G . O A R S . M I S H A . M D S E
A L I M A C G R A W . A N N A S . T I K I
B I G A P P L E C I R C U I T S . F E E S
A D O . E R E . C S H A R P . A M U S E
T E T E S . L O S E O N E S M O J I T O
. G A Z E B O . S R O . T I R E S
P O L I T E D A N C E R . S A H L . A R I
A R E S . B U R . H A E . P E E R E S S
R A S . S R A S . O R A T E . L Y E
S C H O L A R . P U L P I T F I C T I O N
E L A T E . D N A . D E A . R A M B O
C E N T E R O F G R A V Y . L A U G H I N
. O P E . L E I C A . L A K E . E T C
O R B I T A L . A R C . I F I . O R E O
D E O . I D I G . L E A R N E R S P E R M
I D T A G . E E K . A U L A I T
C L A S H O F T H E T A N S . G S T A R
. A N I T A . S A L A M I . S S N . I S O
A B I T . S M O K E Y A N D T H E B A N D
D E S I . T O R I C . S T R E E T C R E D
A L T S . S E E S T . S O Y S . S C A R Y
```

27

28

```
B U B B E ■ ■ A L O P ■ N B C ■ ■ S L O B
A L L E N S ■ S A R I ■ A R O O ■ P O U R
N E A R T O ■ S W E E T B I R D O F U T E
D E B T I N V E N I C E ■ G O I N S I D E
■ ■ ■ C R E E S ■ D E N ■ A N N E ■ S O D
T A H O E ■ A S M A D ■ A D A G I O ■ ■
A R O N ■ G L E E ■ ■ R Y E S ■ N A D I A
B U S T L E ■ S H A M A N ■ ■ A C H I N G
O B E R O N ■ ■ B A T R O O M H U M O R
R A D O N ■ T O M E I ■ A L A I ■ ■ S N O
■ ■ ■ L I K E P U L L I N G T E A T ■ ■
A B S ■ A R I E ■ C O D A S ■ R A V E N
C R O S S O N E S P A T ■ ■ L A B I L E
T A U N T S ■ ■ L A R A M S ■ A L L N E W
S Y R I A ■ A R I D ■ ■ I C K Y ■ E N N E
■ ■ P R O L I X ■ A T A R I ■ ■ R O Y A L
A A A ■ D R I P ■ E R R ■ A N G E R ■ ■
S C R O O G E S ■ Y O U A N D M E B O A T
W E L T M A N A G E M E N T ■ E V O N N E
A L E R ■ N E W T ■ A S T O ■ N E O C O N
N A S A ■ E S O ■ S T A N ■ ■ S T E N T
```

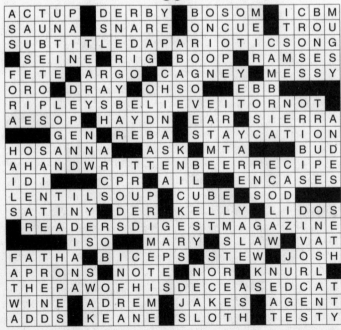

```
A C T U P ■ D E R B Y ■ B O S O M ■ I C B M
S A U N A ■ S N A R E ■ O N C U E ■ T R O U
S U B T I T L E D A P A R I O T I C S O N G
■ S E I N E ■ R I G ■ B O O P ■ R A M S E S
F E T E ■ A R G O ■ C A G N E Y ■ M E S S Y
O R O ■ D R A Y ■ O H S O ■ E B B ■ ■
R I P L E Y S B E L I E V E I T O R N O T
A E S O P ■ H A Y D N ■ E A R ■ S I E R R A
■ ■ G E N ■ R E B A ■ S T A Y C A T I O N
H O S A N N A ■ A S K ■ M T A ■ ■ B U D
A H A N D W R I T T E N B E E R R E C I P E
I D I ■ C P R ■ A I L ■ E N C A S E S
L E N T I L S O U P ■ C U B E ■ S O D ■
S A T I N Y ■ D E R ■ K E L L Y ■ L I D O S
■ R E A D E R S D I G E S T M A G A Z I N E
■ ■ I S O ■ M A R Y ■ S L A W ■ V A T
F A T H A ■ B I C E P S ■ S T E W ■ J O S H
A P R O N S ■ N O T E ■ N O R ■ K N U R L
T H E P A W O F H I S D E C E A S E D C A T
W I N E ■ A D R E M ■ J A K E S ■ A G E N T
A D D S ■ K E A N E ■ S L O T H ■ T E S T Y
```

31

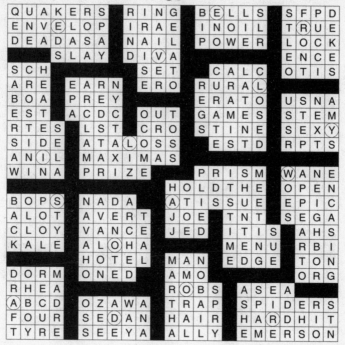

32

33

```
A C E   A S C A P   C O R A L   N O A H S
M R X   S M A R T   A R E T E   O P R A H
B O X S C O R E S   N I S E I   T E T R A
L O O P H O L E   R A S C A L   O N E A L
E N N E   C A L L E D O U T A T F I R S T
      W A H   I N A N E     A T T Y S
  S T E P   C A P E     R O P E
F A I R B A L L   W A L K E D I N A R U N
E L M S   M A O   S L E N D E R   L U K E
Z E E   P I N O N   I C E   C O B R A
  S W I N G F O R T H E F E N C E S
S P L A T     S E T   L I L A C   I N K
O D O R   E N F I E L D   E I N   S T A G
B A T T I N G O R D E R   F O U L T I P S
    D O O R     Y E S T   I O N A
  N O S E R   A S T O R   C E O
B O T T O M O F T H E F I F T H   P L E A
R E O R G   B E L I E F   R E A L T O R S
A V O I R   A D A R N   F U L L C O U N T
G I L D A   M I S T S   A I L E D   T I E
G L E E M   A N T S Y   S T A T S   S E R
```

34

```
W I N   D O W N S   A D A P T   C S I S
A N A S   A W A I T   V O T R E   R A N K
R U I N   T E S S A   O R T O N   A L O U
D I V I D E D H I G H W A Y   P A C E R
S T E V E     G E E   S M I R K S
    E V I L   B E A D S   I N P E R I L
F A L L E N A P A R T   L A S S   D O L L
L I E   L A T I N S   R O M E   S W O R D
A R M B O N E S   S E V E R   L I M E S
B E A R P I T   A C U M E N   I O N
  S N O   T O R N A S U N D E R   D S T
    K E Y   H A R A S S   R E T O T A L
H I D E R   G O T O N   E M P O W E R S
I S I N G   I D O L   T O R I E S   A S A
G A R P   E G A L   B A N A N A S P L I T
H O T R O L L   E B O L A   E T U I
  B O R G I A   O A K   P C L A B
  T I M E R   F R A C T U R E D S K U L L
W I K I   E A T A T   O D E T O   E N D E
A V E S   C U R I E   M O T T O   R N A S
Y O R E   O F A L L   E N D E R   S S S
```

```
L E G R E S T S ■ O C A S E Y ■ F A T A L
A W E A T H E R ■ R U F F L E ■ A G O G O
L E T T H E T I M E S R O L L ■ B O W E R
A R S E N E ■ U L A ■ E L B E ■ N N E
■ A D O S ■ D E S C R Y ■ O R E I D A
L O G ■ H O U S E K E E P I N G S E A L
P A R A S ■ W A L ■ A R O U S E S ■
S H I P L O L L I P O P ■ R D A ■ F E M
■ U P T O N ■ O N S E T ■ I G U A N A
■ E V E S ■ M R T ■ R A D ■ A K R O N
Y O U R E A M A N C H A R L I E B R O W N
A P L A N ■ U T E ■ E L S ■ A L F A
D U L L E A ■ O M E G A ■ H E I R S
A S A ■ N A N ■ N O N E W S I S N E W S
■ D A S B O O T ■ V I A ■ T E N A M
T H E E R A O F F E E L I N G S ■ D N A
R E N O I R ■ T R A I T S ■ A L L E
I T S ■ G A M E ■ S T E ■ F A E R O E
V E L M A ■ I M I N T O S O M E T H I N G
E R E C T ■ M I L I E U ■ C O S T A N Z A
T O R S O ■ I N S E R T ■ D E T E R G E D
```

```
H I P P O ■ S T E M ■ A T T A R ■ D A L I
A L A I N ■ T I T O ■ B A H A I ■ E L A N
S L I C E S I N T O ■ E B E R T ■ G I G A
■ N O T E N O U G H T O R E T I R E O N
A S K ■ O A K ■ E T U I ■ D E N S E
G O I N G T O B E A R E L A T I V E ■
E L L I O T ■ A F L ■ D I L A T E ■ F A X
G A L L ■ L C D T V S ■ T I L ■ S A T E
A C E ■ S E A L ■ A I R P O L L U T I O N
P E R O T ■ L O W ■ R A E ■ D H A R M A
■ L E T I T A L L H A N G O U T ■
A Z A L E A ■ C I O ■ T A O ■ R E E K S
F I N A L L Y G O T I T ■ D U M A ■ A I T
A N T S ■ C I R ■ N O L I T A ■ I S M E
R E E ■ R E P U T E ■ R A N ■ F A C T O R
■ R E D E F I N E T H E M I S S I O N
S A L E S ■ F L A W ■ O O P ■ N N E
T H A T H A S N T B E E N W A S H E D ■
Y E T I ■ L I E S L ■ A M I N O A C I D S
L A I N ■ A N S A E ■ S E R E ■ L H A S A
E D N A ■ N E S T S ■ E X E D ■ T O N T O
```

37

38

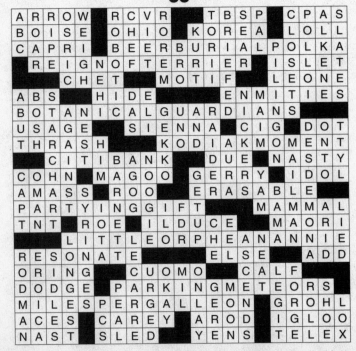

39

Grid 39:

A	R	T	S	■	L	E	A	F	L	I	K	E	■	■	T	S	G	A	R	P
N	E	H	I	■	L	E	N	A	O	L	I	N	■	S	H	E	L	T	E	R
G	A	E	L	I	C	W	A	R	N	I	N	G	■	H	A	V	A	R	T	I
E	L	I	O	T	■	■	■	E	G	A	D	■	A	R	T	E	S	I	A	N
R	A	S	■	C	L	A	S	S	I	C	A	C	T	I	O	N	S	U	I	T
E	L	L	■	H	U	G	O	■	■	■	L	I	E	N	■	■	M	L	S	■
D	E	E	D	■	R	U	S	T	I	C	B	U	C	K	E	T	S	■	■	■
■	■	O	S	A	K	A	■	A	B	O	M	B	■	■	A	L	C	A	N	■
U	P	F	O	R	■	U	N	S	E	T	■	L	A	I	L	A	A	L	I	■
S	U	M	■	S	C	A	N	N	E	D	■	K	I	N	G	L	Y	R	I	C
E	R	A	T	■	R	O	D	I	N	■	C	N	O	T	E	■	S	P	E	E
F	I	N	E	T	U	N	I	C	■	P	R	O	N	E	T	O	■	E	N	T
U	T	I	L	I	Z	E	D	■	B	E	E	T	S	■	■	P	A	N	S	Y
L	Y	C	E	E	■	■	I	R	E	S	T	■	Z	I	P	I	T	■	■	■
■	■	■	O	R	I	G	I	N	A	L	C	Y	N	I	C	■	L	E	V	I
S	O	O	■	■	W	I	S	C	■	■	■	O	T	O	E	■	R	A	M	■
T	O	P	I	C	O	F	T	H	E	M	O	R	N	I	N	G	■	A	R	P
A	L	I	M	E	N	T	S	■	C	E	R	A	■	■	G	O	N	N	A	■
M	A	N	M	A	D	E	■	G	R	E	A	T	L	Y	M	Y	S	T	I	C
P	L	E	A	S	E	D	■	P	U	T	T	O	S	E	A	■	L	I	S	T
S	A	D	D	E	R	■	■	A	S	S	E	N	T	T	O	■	O	C	H	S

40

Grid 40:

B	R	A	S	S	■	S	T	R	A	W	■	S	O	P	■	G	R	A	S	S
R	A	B	A	T	■	T	R	O	T	H	■	T	W	A	■	T	O	V	A	H
A	C	E	L	A	■	R	O	S	E	A	G	A	I	N	■	O	T	E	R	O
S	K	E	T	C	H	O	U	T	■	T	H	I	N	G	S	■	C	R	A	P
■	■	■	S	K	I	P	P	E	D	■	I	N	G	R	A	M	■	A	L	P
P	A	P	■	S	P	H	E	R	I	C	■	S	T	A	V	E	■	G	E	E
O	N	A	T	■	S	E	R	E	N	E	R	■	O	V	E	R	S	E	E	R
P	A	R	E	N	T	■	■	D	A	T	E	D	■	Y	A	L	L	■	■	■
S	T	A	M	B	E	R	G	■	H	U	N	C	H	■	S	O	A	R	E	D
T	O	D	■	C	R	O	O	K	■	S	I	T	O	N	■	T	W	I	N	E
A	L	I	T	■	S	T	I	E	S	■	N	E	V	I	L	■	S	P	E	W
R	I	G	H	T	■	S	N	I	T	S	■	N	E	N	E	S	■	P	R	Y
S	A	M	E	A	S	■	G	R	A	T	E	■	R	E	T	R	I	E	V	E
■	■	■	U	N	T	O	■	A	L	E	P	H	■	■	S	A	D	D	A	Y
J	O	H	N	G	A	L	T	■	E	A	S	E	F	U	L	■	S	I	T	E
U	N	E	■	L	Y	D	I	A	■	M	O	R	O	N	I	C	■	T	E	D
M	E	W	■	E	E	L	E	R	S	■	■	M	E	R	I	D	I	A	■	■
P	H	E	W	■	R	A	G	T	O	P	■	W	A	T	E	R	D	R	O	P
I	O	D	I	C	■	T	A	L	L	A	D	E	G	A	■	C	A	I	R	O
N	U	T	S	O	■	I	M	A	■	S	A	G	E	R	■	U	P	P	E	R
G	R	O	P	E	■	N	E	B	■	S	W	O	R	D	■	S	T	E	N	T

41

42

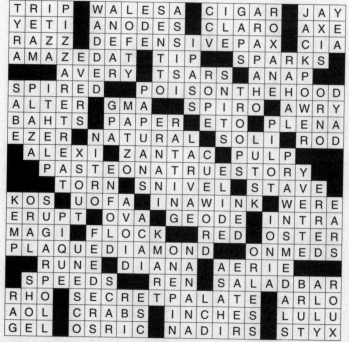

45

46

```
S A M E H E R E ■ O P A Q U E ■ P A I L S
T R A V E L E D ■ M E D U S A ■ E L L I E
A N G E L M A N A G E M E N T ■ N I T T I
G O I N ■ S P A R ■ R I B ■ S E N O R A S
■ ■ T E T E ■ M A S T E R ■ G A T O ■
S H A U N ■ D O R M ■ S C A L Y M O V I E
S A L A D A ■ N E A P ■ P I P E ■ A M A
T H E L I G H T S T U F F ■ M T S ■ T E S
S A X ■ C A W ■ T I N L I K E ■ J O L T
■ D O T Y ■ C O S I ■ H A I R D O
P I L A T E S O F T H E C A R I B B E A N
A G E N T S ■ V I A L ■ E N D S ■
Y U N G ■ P I E D I S H ■ C G I ■ M S G
C A N ■ T W O ■ F A N T A S T I C F O U L
U N O ■ V O L E ■ E Y R E ■ S A L O M E
T A X I D R I V E L ■ E M A J ■ T E R S E
■ L O I S ■ A R I O S I ■ A B E T ■
F I E N N E S ■ O E R ■ N A C L ■ C H A P
E D W I N ■ W E D D I N G C L A S H E R S
S E I Z E ■ A R E T O O ■ H Y S T E R I A
T A S E R ■ M A S O N S ■ S N E E R S A T
```

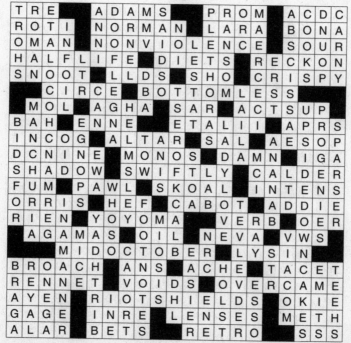

```
T R E ■ A D A M S ■ P R O M ■ A C D C
R O T I ■ N O R M A N ■ L A R A ■ B O N A
O M A N ■ N O N V I O L E N C E ■ S O U R
H A L F L I F E ■ D I E T S ■ R E C K O N
S N O O T ■ L L D S ■ S H O ■ C R I S P Y
■ C I R C E ■ B O T T O M L E S S ■
■ M O L ■ A G H A ■ S A R ■ A C T S U P
B A H ■ E N N E ■ E T A L I I ■ A P R S
I N C O G ■ A L T A R ■ S A L ■ A E S O P
D C N I N E ■ M O N O S ■ D A M N ■ I G A
S H A D O W ■ S W I F T L Y ■ C A L D E R
F U M ■ P A W L ■ S K O A L ■ I N T E N S
O R R I S ■ H E F ■ C A B O T ■ A D D I E
R I E N ■ Y O Y O M A ■ V E R B ■ O E R
■ A G A M A S ■ O I L ■ N E V A ■ V W S
■ M I D O C T O B E R ■ L Y S I N
B R O A C H ■ A N S ■ A C H E ■ T A C E T
R E N N E T ■ V O I D S ■ O V E R C A M E
A Y E N ■ R I O T S H I E L D S ■ O K I E
G A G E ■ I N R E ■ L E N S E S ■ M E T H
A L A R ■ B E T S ■ R E T R O ■ S S S
```

49

```
NORMANS   SGT   ASP    OBJ
OVERLAY   DUOS  BORN   MAO
PUPILSSLIPUP   BLOOPERS
EMO   STAMEN   BEACHBABE
   ADA   PERSEUSSUESREP
WANTOUT   BAIT   TRA   ATH
EQUIP   AUPAIR   OYERS
BUTTRESSEDDESSERTTUB
BAS   LENZ   AHA    URLS
   LIBRA   SUBPARRAPBUS
ELTORO   AUNTS   ARISEN
WARSAWWASRAW   LASED
EPEE   HIT   DENT   UFO
  DEROGATIVEEVITAGORED
  SPOTS   EXTRAS   AWGEE
UMA   UPA   PAPA   YESLETS
GIGOLOSSOLOGIG   RPS
SCENESHOP   SENTRA   TWA
ORIENTAL   XERXESSEXREX
MOS   TAME   ITES   VENTURE
EST   LES   SOS   PROCEED
```

50

```
ATP   FRET   DUNN   LOCKER
DAN   LEDE   MARIO   INHOME
ABE  0/3 DGRAPHICS   DEERES
PLUS   BARNES   HTS   ARENT
TEMP   IRING   HOREB   RADS
  FOYERS   D/4 ELICACY
PONIED   PREMEAL   BR U/7 TES
BRINKS   REBIDS   BYTURNS
S W/2 AG   OMENS   CAL   PITT
  OBV   BERU   WAROF   ERA
PUTN I N/6 ELETTERSINORDER
OSE   TENET   EXIT   T/5 OO
DIED   NOM   SMITE   TIVO
INNINGS   COILER   ALANIS
AGASSI   WAILERS   POTATO
  TANGIBLE   SONOMA
SCAR   EARLS   PARES   ROMA
PARIS   GEE   HUBERT   SRIS
AMECHE   MAGIC 0/8 BALL   ANS
MENTAL   ACUTE   EPEE   TBA
SLA C/9 KS   NETS   LESS   A N/1 Y
```

FINAL ANSWER: COUNTDOWN (9-8-7-6-5-4-3-2-1)

51

```
DEMO █ SHINE █ HOMER █ RAMA
OLAV █ ABNER █ ENOLA █ OFIT
RIDE █ HOTANDHEAVY █ URGE
KHAN █ AMELIA █ STEGOSAUR
SUMMERBREEZE █ SUDSIER
█ ITA █ ENDS █ NEEDLE
FILTH █ HARI █ AAHS █ SAO
UNIT █ MOROSE █ YOUD █ UFOS
MSG █ CONSULS █ DONNA █ TRE
ATH █ ATE █ GAP █ RIYAL █ HAT
NAT █ RHYTHM █ SENATE █ ELP
CTA █ LEMON █ PEA █ TEN █ DEI
HES █ ARONI █ ENMASSE █ AXE
USAF █ SONG █ USENET █ TRAC
█ FOB █ NEHI █ ERIN █ ASKME
SHERYL █ STDS █ SHU
COASTAL █ OLDMANWINTER
ONTHENOSE █ ARCHIE █ AWRY
OSHA █ CAUGHTACOLD █ MIRA
THEM █ INIGO █ BOYLE █ IRON
SURE █ ASTON █ SOSAS █ SLRS
```

52

```
DESKS █ IPOD █ CLAMS █ ANAP
ALCOA █ NILE █ AARON █ NOLO
DIARYQUEEN █ PRISONGRAB
SARA █ UNDO █ SASS █ URANO
█ ENIAC █ APB █ EARLYDAY
BED █ INTERNALANGEL █
EUCLID █ DOOMED █ LASHOUT
EROO █ AMISS █ OWED █ ESTE
BOWSPRITS █ MARITALARTS
█ TRYTO █ GIBED █ EDIES
MOSHE █ TREASURED █ ACCRA
INTEL █ INLET █ BOFFO █
TRIALBLAZER █ LEGISLATE
EYER █ OILY █ MOREL █ DREA
RESTORE █ MYFOOT █ MESMER
█ ROUGEELEPHANT █ YSL
DIGSINTO █ SON █ COSEC
IRATE █ FROG █ ANTI █ FRAU
DEVILSLIAR █ TROTREFORM
ONEL █ EOSIN █ SLOW █ RIPUP
KALE █ ETHNO █ KOKO █ RESTS
```

53

H	A	H	A	S		E	L	C	I	D		E	L	S	E		E	B	B	S
I	M	U	S	T		J	O	U	L	E		M	O	M	A		S	L	A	P
C	O	M	P	U	T	E	R	R	O	R		E	S	A	U		C	A	R	R
		D	E	D	U	C	E	S			O	R	T	S			A	N	T	I
G	A	R	R	E	T	T		E	N	G	L	I	S	H	E	E	P	D	O	G
E	M	U		N	E	E	R		A	T	I	L	T		F	R	E	A	K	S
L	I	M	I	T	E	D	E	D	I	T	I	O	N		E	S	T	O	P	
		S	A	S		V	O	L			H	A	W		T	O	P	P	S	
	B	A	L	I		D	A	I		P	R	I	M	E	R	I	D	I	A	N
T	R	E	A	D	M	I	L	L		O	P	S		R	E	C		C	L	E
R	A	N		C	A	S	E	N	S	I	T	I	V	E			O	L	E	
U	S	E		A	X	L		T	I	E		O	N	E	S	E	A	T	E	R
S	C	I	E	N	C	E	N	T	E	R		R	V	S		L	U	S	T	
T	O	D	A	Y		C	E	E		V	I	A		R	E	D				
		S	H	U	T	S		P	L	A	C	I	D	O	M	I	N	G	O	
O	R	A	T	O	R		T	W	O	A	M		N	I	T	E		O	U	R
P	E	R	S	O	N	A	L	I	T	Y	P	E		V	I	N	R	O	S	E
U	G	L	I		L	I	D	S			T	A	I	N	T	E	D			
S	E	E	D		L	I	N	E		G	U	A	R	D	I	A	N	G	E	L
E	N	N	E		E	G	G	S		O	P	I	N	E		R	E	E	V	E
S	T	E	R		I	N	S	T		P	I	L	E	D		Y	E	S	E	S

54

C	A	R	P	O	R	T		M	A	M	B	A			J	O	B	J	A	R
O	V	E	R	P	A	R		U	S	U	A	L		B	A	D	M	O	V	E
M	E	N	O	T	T	I		S	O	S	H	A	L	L	Y	E	W	E	E	P
E	D	E	N			S	P	I	C	E	S		E	O	N	S		C	R	U
T	O	W	E	L	W	H	A	C	K	S		D	A	T	E		F	O	A	L
O	N	S		O	M	A	R				P	O	S	T		S	L	O	G	S
		S	A	D		T	H	E	L	I	F	E	O	F	W	I	L	E	E	
D	O	Z	E	N	S		B	E	L	I	E	F	S		I	A	M			
O	R	A	R	E			D	I	A	L	S		B	B	L		V	A	C	
N	A	D	E	R	S	W	A	D	E	R	S		T	R	U	E	L	O	V	E
A	T	O	N		H	O	Y	A			E	V	I	L		C	L	A	M	
T	O	R	E	D	O	W	N		T	H	I	N	A	S	A	W	H	A	L	E
E	R	A		O	W	S		D	H	O	T	I				A	A	R	O	N
			A	I	M		I	R	A	N	I	A	N		O	R	I	E	N	T
G	A	R	G	L	E	A	N	D	W	I	N	C	E		I	B	M			
E	V	E	R	Y		S	A	R	S			S	T	L	O		S	A	C	
N	O	V	A		F	I	F	E		F	I	L	T	H	Y	W	I	T	C	H
E	C	O		T	I	T	O		C	A	M	I	S	E			D	E	C	O
T	A	K	E	A	B	I	G	W	H	I	S	K		L	I	E	O	V	E	R
I	D	E	A	T	E	S		P	U	R	E	E		O	L	D	L	I	N	E
C	O	S	T	A	R			A	B	E	T	S		T	E	A	S	E	T	S

55

56

57

```
ONIONS   SCALIA    PESCI
SKISUIT  TALONS    ETHAN
WEIGHTHREEKINGS    WOOLF
ANNE    AWRY    LUVS  PLO
SHARPEIPEN   CREMA  SPAR
NOW  ARC  SASHA   ELITISM
TRAPDOOR   LIENS    EDEN
    IRONED   CZAR   TANGLE
BITTE   FIFED   SIGHTSAW
ACHY   JOECAMEL   TIO PHI
RHE  HARDEN   VISORS  RON
RIG  EYE  SCHIPHOL   SARG
ERICSSON   YALIE    HAYES
LOVETT   RAFT   DETOUR
   ILER   AGREE   REDBARON
CENTRIC   AARGH   LEB  ECO
ORGS   NOBLY  GENERALLEI
RAT  IGOR   ATRA     DADS
OSRIC   TOBAYORNOTTOBAY
NEALE   INURES   CRIMPER
ASYET   EXCESS   ESPIAL
```

58

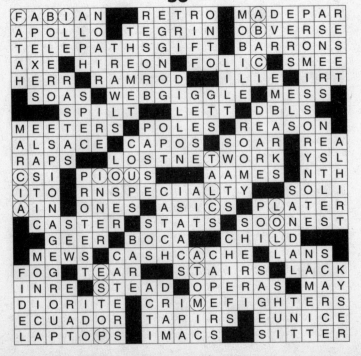

```
FABIAN   RETRO   MADEPAR
APOLLO   TEGRIN  OBVERSE
TELEPATHSGIFT   BARRONS
AXE  HIREON  FOLIC  SMEE
HERR  RAMROD   ILIE   IRT
SOAS  WEBGIGGLE   MESS
    SPILT   LETT   DBLS
MEETERS   POLES   REASON
ALSACE   CAPOS  SOAR  REA
RAPS   LOSTNETWORK   YSL
CSI   PIOUS   AAMES   NTH
ITO   RNSPECIALTY   SOLI
AIN  ONES   ASICS  PLATER
CASTER   STATS   SOONEST
   GEER   BOCA   CHILD
MEWS   CASHCACHE   LANS
FOG  TEAR   STAIRS   LACK
INRE   STEAD   OPERAS  MAY
DIORITE   CRIMEFIGHTERS
ECUADOR   TAPIRS   EUNICE
LAPTOPS   IMACS   SITTER
```

59

Puzzle 59 (completed grid):

```
G O G O L ■ M A S H ■ S A N E ■ S R T A S
A D A N O ■ T R I O ■ D E A R ■ P E A R S
M A Y I T E V E R B E S O S O ■ I C B M S
■ P N I N ■ N E O N ■ L A S ■ N O L O S
I S R ■ S P A S ■ T O I L ■ U D D E R S
A T I S S U E ■ I R M A ■ G C L E F ■
M E D I T E R R A N E A N S I S I ■ O S A
S W E E P ■ M I T T E N ■ M A D E I R A S
■ N A M A B L E ■ P U N ■ R O T C S
M A R A U D ■ U N L E A R N T ■ C U R E
O T E ■ L I C E N S I N G F I F I ■ T U T
B O N D ■ V I N C E N T E ■ A L B U M S
I N T E L ■ N T H ■ R A S S L E R ■
L E O N A R D O ■ S T A N C E ■ N A N C E
E R R ■ T H E M A N W I T H T H E H O H O
■ B R I E R ■ S O O N ■ B A S E T E N
D A Y O N E ■ C O B B ■ P H Y S ■ Q R S
I B E A M ■ U H F ■ I D E E ■ T A B U ■
C O B R A ■ D O N T T R E A D O N M I M I
T R Y A S ■ O R O N ■ O R T S ■ T A T A R
S T E T S ■ N E W T ■ P S S T ■ E J E C T
```

60

Puzzle 60 (completed grid):

```
P A P A ■ I R A E ■ A D D S ■ H A N D E L
A G I N G B U L L ■ D O O M ■ O V E R L Y
T H E G U M B A L L A L L Y ■ L O R A I N
S A D L Y ■ B R I O ■ P E T T Y W O M A N
■ P E S C I ■ S E T H ■ H E S ■ L A N E
O T I S ■ A S H ■ S E I ■ R E L I C ■
L O P ■ A T H O U S A N D A C E S ■ R C A
A R E N D T ■ C H E ■ I V E ■ A R I A S
F I R E M A N ■ F R A C T A L ■ T I T U S
■ C I L I A ■ N A T L ■ V I L E
B E D K N O B S A N D B O O M S T I C K S
U N I T ■ S L U R ■ N O T R E ■
R O S I E ■ G I B B E R S ■ D I A R I S T
P L I E S ■ U S E ■ E A T ■ C L A N C Y
S A N ■ M Y F I E N D F L I C K A ■ G A P
■ C L E E F ■ E Y E ■ C U E ■ N E M O
T A L E ■ W A S ■ T E R R ■ T R I E S ■
O L I V E T W I S T ■ T O I L ■ M E T A L
T I N E A R ■ M U L H O L L A N D D I V E
A V E R S E ■ O R E O ■ F I S T B L O O D
L E S S E E ■ N E S T ■ S A S H ■ E N N A
```

61

```
■ B O O E D ■ ■ V E L M A ■ P R A M S ■
P O O H B A H S ■ A L A R M ■ A I S L E S
A R M Y B R A T ■ C A R B O N D A T I N G
C A P E ■ K S U ■ P A I N E D ■ R I O T ■
E X H A U S T F A N S ■ G R A Y H A I R S
■ ■ ■ H R H ■ ■ L O E B ■ A R F S ■ ■ ■
O C H ■ L A T E M O D E L ■ ■ I N T R O ■
M O A B ■ D A N S K ■ N E A L E ■ K E N T
I N S I D E J O B ■ K I T T Y L I T T E R
S T A K E ■ ■ O R I G ■ W E D S ■ U P I ■
S I C E M ■ M I X E D N U T S ■ A K R O N
I N A ■ U S A F ■ V A I N ■ ■ A I N T I ■
O U T E R P L A N E T ■ Q U I C K R E A D
N E C K ■ L I T E R ■ B U L G Y ■ S E T A
■ S H E B A ■ ■ D I P L O M A C Y ■ S O D
■ ■ O T T S ■ E R A T ■ ■ L A Z ■ ■ ■
S P E E D T R A P ■ U S E D V E H I C L E
O L E S ■ E A G L E D ■ ■ R I C ■ G R O G
W I N T E R X G A M E S ■ Y E A R Z E R O
S E S A M E ■ E Z I N E ■ S T R E A M I N
■ S Y N O D ■ D A R T S ■ ■ S A G E S ■
```

62

```
C A L C ■ M C A T ■ G E I C O ■ A T P A R
O R E O ■ A R G O ■ O X F A M ■ C H O S E
M E A S U R I N G S N O O P S ■ H E M I N
P A R T B ■ S O S O ■ C R A K E ■ P E A T
■ ■ A U N T S ■ J P E G ■ ■ S T O L G A
S T A N ■ O A T ■ O U T O F T H E P O O L
P R I Z E S L I P U P ■ T I R A N E ■ ■
A E R A T E ■ C O R A L ■ C U R D ■ T O T
T A J ■ A G E ■ I N T U I T ■ P I S A N O
■ S O X ■ A A H ■ E L C I D ■ N I C E R
T U R K E Y T O R T ■ L I V I N G M O O R
A R D E N ■ S L O E S ■ E R E ■ S S R ■
B E A S T S ■ S T E P P E ■ T U N ■ A M A
U R N ■ R I F T ■ M Y R N A ■ T A I L O R
■ ■ P E N D E D ■ C O S M O R E M A R K
I N D I A N A R E C A P ■ I N A ■ I D E S
T O D A T E ■ ■ L I M A ■ W E L D S ■ ■
S I R S ■ R A B I D ■ N E R O ■ A S A D A
E D I T H ■ L O V E M E L O V E M Y G O D
L E V E E ■ A Z E R A ■ K N E W ■ O U Z O
F A E R Y ■ N O R S E ■ O G R E ■ U E Y S
```

63

A	S	S		M	O	O	G		A	D	D	T	O		B	O	A	T	E	R
L	E	T		A	A	R	E		N	E	O	N	S		U	N	L	A	S	H
B	E	[ARM]	A	R	K	E	T		T	A	T	T	L	E	T	A	[LEG]	R	A	Y
U	M	A	S	S		O	S	C	I	N	E		I	N	C	R	E	A	S	E
M	E	N	T	H	E		A	H	H		L	A	N	D	H	O				
		R	E	G	U	L	[ARM]	E	A	L	S		L	E	I	C	A			
F	R	A		S	E	L	L	E	R	S		G	A	S	P	L	A	N	E	T
L	E	I	A		S	E	A	D	O	O		O	T	O	H		T	O	R	A
A	C	O	L	Y	T	E	S		D	O	U	B	[LEG]	L	A	Z	E	D		
S	O	L	[ARM]	A	S	S		M	O	N	O	D	R	A	M	A				
K	N	I	S	H		O	A	T	B	R	A	N		M	B	E	K	I		
	O	I	L	S	L	I	C	K	S		B	U	B	B	[LEG]	U	M			
W	[ARM]	E	M	O	R	I	A	L	S		P	A	S	S	L	I	N	E		
H	A	L	E		M	E	G	A		S	E	A	R	L	E		S	E	T	A
I	N	K	E	R	A	S	E	R		U	N	L	O	O	S	E		S	A	N
T	I	E	T	O		M	I	D	D	[LEG]	R	O	U	N	D					
	L	E	S	S	E	N		O	R	A		P	R	I	N	T	S			
P	R	O	F	O	R	M	A		S	T	R	A	T	A		O	P	E	R	A
C	A	L	E	N	D	[ARM]	O	N	T	H	S		I	D	[LEG]	O	S	S	I	P
B	R	A	N	D	O		N	O	I	R	E		N	E	A	T		T	A	P
S	E	N	N	A	S		E	R	R	O	R		G	E	L	S		S	L	Y

64

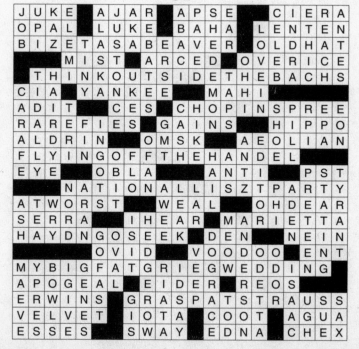

J	U	K	E		A	J	A	R		A	P	S	E		C	I	E	R	A
O	P	A	L		L	U	K	E		B	A	H	A		L	E	N	T	E	N
B	I	Z	E	T	A	S	A	B	E	A	V	E	R		O	L	D	H	A	T
	M	I	S	T		A	R	C	E	D		O	V	E	R	I	C	E		
	T	H	I	N	K	O	U	T	S	I	D	E	T	H	E	B	A	C	H	S
C	I	A		Y	A	N	K	E	E		M	A	H	I						
A	D	I	T		C	E	S		C	H	O	P	I	N	S	P	R	E	E	
R	A	R	E	F	I	E	S		G	A	I	N	S		H	I	P	P	O	
A	L	D	R	I	N		O	M	S	K		A	E	O	L	I	A	N		
F	L	Y	I	N	G	O	F	F	T	H	E	H	A	N	D	E	L			
E	Y	E		O	B	L	A		A	N	T	I		P	S	T				
	N	A	T	I	O	N	A	L	L	I	S	Z	T	P	A	R	T	Y		
A	T	W	O	R	S	T		W	E	A	L		O	H	D	E	A	R		
S	E	R	R	A		I	H	E	A	R		M	A	R	I	E	T	T	A	
H	A	Y	D	N	G	O	S	E	E	K		D	E	N		N	E	I	N	
	O	V	I	D		V	O	O	D	O	O		E	N	T					
M	Y	B	I	G	F	A	T	G	R	I	E	G	W	E	D	D	I	N	G	
A	P	O	G	E	A	L		E	I	D	E	R		R	E	O	S			
E	R	W	I	N	S		G	R	A	S	P	A	T	S	T	R	A	U	S	S
V	E	L	V	E	T		I	O	T	A		C	O	O	T		A	G	U	A
E	S	S	E	S		S	W	A	Y		E	D	N	A		C	H	E	X	

B	A	D	E	N		D	I	M	L	Y		D	A	W	N		C	A	R
U	T	E	R	O		A	E	N	E	A	S		E	R	A	T		O	L	E
D	R	E	S	S	I	N	G	O	N	T	H	E	S	I	D	E		R	I	M
D	I	S	T	E	N	D		N	O	T	A	R	I	Z	E	S		N	C	O
			C	H	I	S			E	P	I	C		S	T	R	E	E	T	
S	Q	U	A	R	E	M	I	L	E		E	N	A	M	I		E	R	S	E
E	I	S	N	E	R		M	I	S	C			A	N	T	E	S			
A	N	G	S	T		T	E	A	T	A	S	T	E	R		A	F	T	E	R
	G	A	P		R	O	O	M	A	T	T	H	E	T	O	P		O	K	E
		A	D	A	R	N		E	L	A	N		L	I	O	N	E	L		
S	I	M	C	I	T	Y		A	A	R	O	N		K	E	N	N	E	D	Y
H	E	E	H	E	E		E	S	C	E		S	L	O	G	S				
E	R	N		S	L	A	N	T	E	D	L	I	N	E	S		T	O	V	
R	E	T	I	E		H	E	A	D	T	O	T	O	E		N	A	N	C	I
	A	D	L	A	I			O	M	O	O		G	O	F	E	R	S		
M	C	L	I		N	S	T	A	R		B	O	T	T	O	M	F	I	S	H
A	A	B	O	N	D		E	G	E	R		S	E	L	A					
Y	S	L		O	T	H	E	R	S	H	O	E		P	E	D	I	C	A	B
O	S	O		T	H	E	M	A	N	I	N	T	H	E	M	I	D	D	L	E
R	I	C		M	E	M	E		I	N	M	A	T	E		S	E	R	I	N
S	A	K		E	N	I	D		K	E	E	L	S		M	A	S	T	O	

O	H	G	O	D		I	C	H	A	T		B	A	S	E	D		S	A	C
P	O	L	L	O		N	E	R	V	E	C	E	N	T	E	R		P	R	Y
T	R	A	I	L	O	F	T	H	E	C	E	N	T	U	R	Y		I	N	C
E	N	R	O	L	L	E	E		C	H	O	S	E	N			O	R	A	L
D	Y	E		I	D	A	R	E			S	T	A	R	G	A	Z	E		
			T	E	H	R	A	N	R	A	I	N		S	C	U	L	L		
F	R	I	E	D	A		G	A	R	N	E	T		T	I	E	S	O	N	
R	E	C	T		T	E	S		D	O	R	I	A		O	N	S	I	D	E
A	L	O	H	A		T	H	E	L	O	I	N	K	I	N	G		T	O	W
N	I	N	E	S		H	A	R	E	M		E	N	E		W	A	R	T	
	E	C	R	U		E	V	R	Y		M	I	S	E		I	H	R	E	
U	F	O	S		A	N	I		O	A	S	T	S		C	O	C	A	S	
S	M	L		F	R	E	N	C	H	F	I	R	E	S		S	K	A	T	E
G	A	L	O	R	E		G	R	A	F	T		N	E	S		N	S	E	C
A	P	E	M	E	N		S	A	V	E	A	S			C	H	E	E	R	Y
	C	A	R	O	B		M	A	R	I	T	A	L	L	A	W				
A	T	T	H	E	T	O	P			A	S	E	E	D		T	A	W		
L	E	I	A		S	I	E	N	N	A		S	C	R	A	M	B	L	E	
E	X	O		D	O	N	T	T	O	U	C	H	T	H	A	T	D	A	L	I
V	A	N		S	W	I	T	C	H	B	L	A	D	E		I	L	L	E	R
E	S	S		L	E	A	S	H		S	U	G	A	R		T	I	L	E	D

67

PSHAW · PAPER · IMMAD · DOS
ALONE · AIOLI · SCARE · AKC
PORKBARRELPROJECT · YEA
· SHAPE · KAPOW · OSTER
ACE · PREPARETOBECUTOFF
POPUPS · IRONED · SHRINES
ALLS · INCA · STEER
COASTONTHROUGH · EDSELS
ERY · OPS · YESMAAM · TOE
· FUR · ROADRAGEZONE
MAHARAJAS · SEROTONIN
GOODSHORTCUT · THO
RNA · STANDUP · ATO · HAG
SERAPH · IGNORETHISSIGN
· LOOSE · TARA · ASEA
BASETWO · PHILLY · HUMANS
LEAVEIFYOUSEEACOP · NTH
INREM · TILTS · ASSAD
GET · KEEPITUNDEREIGHTY
HAR · IMSET · ERWIN · DREAD
TSE · NUTSY · RAINY · EARNS

68

LISA · ASTIN · PERMA · CHEF
AGUA · THANE · ACERB · AUTO
WNBA · HAIRS · CONW8WITTY
NOW · OODLES · ANTI · INSET
CR8 · ALOG · EZINE
HARKS · W8UNTILDARK · FDA
ANANIAS · SOHOT · RAEDAWN
ICIEST · ATTEND · DEDUCED
RENE · MIRE · LESS · SEER
· LIFTEDW8S · TESTTUBE
BUC · BEAN · ALC · ALEE · PSI
EPHEMERA · P8ONPLACE
ANAP · SRIS · OLAV · FROM
MEFIRST · ETHANE · ERIEPA
EXECUTE · DIONE · GRILLER
RTS · B8ANDSWITCH · TEENY
· VASCO · HERE · ATA
LIMIT · AONE · SMORES · SRS
SK8BOARDER · TIKKI · BEAT
TEAR · STLEO · ACEIN · IDDO
SAGA · USERS · TERNS · G8ER

71

```
S A V A L A S ■ J A M J A R ■ ■ P L E B E
I G I V E U P ■ A M O E B A ■ R E E V E S
R E S I S T I N G A R E S T ■ A R D E N T
■ S T O R E ■ T A R O T ■ M E A N I E
D I E ■ R I P S ■ Y E L L S A T ■ I N S
U N D E R A T A C K ■ D U E T ■ T O N ■
A D E X E C ■ L U N G ■ T O I L I N G A T
D Y N A M I C ■ M O O T ■ N E U ■ B A D E
■ M A N E S ■ X O U T ■ S A T A T O P
M E R ■ I G L O O ■ D R E W ■ U R S I N E
O D E O N ■ L O V E A F A I R ■ A E R I E
E I T H E R ■ N U T S ■ K N E A D ■ E S S
S T U D D E D ■ M O N O ■ K A L E L ■
H E R E ■ P E P ■ N E A P ■ P O W E R P C
A D N A U S E A M ■ W H I M ■ H A V A S U
■ A R M ■ P R O F ■ U P O N A R I V A L
A N D ■ P I S T O L S ■ E R O S ■ I T T
D E R M I S ■ I C E A X ■ O U T E R ■
O M E A R A ■ C H E C K I N G A C O U N T
L E S L E Y ■ L E C H E R ■ A T O M M A N
F A S T S ■ E D E S S A ■ T E N P A S T
```

72

```
B E T A S ■ A C R E ■ P S H A W S ■ C B S
O V E R P A S S E D ■ R O A D E O ■ O A T
B E D R O C K A N D B E D R O L L ■ M B A
■ A O N E ■ A I R ■ A B C ■ O M A N
■ F I R E W A T E R F I R E H A Z A R D
L A R G E ■ L A D ■ O R E S ■ B A N ■
I N U N D A T E ■ B R A ■ G A R D E N
M O I ■ B U C K N A K E D B U C K E Y E
A N T I W A R ■ O A R S ■ R A N K ■ E D S
■ A S S N ■ A T O ■ M U D ■ B R I T
■ B I G W H E E L O F B I G C H E E S E
R E D O ■ D N A ■ S I X ■ H U L L ■
I R E ■ A C T I ■ M O R E ■ E N M A S S E
D E A D W O O D D E A D D U C K ■ H E X
S A L A A M ■ R A P ■ S K Y S C A P E
■ G I S ■ V I E D ■ A M P ■ P O R T S
T R A S H C A N W E T R A S H T A L K ■
R O S Y ■ A L T ■ W A Y ■ O H N O
A X L ■ B L U E C R A B B L U E G R A S S
M I A ■ A V E N U E ■ L E O N A L E W I S
P E W ■ T E S T E D ■ E S T D ■ E R E C T
```

73

B	I	A	S		C	I	V	I	C		H	A	A	S			T	W	A	S
O	R	G	Y		O	N	E	A	L		I	L	S	A		C	H	I	L	L
H	A	U	L		K	A	N	G	A		G	O	T	O		H	A	N	O	I
R	E	A	L	M	E	N	D	O	N	T	H	E	A	T	Q	U	I	C	H	E
			A	I	D	E			G	A	L	S		O	U	R		E	A	R
L	E	T	B	E		E	C	O	L	I			M	A	C	H				
I	T	H	I	N	K	T	H	E	R	E	F	O	R	E	I	H	A	M		
N	A	E		N	A	S	A			E	O	E		D	Y	N	A	S	T	
G	L	E	A	S	O	N		S	A	S		O	W	L		D	R	E	A	
		R	E	B		D	E	L	T	A	H	A	I	R	L	I	N	E	S	
A	D	O	R	A	B	L	E		P	A	C		S	P	O	U	T	E	R	S
S	E	V	E	N	Y	E	A	R	H	I	T	C	H		P	V	T			
A	M	E	S		O	R	E		D	E	N		R	E	S	O	R	T	S	
P	O	R	T	A	L		M	D	S		O	N	E	I		I	O	U		
	S	E	T	O	N	E	S	T	E	E	T	H	O	N	H	E	D	G	E	
	R	E	G	O			P	A	N	E	L		U	V	E	A	S			
S	T	U		L	O	U		S	E	C	T		E	T	N	A				
H	E	R	R	I	N	G	O	N	T	H	E	R	I	G	H	T	S	I	D	E
A	R	G	U	E		A	L	E	E		B	O	N	G	O		I	M	A	X
F	R	E	E	R		T	E	A	R		B	A	T	E	S		O	H	M	E
T	E	S	S		S	O	D	S		E	R	O	D	E		N	O	E	S	

74

G	E	T	S	A	N	A		I	D	A	H	O			S	T	R	I	N	G	S
A	C	H	E	F	O	R		S	E	V	E	R			T	O	O	S	O	O	N
B	L	E	A	T	E	D		A	L	L	ON	R	E	D		I	N	C	A	R	G	O
S	A	W		E	N	O		L	A	M		H	O	E		R	I	K		W	O	W
	T	E	A	R	D	R	O	P		ON	I	ON		V	I	S	C	E	R	A	L
	D	R	T		S	O	F	T	C	O	L	O	R			F	E	Y			
S	U	N	C	H	I	P	S		ON	E	I	R	ON		A	S	S	E	S	S	A	S
N	N	E		A	F	R	A	I	D			G	R	E	T	E	L		P	G	A
A	B	S	E	N	C	E		ON	A	U	C	T	I	ON		A	L	L	E	R	G	Y
K	O	D	A	K		P	M	S		K	O	A		E	B	B		E	T	U	I	S
E	L	A	P	S	E		ON	T	H	E	B	U	T	T	ON		G	R	A	C	E	S
S	T	Y		G	E	C	K	O	S		A	T	O	M	I	C		E	S	O
		B	I	G	ON		R	I	B	C	A	G	E		ON	S	E	T			
R	A	J	I	V		M	G	M		L	A	S		S	H	A		N	A	C	H	O
E	M	O	T	I	ON	A	L		C	O	N	A	N		I	M	ON	T	O	Y	O	U
M	E	L		N	A	N	U		Y	A	Y	M	E		R	I	S	E		N	U	S
O	B	L	ON	G	S		T	ON	Y	T	ON	I	T	ON	E		I	R	ON	I	S	T
P	A	Y	S		P	E	S	T	O			I	B	E	A	M		A	C	E	S
	W	A	R	D		H	U	E		T	Z	U		S	M	U	T				
S	T	R	I	F	E	S		E	N	T	E	R	E	D		L	E	T	I	T	B	E
T	H	E	T	R	E	E	L	I	G	H	T	I	N	G	C	E	R	E	M	O	N	Y
A	A	M	C	O		L	O	C		N	ON	E		E	V	E		S	E	G	E	R
G	I	S	H		S	U	E		O	S	S		T	S	P		R	A	G	E	

Q	U	A	F	F	S	■	■	O	M	A	H	A	■	S	A	P	P	I	E	R
A	N	G	O	L	A	■	A	S	E	V	E	R	■	I	N	A	H	O	L	E
T	E	R	R	O	R	■	C	U	T	O	N	B	O	L	D	L	I	N	E	S
A	V	E	■	P	A	R	T	■	E	N	S	■	R	V	S	■	L	I	M	E
R	E	E	K	■	J	E	S	T	S	■	■	O	N	E	O	F	■	Z	E	N
I	N	D	O	■	E	B	O	N	■	S	A	P	O	R	■	I	D	E	N	T
■	■	I	N	V	E	N	T	■	H	U	R	T	■	E	X	I	S	T	S	■
N	A	M	■	A	O	L	■	B	O	N	A	■	I	D	E	S	■	■	■	■
O	P	E	N	S	■	S	H	A	D	E	T	H	E	C	I	R	C	L	E	S
D	O	N	O	T	■	■	O	M	A	R	■	V	E	T	■	O	L	L	A	■
O	L	D	S	■	S	E	P	O	Y	■	B	O	O	T	S	■	L	A	P	D
F	L	E	E	■	O	R	O	■	■	C	A	S	K	■	N	O	M	A	D	■
F	O	L	D	A	L	O	N	G	D	A	S	H	E	S	■	E	R	A	S	E
■	■	I	V	E	S	■	L	I	N	K	■	■	A	G	O	■	S	O	N	■
P	E	E	V	E	S	■	C	O	R	D	■	O	O	L	O	N	G	■	■	■
R	U	L	E	R	■	P	H	O	T	O	■	O	N	T	O	■	A	S	P	S
E	R	E	■	S	C	R	A	M	■	■	S	H	R	E	D	■	G	E	L	T
S	A	V	E	■	A	I	R	■	J	A	I	■	U	R	N	S	■	W	A	R
U	S	E	T	A	P	E	O	N	E	D	G	E	S	■	E	N	L	A	C	E
M	I	N	U	T	E	S	■	O	H	O	H	O	H	■	S	I	E	G	E	S
E	A	S	I	E	S	T	■	B	U	S	T	S	■	■	S	P	E	E	D	S